TYPICAL SMALL HOME WORKSHOP

CARPENTRY FOR BEGINNERS

HOW TO USE TOOLS, BASIC JOINTS
WORKSHOP PRACTICE
DESIGNS FOR THINGS TO MAKE

Edited by
CHARLES H. HAYWARD

Martino Publishing
Mansfield Centre CT

Martino Publishing
P.O. Box 373,
Mansfield Centre, CT 06250 USA

web-site: www.martinopublishing.com

ISBN-13: 978-1-57898-764-1 (hardcover: alk. paper)
ISBN-10: 1-57898-764-4 (hardcover: alk. paper)
ISBN-13: 978-1-57898-765-8 (pbk.: alk. paper)
ISBN-10: 1-57898-765-2 (pbk.: alk. paper)

Library of Congress Cataloging-in-Publication Data

Hayward, Charles Harold, 1898-
Carpentry for beginners: how to use tools, basic joints, workshop practice, designs for things to make edited by Charles H. Hayward.
p. cm.
Reprint. Originally published: Philadelphia, Pa.: J.B. Lippincott Co., 1949.
Includes index.
ISBN-13: 978-1-57898-764-1 (hardcover: alk. paper)
ISBN-10: 1-57898-764-4 (hardcover: alk. paper)
ISBN-13: 978-1-57898-765-8 (pbk.: alk. paper)
ISBN-10: 1-57898-765-2 (pbk.: alk. paper)
1. Woodwork--Amateurs' manuals. I. Title.

TT185.H39 2009
684'.08--dc22 2009019113

Cover design by T. Matarazzo

Printed in the United States of America On 100% Acid-Free Paper

CARPENTRY FOR BEGINNERS

HOW TO USE TOOLS, BASIC JOINTS
WORKSHOP PRACTICE
DESIGNS FOR THINGS TO MAKE

Edited by
CHARLES H. HAYWARD

J. B. LIPPINCOTT COMPANY
Philadelphia New York

INTRODUCTION

THIS book is intended for the home craftsman who wants to make all sorts of things in wood from a table lamp to a rabbit hutch. To the tradesman carpentry refers to the constructional woodwork of a house—the roof, flooring, and so on. To the man in the street, however, it generally means the making of almost everything in wood; hence the general character of the designs we give.

Woodwork is one of the most interesting as well as the most useful of crafts. Wood is a pleasant material to work; it can be used for a tremendously wide number of articles; and whilst simple things call for no great ability, they need care in setting out and working, and thus present enough difficulties to be thoroughly interesting. Most men have in them the urge to construct, and skill in woodwork enables them to gratify this and at the same time produce useful and attractive items for the home.

We give a range of comparatively simple designs for objects to make which we know from experience to be in everyday demand; small general items, pieces of furniture, and garden woodwork. These are followed by instructions on the use of tools, and the everyday processes involved in woodwork—making doors, hingeing, fitting locks, cutting joints, and so on. Those who wish to follow a more specialized branch of work should see other works in this series; CABINET MAKING FOR BEGINNERS, TOOLS FOR WOODWORK, PRACTICAL VENEERING, STAINING AND POLISHING, TIMBERS FOR WOODWORK, LIGHT MACHINE TOOLS, JOINTS IN WOODWORK, and ENGLISH PERIOD FURNITURE.

PRINTED IN GREAT BRITAIN BY WILLIAM CLOWES AND SONS LIMITED
LONDON AND BECCLES
PR 3317

CONTENTS

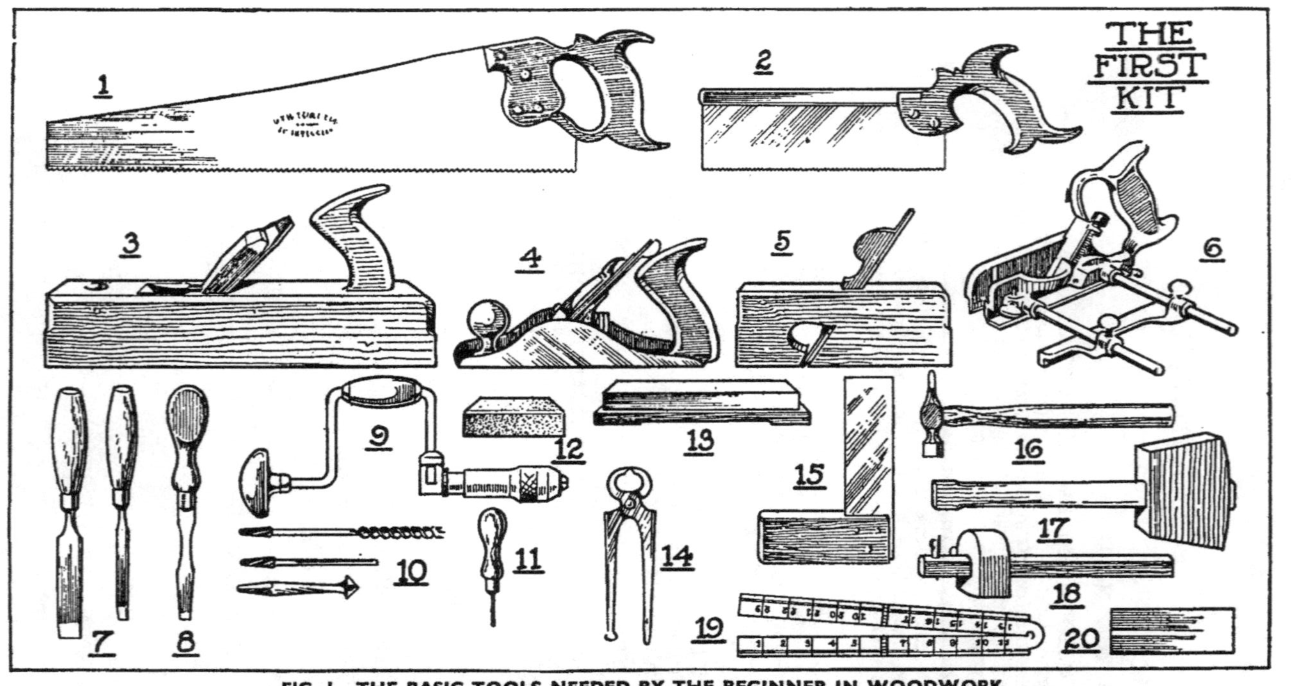

FIG. 1. THE BASIC TOOLS NEEDED BY THE BEGINNER IN WOODWORK.

1. Hand-saw, 20–22 in., cross-cut, about 9 points per inch.
2. Back-saw, 10 in., 14–16 points per inch.
3. Jack plane, 14–16 in., cutter 2–2¼ in.
*4. Smoothing plane, 9 in., 2-in. cutter ; or 10 in., 2⅜-in. cutter.
*5. Rebate plane, 1-in. cutter.
*6. Plough, metal or wood.
7. Chisels, ¾-in. and ¼-in., firmer
8. Screwdriver, 6-in. blade, London or Cabinet pattern.
9. Brace, 8 in.–10 in. sweep, ratchet.
10. Bits, ⅜-in. twist, ¼-in. shell, ½-in. snail countersink.
11. Bradawl, medium.
12. Cork rubber.
13. Oil-stone, 8 in. by 1¾ in.–2 in. India, Carborundum, or Aloxite, fine grade.
14. Pincers, medium size.
15. Try-square, 6-in. blade.
16. Hammer, Warrington or London, 11–12 oz. including handle.
17. Mallet, 5-in. head.
18. Gauge, cutting.
19. Rule, 2–3 ft. folding.
*20. Scraper, 5 in.

The tools marked with an asterisk can be bought later if preferred.

CARPENTRY FOR BEGINNERS

THE TOOLS YOU NEED

TO do any woodwork at all you must clearly have certain elementary essentials, and you will find these illustrated on the opposite page. Particular work may call for special tools, but you will not go far wrong with this nucleus. Some may be unnecessary for the more elementary jobs that you will tackle, but with them you will be able to undertake a fair range of woodwork. As you progress you can add others; some of those on page 2, for instance; but do not cumber yourself with an unnecessarily large kit at the outset. It is better to master the few basic tools and purchase others as the necessity arises. Be sure, however, to get good tools. The shilling or two that you may save in buying tools of inferior metal or design is soon lost, and you are under the constant handicap of having to allow for inaccurate or rough work. Go to a tool shop and pay the proper listed price, and you will at least put yourself beyond the temptation of blaming the tools when things do not turn out as well as had been hoped. Having got good tools, look after them. Keep them sharp, avoid rust, and do not use them for work for which they were not intended.

So far as the sizes and kinds of tools are concerned you need not accept the suggested list too rigidly. A tool of different size from that given will probably do the work perfectly well, and for some work may even be better. Then, again, if you anticipate doing finer work eventually, you could with advantage vary the list straightway by getting two back-saws instead of one. In this case it would be better to get an 8-in. dovetail-saw and a 14-in. tenon-saw in place of the suggested 10-in. saw.

Several tools you can make yourself, and some of them are so essential that you could usefully start on them as your first essay in woodwork. These are listed on page 3. In addition, there is the question of a bench. If you have the space most certainly make or buy one. It makes a tremendous difference to the pleasure you will get out of your work. Lastly, you need a chest or some other accommodation for tools It does not matter much what you have, but remember to allow for tools that you will buy later.

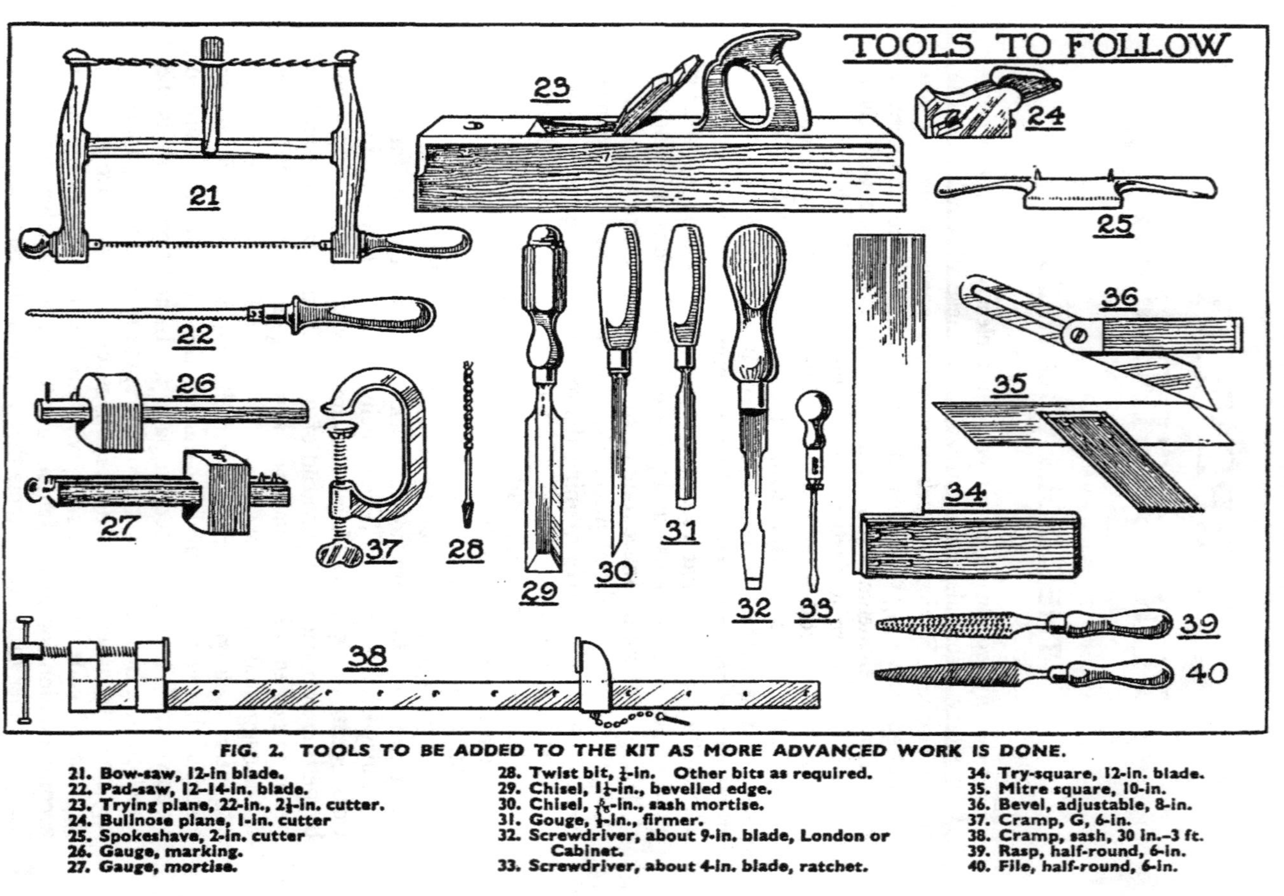

FIG. 2. TOOLS TO BE ADDED TO THE KIT AS MORE ADVANCED WORK IS DONE.

21. Bow-saw, 12-in blade.
22. Pad-saw, 12–14-in. blade.
23. Trying plane, 22-in., 2⅜-in. cutter.
24. Bullnose plane, 1-in. cutter
25. Spokeshave, 2-in. cutter
26. Gauge, marking.
27. Gauge, mortise.
28. Twist bit, ¼-in. Other bits as required.
29. Chisel, 1¼-in., bevelled edge.
30. Chisel, 5/16-in., sash mortise.
31. Gouge, ½-in., firmer.
32. Screwdriver, about 9-in. blade, London or Cabinet.
33. Screwdriver, about 4-in. blade, ratchet.
34. Try-square, 12-in. blade.
35. Mitre square, 10-in.
36. Bevel, adjustable, 8-in.
37. Cramp, G, 6-in.
38. Cramp, sash, 30 in.–3 ft.
39. Rasp, half-round, 6-in.
40. File, half-round, 6-in.

CARE OF TOOLS

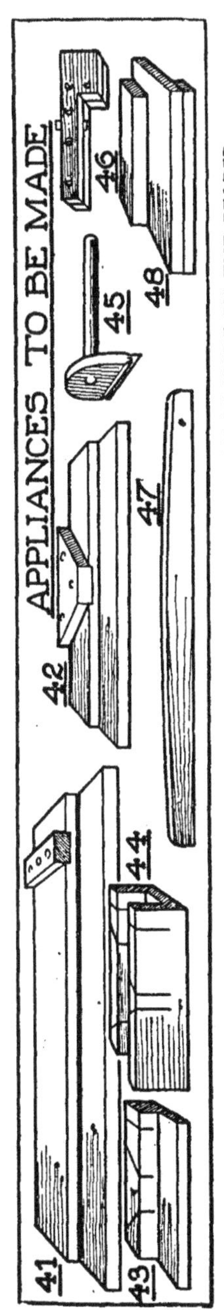

FIG. 3. ALL OF THESE ARE INVALUABLE IN THE WORKSHOP AND CAN BE MADE BY THE READER.

41. Shooting-board, 30 in.–3 ft.
42. Mitre shooting-board, 20-in.
43. Mitre block, 9 in.
44. Mitre box, 14-in., to take 4 in. width.
45. Veneering hammer, blade 6–7 in.
46. Scratch, 6 in.
47. Straight-edge, 3 ft. and 6 ft.
48. Bench hook, about 9 in.

Chapters on the use of tools begin on page 92.

Here are a few notes on the care of tools that you can follow with advantage.

Keep a pad of cotton-wool soaked in linseed oil handy on the bench and rub the sole of the plane or the blade of the saw across it occasionally. This lubricates it and makes the working much sweeter.

Do not oil twist bits to be used for dowelling, as oil is transferred to the hole, preventing the glue from sticking.

Wipe the steel parts of tools with an oily rag from time to time. It prevents rust.

Do not pile edge tools on the bench or in the chest. The edges are easily damaged.

Avoid striking chisels with the hammer. Use the mallet.

If the floor in front of the bench is shiny so that you are inclined to slip shake a little plaster of paris over it.

Then, a final note on the care of your own hands. Keep them always behind the cutting edge of the tool you are using. It is easily the best safeguard against cutting yourself.

SIX ATTRACTIVE ITEMS WHICH DO NOT CALL FOR ADVANCED SKILL IN WOODWORK.

Magazine stand, 18 in. wide, 18 in. high, 14 in. deep ; Tray, 20 in. by 15 in. ; Fire-screen, 22 in. by 19 in. sight ; Clockcase, 12 in. by 9 in. ; Book rack, 7 in. by 6 in. ends ; Lamp stand, 8–9 in. high by 6 in. base.

DESIGNS SECTION

I. SMALL INCIDENTAL ITEMS

SIX SMALL THINGS FOR THE BEGINNER

Magazine stand ; Tray ; Fire-screen ; Clockcase ; Book rack ; Lamp stand.

ALTHOUGH definite sizes are given in the accompanying diagrams there is no need to keep too rigidly to them. They may have to be varied to suit any special fittings that may be available, or in accordance with the wood available.

Magazine stand (Fig. 1). The ends (A) and bottom (B), are about ⅝ in. thick, lap-dovetailed together. Each end is trenched across, stopping about ¼ in. from each edge, for the shelves (C). The vertical divisions (D) are in ¼-in. thick plywood fitting into grooves worked in the ends (A). The number of these can be reduced if desired to four or three, thereby making the stand somewhat narrower. The shelves can be glued in upon assembly, but the vertical divisions should be left dry in the grooves in order to simplify polishing and subsequent dusting and cleaning. The end scrolls (E) are glued and pinned on and rounded over. The grain runs crosswise. The bases (F) have rounded ends and are screwed up underneath.

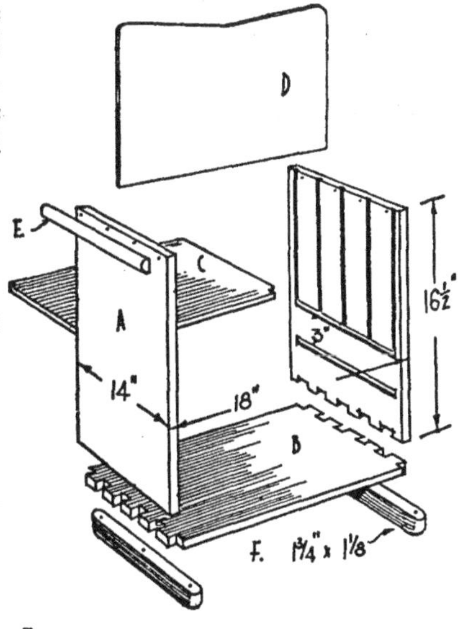

CUTTING LIST

		Long ft.	Long in.	Wide in.	Thick in.
A	2 Ends	1	5	14¼	⅝
B	1 Bottom	1	6¼	14¼	⅝
C	2 Shelves	1	6	14¼	⅝
D	5 Divisions	1	6	9	¼
E	2 Scrolls		1⅜	14¼	⅝
F	2 Bases	1	2	2	1⅛

FIG. 1. SIZES AND DETAILS OF MAGAZINE STAND.

Tray (Fig. 2). Any odd pieces of thin wood or plywood about the size given make good trays. The stuff should be about ¼ in. thick. If solid wood, the edges could be rounded and screwed directly to the rim without rebating. It is essential that solid wood is seasoned, because any shrinkage will be opposed by the rims. It is always better to make up the rim separately for ease in staining and polishing. After this is done the rim can be screwed to the tray. A suitable handle in ebonized hardwood is indicated. If this is arranged not to project above the rim several trays can be stacked one on top of the other, if required. Rim corners can be dovetailed or mitred.

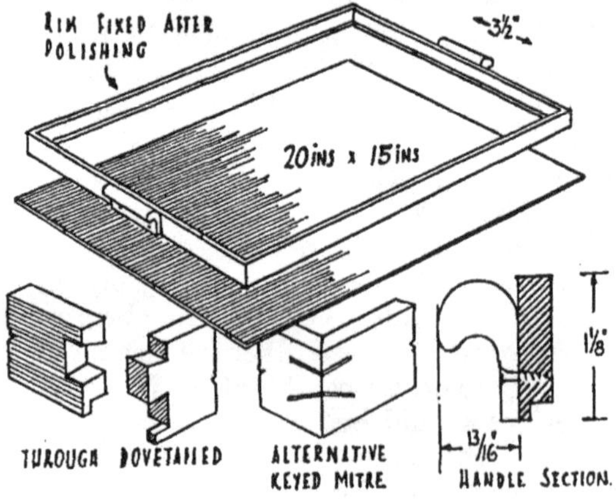

FIG. 2. CONSTRUCTION OF TEA TRAY.

Note that if they are through-dovetailed it is necessary to allow a straight bottom member to project on the dovetailed piece level with the rebate as shown in the diagram. Otherwise a gap will show at the end.

CUTTING LIST

	Long ft.	Long in.	Wide in.	Thick in.
1 Bottom . .	1	8½	15¼	¼
2 Rims . .	1	9½	1¼	5/16
2 ,, . .	1	4½	1¼	5/16
2 Handles .		4	1¼	13/16

Fire-screen (Fig. 3). If you have a piece of needlework, this will fix the size of the frame. As a guide, 22 in. high by 19 in. or 20 in. wide sight sizes, would be good proportion. The frame is from 1-in. wood finishing about ⅞ in. thick, and can be put together in various Always. ternative top joints are shown; also the tenoned joint of the wide bottom rail. The rebate for the glass and panel should be worked first.

The base should be wide enough for stability and firmly screwed to the frame. Ebonized blocks underneath raise it above the hearth. It is better to take the frame to a glass cutter if this cannot be cut at home. Tapestry or any suitable material is stretched over ¼-in. thick plywood and tacked behind. Allowance for the turn-over of

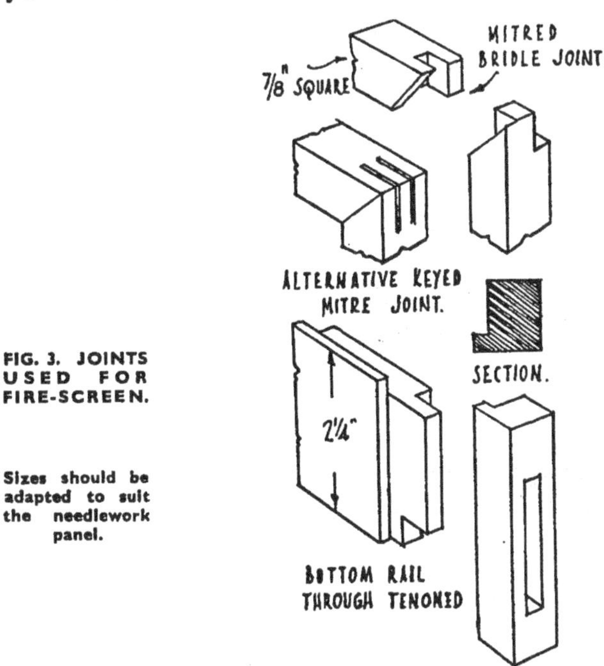

FIG. 3. JOINTS USED FOR FIRE-SCREEN.

Sizes should be adapted to suit the needlework panel.

the material must be made when inserting the panel. It is held with fine beads and a thin back screwed on excludes all dust. If plywood is a difficulty for the panel a light framework can be halved together and the material stretched over this. All sharp edges and corners should be taken off so as not to damage the material.

CUTTING LIST

	Long ft.	Long in.	Wide in.	Thick in.
2 Uprights . .	2	3	1	⅞
1 Rail . .	1	10½	1	⅞
1 ,, . .	1	10½	2¼	⅞
1 Base . .	1	10½	6	⅞
2 Blocks . .		6⅛	2¼	⅞
1 Panel . .	1	10½	20¼	¼

Clockcase (Fig. 4). Sometimes an old clock movement can be fitted with a new dial. It is better to have the clock in hand before making the case. The ends (A) are rebated for the plywood front and back. The front (B) can be glued and pinned, but the back should be left dry and screwed for removal at any time. The bottom (C) is screwed to the ends (A) from beneath. Odd pieces of wood will serve for the domed top. These are mitred and tongued. The moulding should be worked before fixing. Work to the bevel for the front opening and to the clock for the depth of the case. Plain square feet would look quite well. Moulded feet could be worked in a length, as shown, and fret cut to size.

CUTTING LIST

		Long		Wide	Thick
		ft.	in.	in.	in.
A	2 Ends .		9½	4	½
B	1 Front .	1	0½	9¼	¼
	1 Back .	1	0½	9¼	¼
C	1 Base .		10½	5	⅜
	5 Tops .		5	2⅞	5/16
	1 Footstrip .		9	1¾	⅝

Expanding book rack (Fig. 5). This is quite simple and will use up any odd pieces of hardwood in the workshop. The ends (A) are 7 in. high by 6 in. wide by ¾ in. thick. To one end dovetail two rails (B). These rails have bevelled or rounded faces and are connected by a cross-piece (C) at the open end. To the other end (A) a bevelled rail (D) is tenoned. These tenons could be taken through and wedged. Two pieces (E) are bevelled to engage rail (D) and are screwed to rails (B) from beneath. The rack can be made any length up to about 18 in.

CUTTING LIST

		Long		Wide	Thick
		ft.	in.	in.	in.
A	2 Ends .		7½	6¼	¾
B	2 Rails .	1	6½	2¼	½
C	1 Cross-piece		6	2¼	½
D	1 Rail .	1	6½	3¼	½
E	2 Pieces .	1	6½	1¾	½

Sizes are for 18-in. rack.

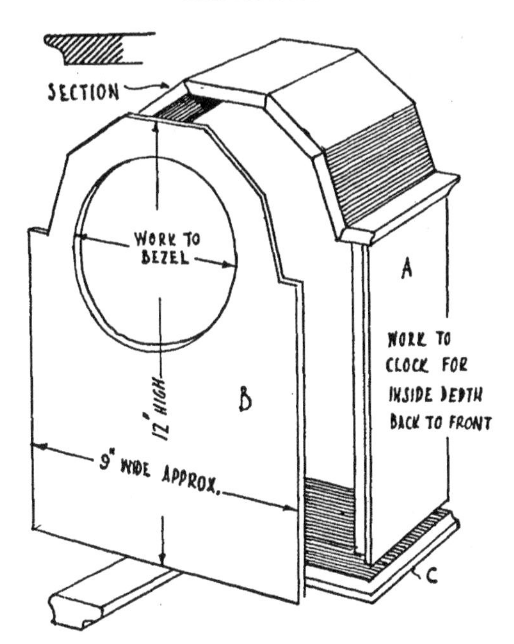

FIG. 4. MAIN SIZES AND CONSTRUCTION OF CLOCKCASE.

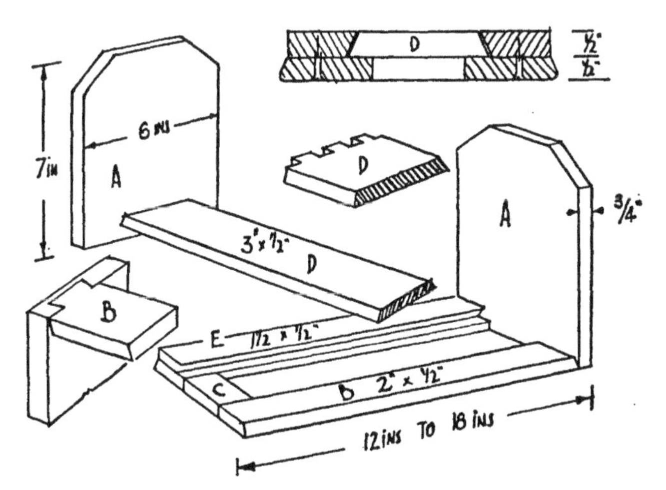

FIG. 5. ADJUSTABLE BOOK RACK AND ITS SIZES

Lamp stand (Fig. 6). This is a novelty in having an ash-tray to the base. The tray is removed by turning button feet underneath. The flex can be carried down behind one of the struts and through the base. Alternatively, the ash-tray can be omitted, the base cut in a circular solid block, and the column taken down to the base, struts being added as a decorative feature afterwards. Prepare a half-template of the shape, reversing about a centre line to mark the

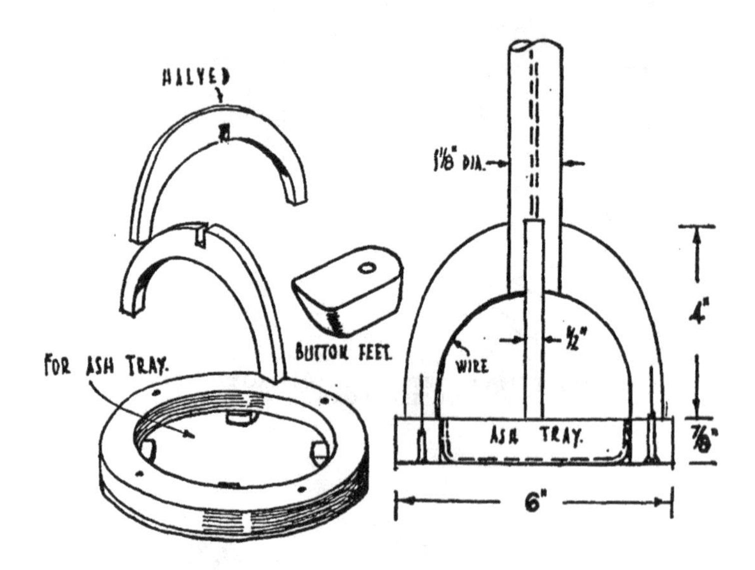

FIG. 6. METHOD OF MAKING LAMP STAND.

whole. Cut out with the bow-saw and clean up with spokeshave. It will be found easier if the marking out and cutting of the halved joint is done before the shapes are cut. Only hardwood should be used for this.

CUTTING LIST

	Long in.	Wide in.	Thick in.
1 Base . .	6½	6¼	⅞
2 Struts . .	6	4¼	½
1 Column .	7	1¼	1⅛
4 Feet . .	1¾	1⅛	⅛

CHILD'S MEAL TRAY

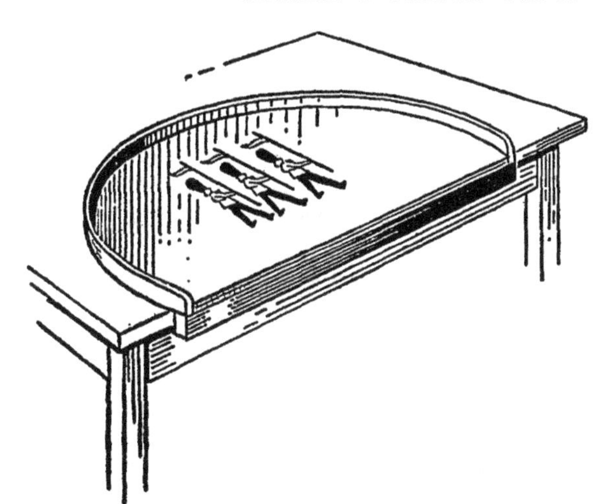

FIG. 1. A REALLY PRACTICAL IDEA FOR THE YOUNGSTER.

The great advantage of this is that no damage is done when the inevitable accident occurs at the table. Cups belonging to others are out of reach, and little harm is done if his own is overturned. The under-lipping at the front edge prevents the whole tray from being pushed forward over the table.

THREE parts only are required: (A) Tray bottom, 18 in. by 10 in., of $\frac{1}{4}$-in. plywood; (B) Rim: a strip of $\frac{1}{8}$-in. ply, 1 in. wide by 33–34 in. long; (C) Lipping, $18\frac{1}{2}$ in. by $\frac{7}{8}$ in. by $\frac{1}{2}$ in.

The tray bottom is shaped as in the diagram, and is cut with bow-saw or fret-saw. The thin plywood rim (B) is easily bent to the curve. It is glued on and pinned. When fixing, allow a little over-hang at each end. Pins may be driven in every 3 in. The rounding over of the ends may be done after the glue is set. Glasspaper the top edge to a smooth, rounded finish.

Lipping (C) is glued on and recess-screwed from below. Alternatively, it may be pinned from above. The finish may be by painting (white), enamelling or lacquering. A nursery-rhyme transfer gives an attractive touch, and serves to engage the child's attention.

It will be seen that the shape of tray bottom (A) provides for the maximum space. At the same time, the rounding of the outer corners minimizes interference with other items on the table.

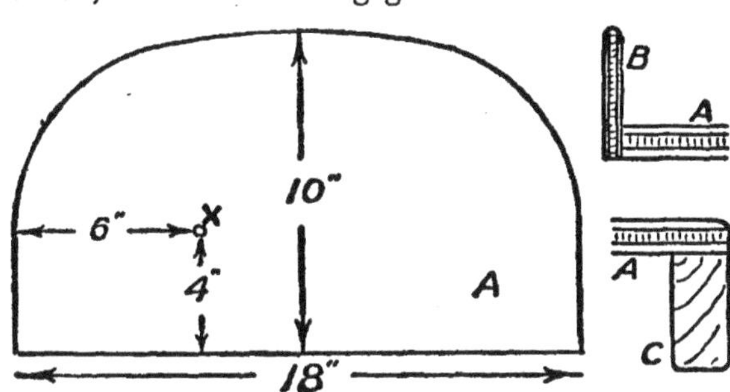

FIG. 2. SHAPE AND SIZES, AND SECTIONS AT EDGES

COMBINED READING LAMP AND BOOK ENDS

CUT out all the pieces and finish to shape, remembering that only one end is cut out on top to receive the lamp-holder block. The bottoms are secured by lap-dovetailing up into the ends. The shaped end brackets are fixed by housing $\frac{1}{4}$ in. deep into the bottoms and $\frac{3}{16}$ in. into the ends, as shown in Figs. 2 and 3. It is inadvisable to go deeper with the housing in the case of the end for fear of fouling the hole that is ultimately bored to take the electric light flex.

FIG. 1. USEFUL ITEM SERVING A DOUBLE PURPOSE.
If the wood is not heavy enough to give stability you can always add a metal plate beneath each end to extend beneath the first few books.

After assembling these pieces the lamp-holder block is fitted by halving as shown. Lastly, the small end piece between the top of the shaped bracket and the bottom of the holder block is fixed. In the case of the other end, this end piece reaches to the top of the end where it is rounded off, as in Fig. 2.

Returning to the lamp-holder end, a $\frac{1}{4}$-in. diameter hole is bored down to take the flex and another to meet it from the back edge of the book end, this reasonably near the bottom. The whole is finished off with a batten-type lamp-holder, which is screwed to the block with small screws.

READING LAMP AND BOOK ENDS

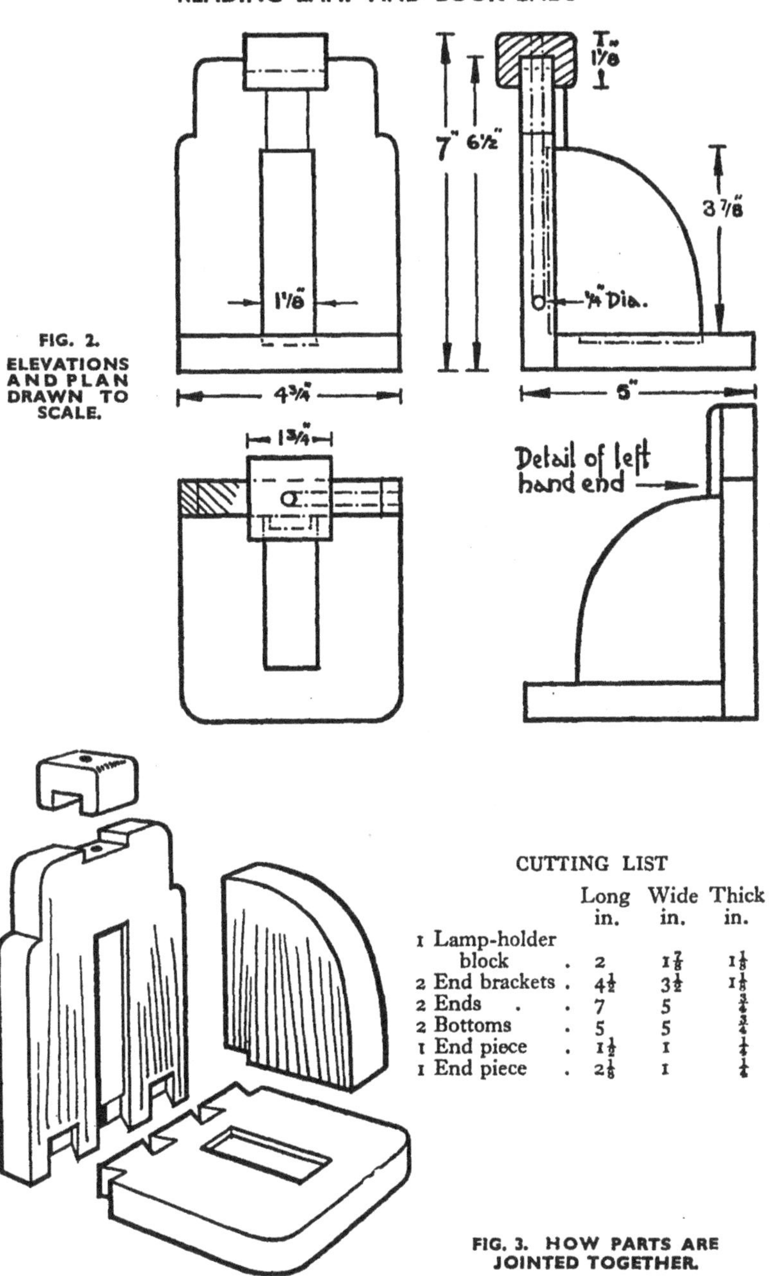

FIG. 2. ELEVATIONS AND PLAN DRAWN TO SCALE.

FIG. 3. HOW PARTS ARE JOINTED TOGETHER.

CUTTING LIST

	Long in.	Wide in.	Thick in.
1 Lamp-holder block	2	1⅞	1⅛
2 End brackets	4½	3½	1⅛
2 Ends	7	5	¾
2 Bottoms	5	5	¾
1 End piece	1½	1	¼
1 End piece	2⅛	1	¼

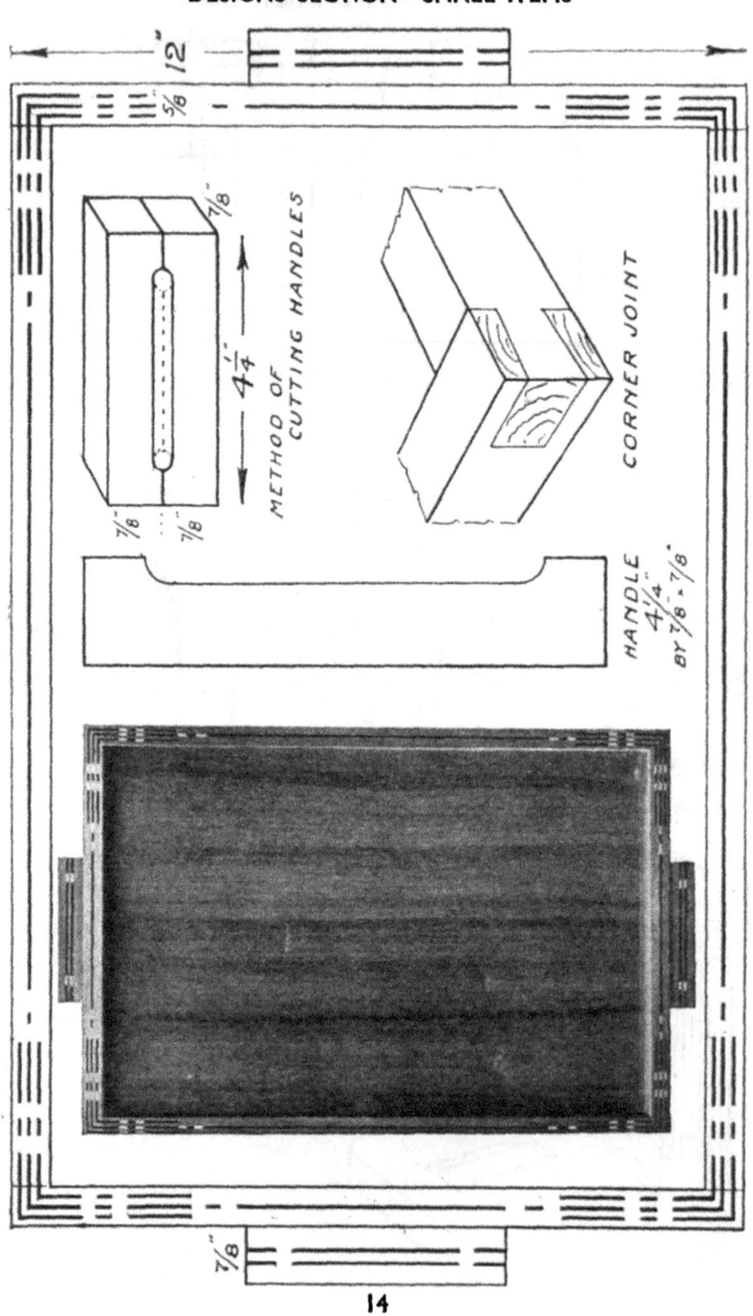
12"
5/8"
7/8"
METHOD OF
CUTTING HANDLES
4¼"
CORNER JOINT
HANDLE
4¼"
BY 7/8" × 7/8"
7/8"

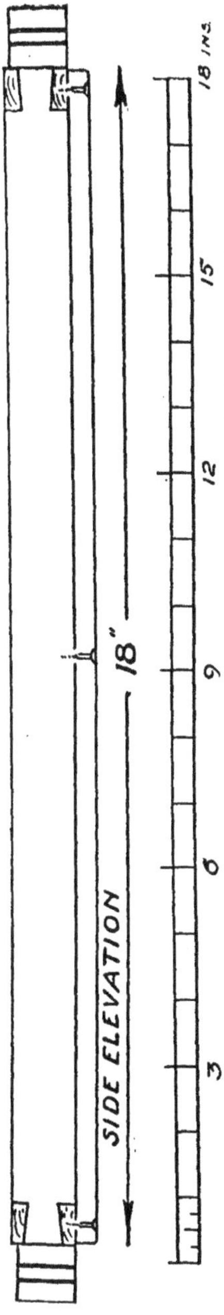

THE TRAY LOOKS EXTREMELY WELL IN WALNUT WITH EBONY AND BOX INLAYS.

TEA TRAY

THERE is an original touch about this tray which makes a pleasant change from the common pattern with moulded edging and metal handles. It has a plain square edging dovetailed together at the corners, with an enrichment of inlay strings at the top, and wooden handles which do not rise above the level of the top. Apart from its making an attractive tray, it is an excellent general exercise, including as it does rub-jointing, dovetailing, string inlaying, slot screwing, as well as general planing and cleaning up.

The stuff for the edging is 1 in. by $\frac{5}{8}$ in. in section, and after squaring up and cutting to the over-all length the ends are gauged for the dovetails, the gauge of course being set to the thickness of the wood ($\frac{5}{8}$ in.). After cutting the joints and gluing up, the corners are levelled, special care being taken to avoid splintering out the wood. To work the inlay grooves a scratch is used, the cutter being filed to make a hand-tight fit for the string. The corners must be marked out so that the scratch does not overrun. A small, thin chisel is handy for cutting in the corners, especially where the grooves run across the grain. A good plan is to use a cutting gauge at these parts before the scratch is used. Lines squared across mark the lengths of the short alternate inlays of ebony and boxwood. After cutting off to length they are glued and rubbed in with the pene of a hammer. Allow as long as possible for the glue to harden so that as the glue dries out it does not pull the inlay below the surface.

The panel can if necessary be rub-jointed to obtain the width. It stands in a little all round and is screwed on. The handles are made from a single block, as shown, and are slot screwed on.

FRUIT TROUGHS

CONSTRUCTION is much the same in all three designs. The bottom is dovetailed to the ends, and the last named are grooved to hold the transparent front and back. If glass is used for the latter the exposed top edge and corners should be rounded to avoid injury. The only alternative is to cover the edge with passe partout or some form of plastic binding to protect it. In the event of *Perspex* being used the edges are easily rounded and polished.

Design A.—Practically any ½-in. hardwood can be used. Mark out the ends from Fig. 2, plotting out the shape map fashion. The main curve can be struck with compasses. As the glass is ¼ in. thick two grooves ¼ in. wide are needed parallel with the sloping sides. They are ¼ in. from the edge and are taken right through. Cut out the bottom 5¼ in. wide, this allowing for the sloping edges. The last named are planed after the whole has been assembled. Lap-dovetails are used and those at the ends should be as close as possible to the corners so that the glass grooves run down into the sockets and so are concealed.

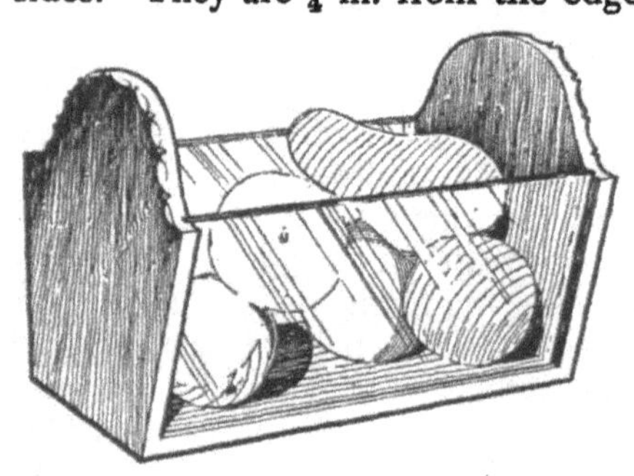

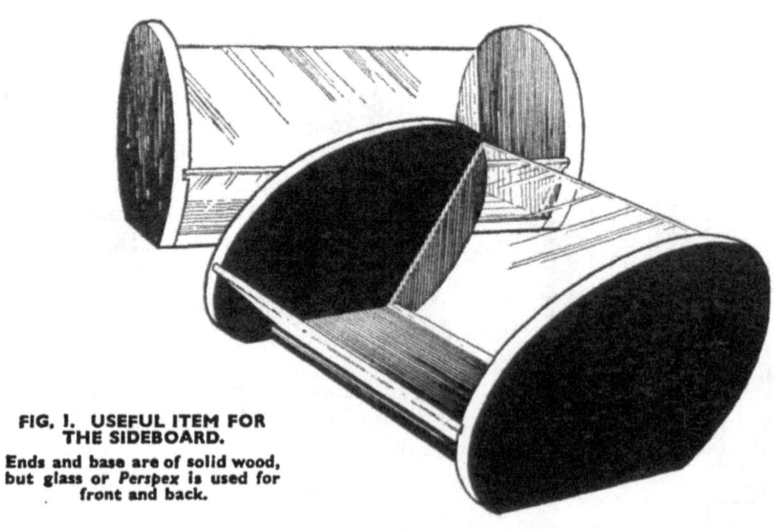

FIG. 1. USEFUL ITEM FOR THE SIDEBOARD.

Ends and base are of solid wood, but glass or *Perspex* is used for front and back.

The joints being cut, the decoration around the curve can be worked with half-round and three-cornered files. Test for squareness when assembling and finally plane the edges of the bottom to align with the ends.

Design B.—The shape here is marked with compasses, leaving a straight portion at the bottom (Fig. 3). The latter is lap-dovetailed in as before and the end dovetails should be at the extreme ends so that the grooves run into the sockets. The joints being cut, the glass grooves can be marked. If the points at which they emerge are pencilled in along the bottom and around the shape it is only a matter of joining the marks with a straight-edge. Both ends can be put together and the edge marks drawn across both. Saw down the sides of the grooves and chisel away the waste. If possible finish off with a router.

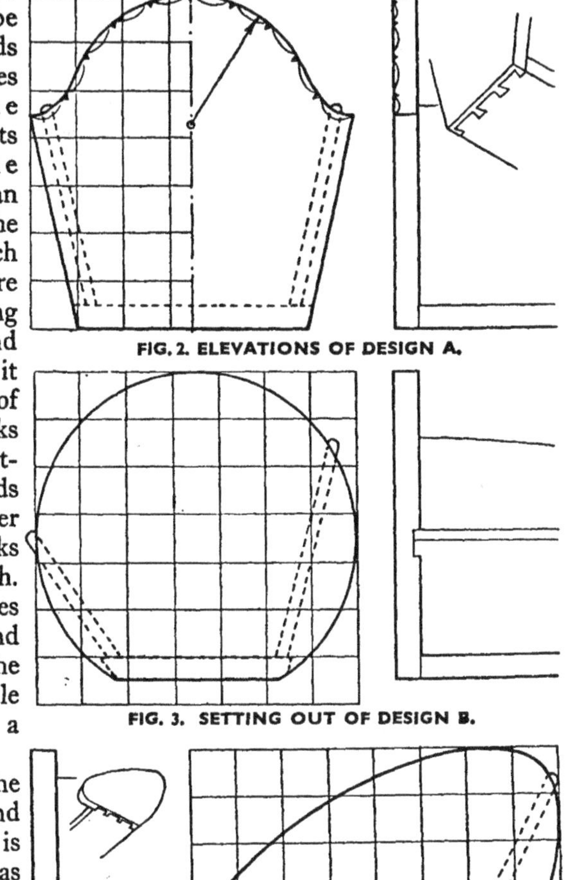

FIG. 2. ELEVATIONS OF DESIGN A.

FIG. 3. SETTING OUT OF DESIGN B.

FIG. 4. HOW DESIGN C IS MARKED OUT.
Length in all cases can be from 12 to 15 in. Squares represent 1 in. each.

Design C.—The setting out and construction is much the same as in the other examples, but the bottom can be in $\frac{3}{8}$-in. wood rather than $\frac{1}{2}$-in. Lap-dovetail the corners as shown in Fig. 4.

COMBINED CIGARETTE BOX AND LIGHTER

THERE is a touch of novelty about this that will appeal to many. A utility lighter is recessed into a block specially provided at one end. Practically any hardwood could be used and it could be veneered if desired. A piece of black plastic could be used for the lid if preferred.

The sides are rebated at one end only to take the thinner of the two ends, as will be seen from the plan in Fig. 2, whilst at the other end of the box the thicker end is rebated to take the sides. This end also has a rebate worked along the top inside edge to support the top itself.

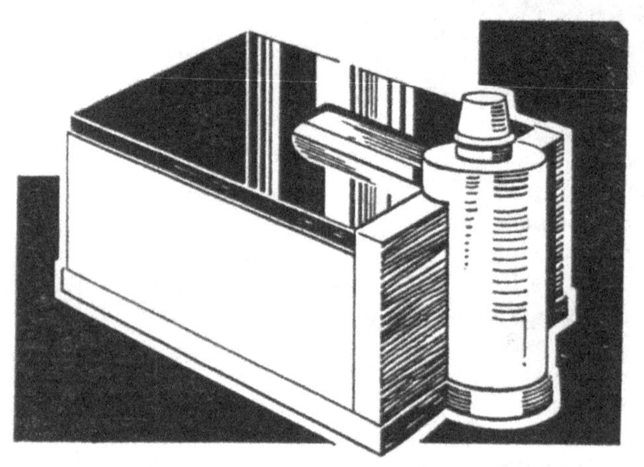

FIG. 1. ATTRACTIVE ITEM WITH A NOVEL TOUCH.
Small oddments of wood can be used to make a small box of this kind. If desired the top can be a plastic material. Over-all length is 6½ in., width 3⅝ in., and height 3⅜ in.

The top is rebated on all four edges to fit over the sides and ends (Fig. 2). The lighter holder is turned or planed to shape (1½ in. diameter), bored out to take the lighter, and finally cut out to fit over the thicker end as shown. It would be advisable to bore the hole first so that the maximum wood is left. If the shape is being planed from a square block, cramps can be applied in both directions to minimize any splitting risk. The holder is fixed in position by gluing and screwing from the inside of the box end. The lighter holder bottom is cut to shape and slightly notched into the end of the box bottom, and the whole secured to the box by gluing and either pinning or screwing. The box itself is put together with glue and fine pins, the handle being secured to the top in a like manner, though of course after the top has been polished.

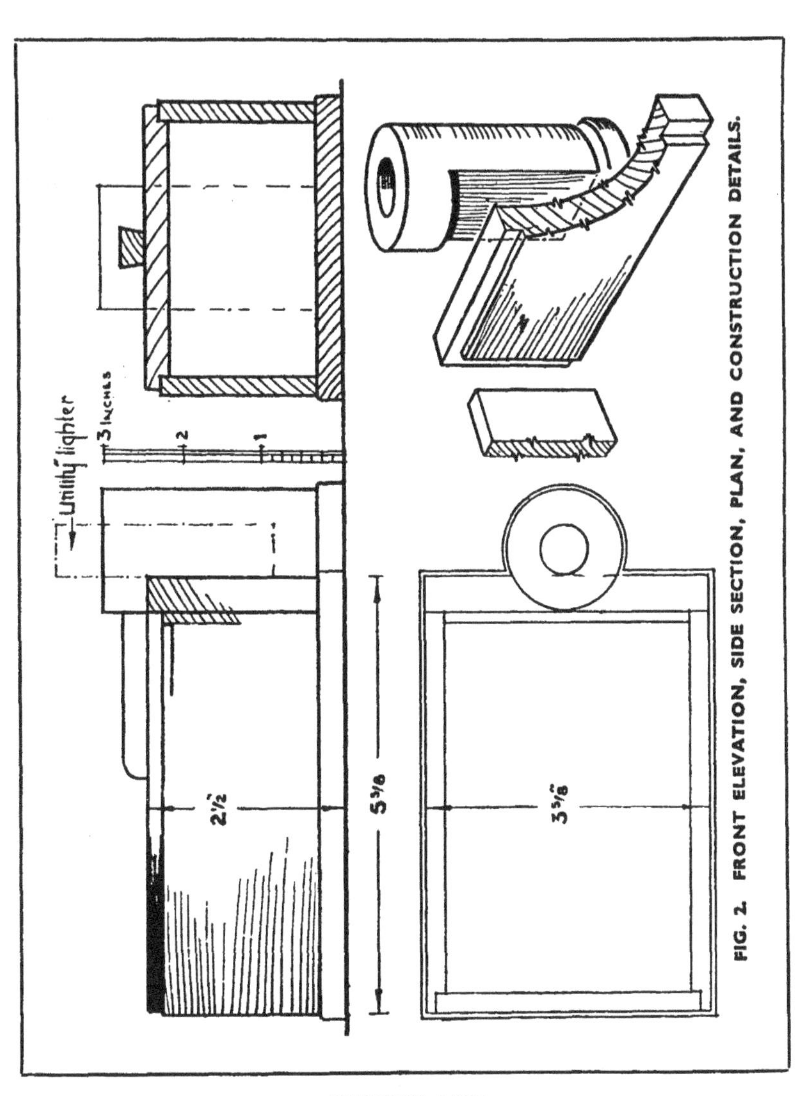

FIG. 2. FRONT ELEVATION, SIDE SECTION, PLAN, AND CONSTRUCTION DETAILS.

CUTTING LIST

	Long in.	Wide in.	Thick in.		Long in.	Wide in.	Thick in.
1 Lighter holder	3	1⅝	1½	1 Top . .	5	3⅝	$\frac{5}{16}$
1 End . .	3⅞	2¼	$\frac{9}{16}$	1 Handle . .	2¼	⅝	$\frac{5}{16}$
1 Bottom . .	5¾	4	$\frac{5}{16}$	2 Sides . .	5⅛	2⅛	¼
1 Lighter holder bottom .	1⅞	1⅜	$\frac{5}{16}$	1 End . .	4	2⅛	¼

All the above sizes are net.

EASY-TO-DUST TRAY

IT will be seen from Fig. 2 that the main tray bottom is rebated around the edges and has an edging hollow-moulded at the inside, thus eliminating awkward square angles. To make the corners easy to dust the ends of the moulding are cut away at an angle at the top level with the tray bottom, and the hollow continued towards the points. In this way there are no square corners anywhere, and dust can be swept right out of the tray at any of the corners.

Tray bottom. For this use ½-in. or ⅝-in. wood. Plywood or laminboard can be used, but should be lipped to give a neat finish. If solid wood is used it is essential that it is quite dry. Mark out the rebate with the gauge, and cut with the rebate plane, working across the grain first.

Moulding. The exact section of the moulding is not greatly important providing that the square at the bottom of the hollow equals the rebate depth of the bottom. A round moulding plane can be used, the bulk of the waste being removed with the ordinary bench plane first. Mitre the corners, making sure that the bottom makes a good joint. The top does not matter so much as it is cut away.

Mark where the parts go, then cut back the top of the corners as at B, Fig. 2. Saw across the grain on the mitre block, and ease away the waste with the chisel to finish just short of the bottom square. To continue the hollow up to the point a gouge of the same curvature as the hollow should be used. Ease away the wood so that a graceful curve is formed, the gouge finishing so that it cuts across the grain at right angles. Cut away the wood above with a chisel so that the flat portion is continued round, and finish off the extreme corner with the file. Follow with glasspaper.

FIG. 1. USEFUL TRAY FOR AFTERNOON TEA AND FOR GENERAL HOUSEHOLD PURPOSES, 20 in. by 13 in.

The hollow moulding makes the bottom in a continuous sweep with the edges. As the corners are cut away all dust and any liquid spilt on the tray can be cleared off easily. A painted or varnished finish is recommended.

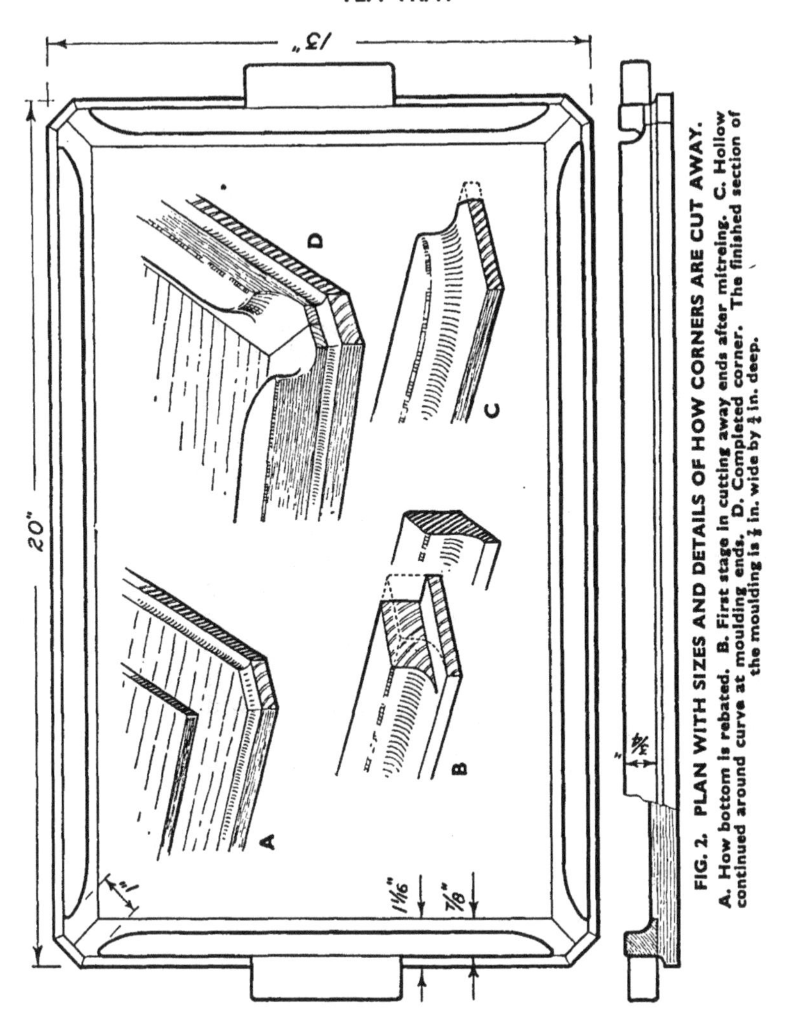

FIG. 2. PLAN WITH SIZES AND DETAILS OF HOW CORNERS ARE CUT AWAY.

A. How bottom is rebated. B. First stage in cutting away ends after mitreing. C. Hollow continued around curve at moulding ends. D. Completed corner. The finished section of the moulding is ⅞ in. wide by ¾ in. deep.

Before screwing on the mouldings, place the last named in position and mark their extent on the rebate. This will enable the small hollow member to be worked round the bottom level with the moulding. The corners can also be taken off, a corresponding projection from the rebate being allowed so that the small hollow can be continued round.

Handles can be blocks hollowed beneath and fixed with slot screws. Alternatively pieces of plastic can be used. Lacquer, paint, or enamel are the best finishes. Choose a heat-proof variety.

STATIONERY CABINET

THIS stationery cabinet is ornamental and useful for odds and ends of letters, bills, etc. It is constructed throughout in oak and decorated with veneer and black lines.

The top is lap-dovetailed to the ends and the bottom housed in, the housing being stopped at the front edge. The ends should be lined before dovetailing. The top and bottom lining may be left till the job is assembled or can be glued on beforehand. It is recommended that the job be assembled dry, the front levelled off and the job taken to pieces before the lines are put in.

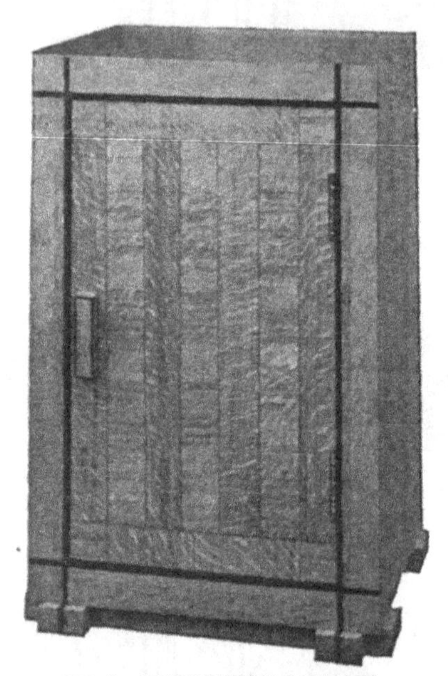

FIG. 1. STATIONERY CABINET.
(Size, 13½ in. by 9 in.)

The door is made of laminated wood preferably, but sound solid wood can be used. It is veneered on both sides, the front being patterned as illustrated. The door is hung with two 1½-in. brass butts and fitted with a ⅜-in. ball catch. The handle is slot-screwed and decorated with a black line as shown.

The ends and top are rebated to take a ⅜-in. back, which is screwed into position. Plywood may be used for the back, but it should be remembered that a cabinet of this kind is generally viewed from all directions and

CUTTING LIST

	Long ft.	Long in.	Wide in.	Thick in.
2 Ends . .	1	0½	7	⅝
1 Top . .		8	7	⅝
1 Bottom . .		8	6⅝	⅝
2 Linings . .	1	0½	1½	⅜
1 Lining . .		6½	1½	⅜
1 Lining . .		6½	1½	⅝
1 Door . .		11	6½	⅝
		(Laminated Wood)		

	Long ft.	Long in.	Wide in.	Thick in.
1 Handle . .		1¾	½	⅝
1 Back . .	1	0½	8	⅜
2 Plinths . .		9	1½	⅝
2 Plinths . .		7½	1½	⅝
Black line . .	4	6	⅛	⅛
” . .		6	1/16	1/16
Oak veneer .	1	0	12	
Interior plywood	1½ square feet			

Thinner stuff may, if preferred, be used for ends, top and back, sizes being adjusted accordingly.

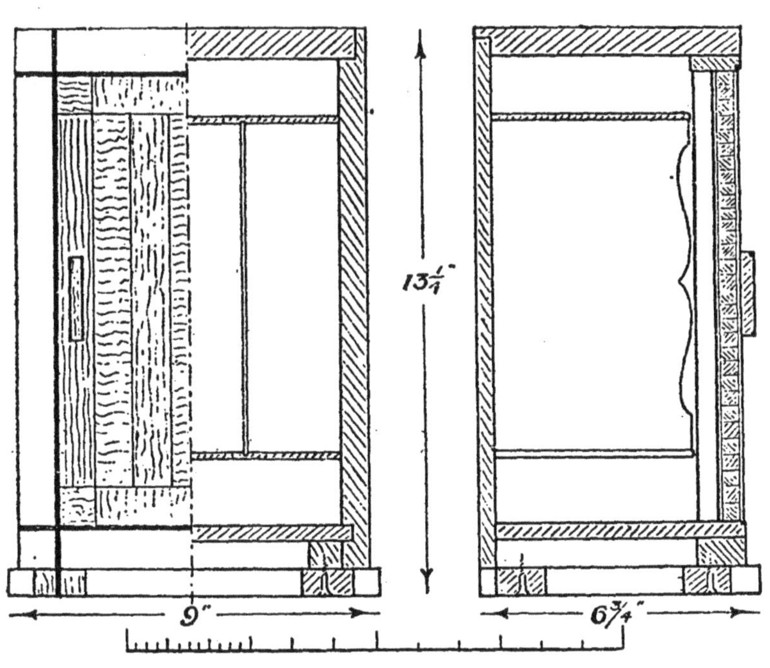

FIG. 2. FRONT ELEVATION.
(Left hand, closed ; Right hand, open.)

FIG. 3. SECTIONAL END VIEW
Showing Stationery Partition.

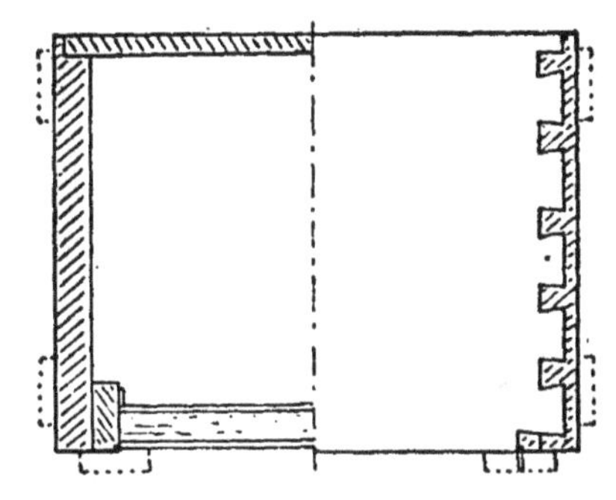

FIG. 4. PLAN OF CABINET.
(Left hand, Sectional Plan ; Right hand, Top dovetailed to end.)

should look well from the rear. The interior partitions may be made from ¼-in. oak, but plywood could easily be substituted. A natural finish is recommended for this cabinet, which could function equally well as a smoker's cabinet if provision is made for pipes and tobacco instead of stationery partitions.

ELECTRIC TABLE LAMP

THE design of this lamp is based chiefly on the octagon, and once this point is realized the marking out is greatly simplified —in fact, it becomes almost obvious. First, however, a word on the construction.

Construction. The upright is joined to the base with a double mortise and tenon joint. This is not only stronger than a single tenon, but has the advantage that the centre hole to take the flex is

FIG. I. LAMP WITH FACETED SIDES.
The faceting suggests work often found on a precious stone. The essential feature is accurate marking out, the actual cutting being simple.

between the tenons, which are thus not weakened. It is marked out with the gauge, the only point to note being that the tenons should be set well in, because all the facets are finished with the plane, and, since the bottom ones slope, the plane must clear the tenons. In practice the shoulders are cut, but not the sides of the tenons, the latter being done after the faceting.

Marking out. Plane the wood to finish 2$\frac{7}{8}$ in. square in section, if necessary jointing two or more pieces together to obtain the thickness. Square round the over-all length (including the tenon), also the shoulder, and cut off to size. It is advisable to trim the top end with the plane. The entire marking out can be done now at the ends if desired, but it involves rather a complication of lines, and it is clearer if the relevant lines for each particular process only are put in before the various angles and facets are planed away, and before the centre hole is bored.

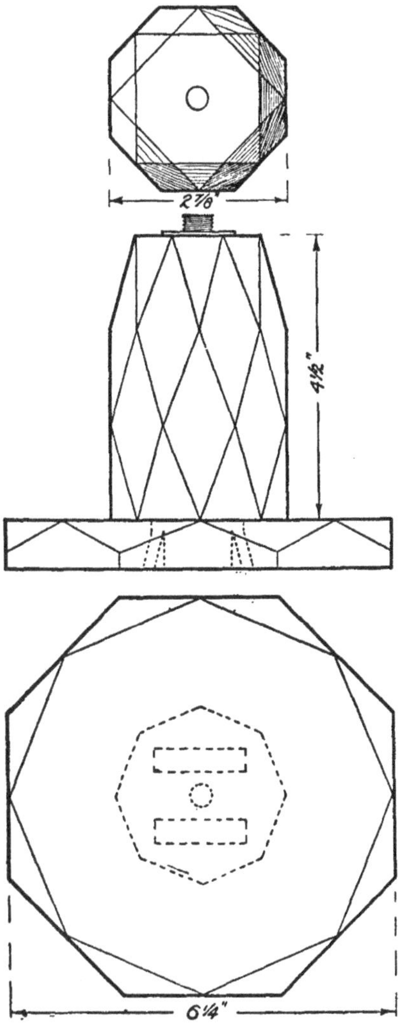

With the gauge put in the centre lines and the two diagonals, and from the centre scribe in a circle with dividers. Where the circle cuts the diagonals draw in lines at 45 degs. These mark the sides of the octagon, as shown in Fig. 3. Parallel lines can be drawn along the sides as a guide when planing, and lines dividing the length into three should be squared round as shown.

Bore the hole ($\frac{3}{8}$ in.) half-way from each end, and mark the tenons with the gauge. The shoulders can then be sawn all round, after which the corners can be planed away to form the octagon. Take care to stop exactly on the line. The work should now appear as in Fig. 4 except for the additional marking-out lines at the end. These now follow.

FIG. 2. ELEVATION AND BASE PLAN.

First facets. As the first facets are at an angle midway

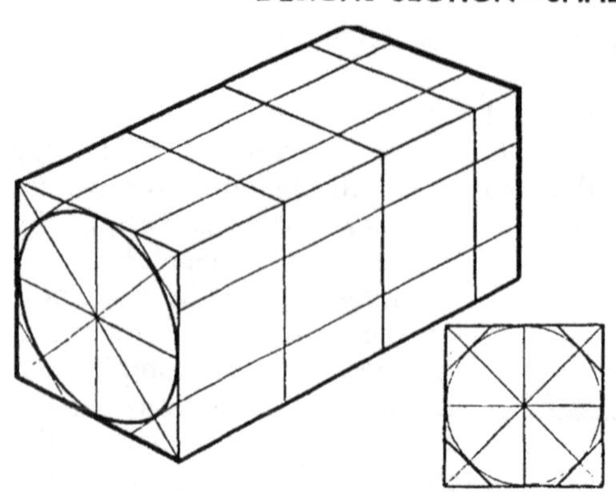

FIG. 3. HOW SQUARE IS MARKED OUT.

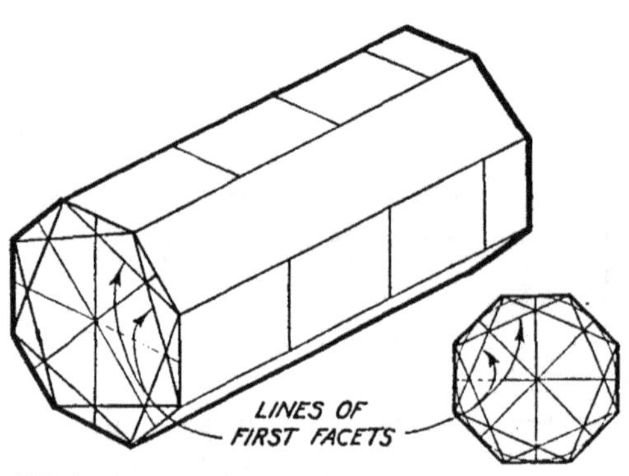

FIG. 4. OCTAGON WORKED AND ENDS MARKED.

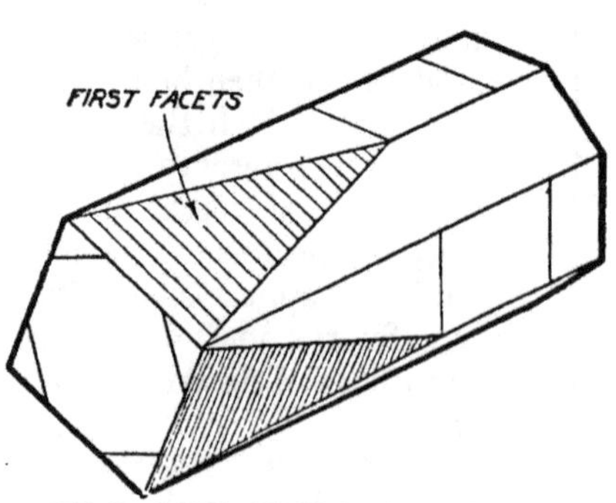

FIG. 5. FOUR OF FIRST FACETS CUT.

between the slope of the sides of the octagon, it is clear that lines joining alternate corners will be at the correct slope. These are drawn in as in Fig. 4 and the waste wood cut away at an angle, first with the chisel, then with the plane, as in Fig. 5. The slope runs back to the second cross pencil line. There is no need to mark, however, because it is merely a case of stopping when the facet reaches the pencil line and the mark at the end. However, lines can be drawn if preferred.

It will be found convenient to deal with opposite faces first, as shown in Fig. 5. In this way the section at the end becomes that of a square. The remaining four corners follow until the work has the appearance shown in Fig. 6. The easiest method is to pare away the wood down to about $\frac{1}{16}$ in. or less of the line, then complete with the plane. A small block plane will prove very handy.

Second facets. These are cut similarly to the first facets, but, being at an angle midway between the last named, they necessarily revert to the original slope of the octagon. The end view in Fig. 6 shows this; also how they reach to the middle of each first facet.

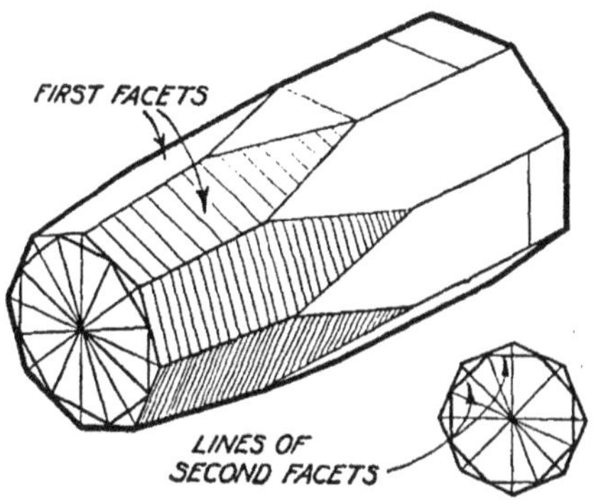

FIG. 6. ALL EIGHT OF FIRST FACETS CUT.

Fig. 6 also shows how they begin at the first squared pencil line. Incidentally this line will have been obliterated by previous faceting and will have to be put in afresh. Mark in the lines and cut with chisel and plane as before, completing opposite facets first.

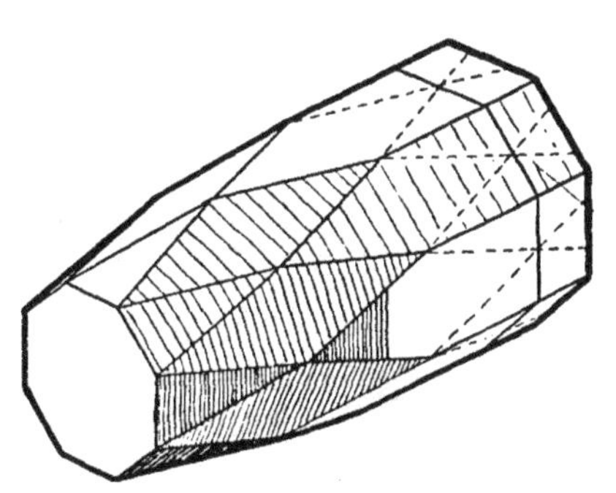
FIG. 7. SECOND FACETS CUT.

Bottom facets. These are similar to the first facets so far as the angle is concerned, but they do not cut in so deeply. The dotted lines in Fig. 7 show how they reach to a point midway across each facet on the shoulder line. Incidentally a convenient method of gripping the work whilst faceting is shown in Fig. 8.

The tenons can now be cut. If the wood has straight grain a chisel can be used to split down up to the gauge line. Otherwise the saw can be used, the waste between the tenons being chopped.

Base. This calls for little explanation. The wood is prepared first as a square, the mortise marked out (*Continued on page* 31).

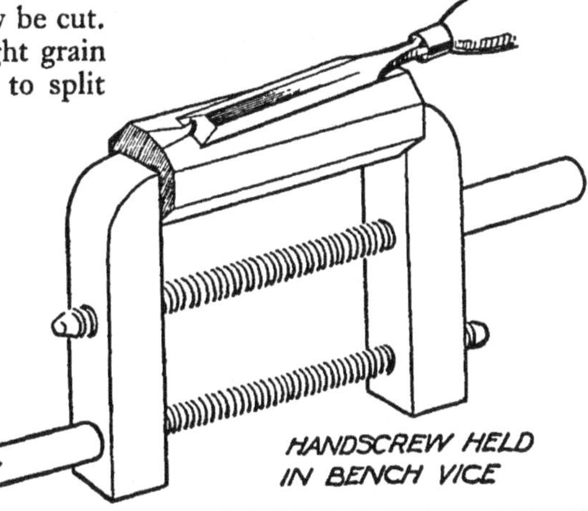

FIG. 8. HOW WOOD CAN BE GRIPPED WHILST WORKING.

2. FURNITURE, ETC.

ADJUSTABLE FIRESIDE CHAIR

THIS type of chair is very comfortable and hard wearing. Being adjustable one can relax in any position, and the loose-cushioned seat and back covers can be cleaned or renewed when they become dirty or worn. The arms may be padded if desired. Hardwood only should be used, such as birch, beech, or similar wood.

FIG. I. CHAIR COMBINING COMFORT WITH SIMPLICITY.
No shaped work is involved in this type of chair, the whole thing being made from plain straight squares and rails. No upholstery is required beyond the loose cushions.

Main framework. The front legs (A) are connected by the seat rail (C) and the stretcher rail (N). Both these rails are tenoned to the legs as shown in Fig. 3. All tenons should be stout and tight fitting and pegged after assembly. The back legs (B) are shorter than the front ones to allow the arms to slope down towards the back, and are also connected by a rail (D) and a stretcher rail (N), similarly to the front. Before gluing up the front and back frames,

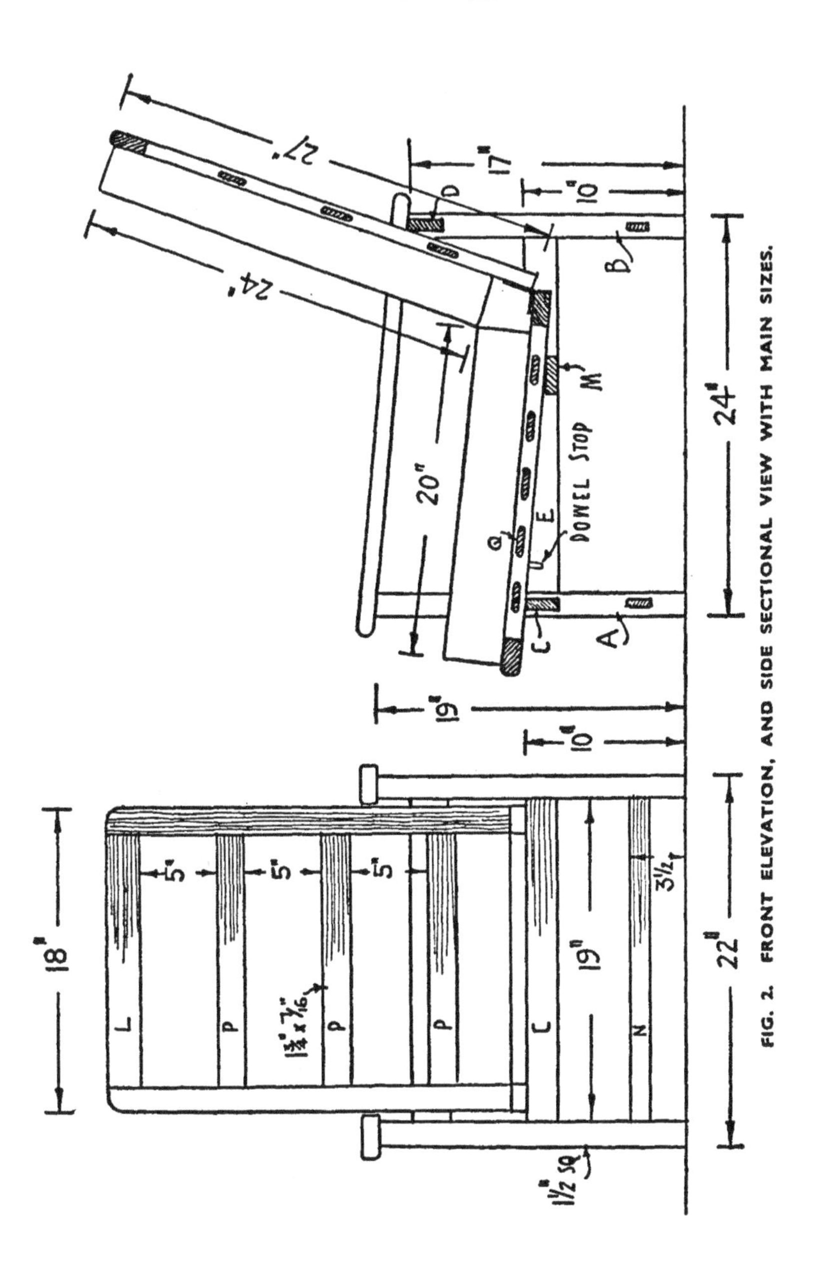

FIG. 2. FRONT ELEVATION, AND SIDE SECTIONAL VIEW WITH MAIN SIZES.

groove the legs from above the top of the seat rails for the plywood panels at the sides. Work to the plywood thickness for the grooves, which should be central in the legs.

The side rails (E), Fig. 3, and the underside of the arms are also grooved for these panels. The side rails (E) may be dowelled or tenoned to the legs. If tenoned mitre the tenons of the front and

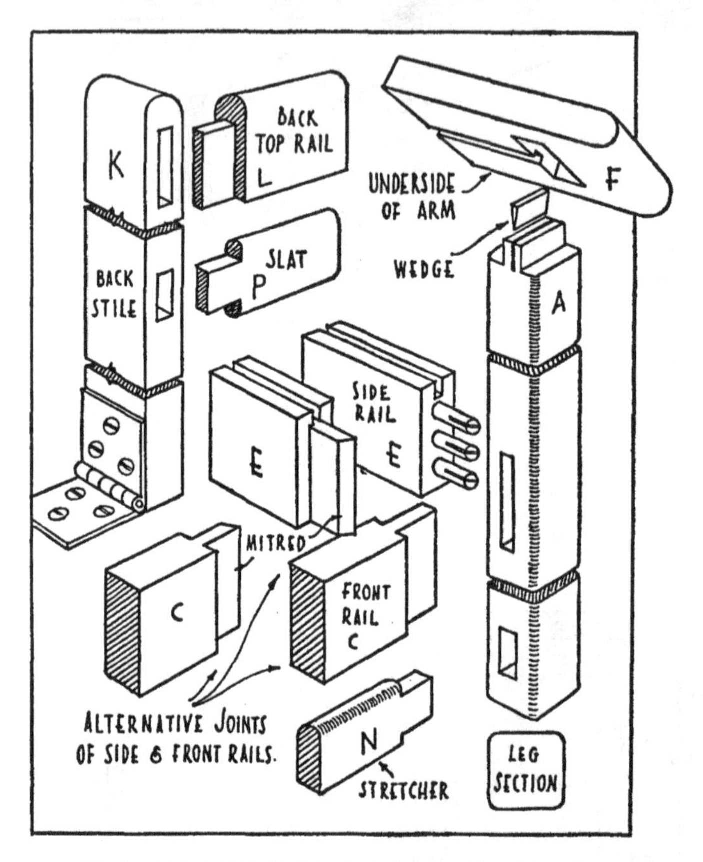

FIG. 3. DETAILED DRAWING OF PARTS AND JOINTS.

side rails in the mortises as indicated in Fig. 3. All shoulders are square and easy to cut. As the chair is usually lifted by the arms they have a tendency to pull away from the front legs unless the joints are very sound. Hence it is advisable either to wedge or peg the tenons that enter them.

It is suggested in Fig. 3 that the mortises gradually increase in size as they enter the arms so that the tenons may be saw kerfed and wedged, thereby ensuring a tight fit. Alternatively the leg tenons could be taken through the arms and be wedged from above. This would be concealed if the arms were padded. Dowelling is not recommended, as the dowels are too short to hold properly. At the rear the arms are screwed, sunk and pelleted.

The cross rail (M), Fig. 2, that supports the seat at the rear must be carefully notched into the side rails (E) and *firmly* screwed, the bottom of the cross rail to be flush with the bottom edge of the side rail. The front corners could be braced.

Seat and back. The seat and back frames are simple to make, the rails (J and L) and the slats (P and Q) being tenoned to the side pieces, the former being shouldered and the latter bare-faced. The rounded edges are cut back, Fig. 3.

The corners of all legs should be well rounded before assembly and all the edges of the rails neatly softened off. It is advisable to fix dowel stops to engage the front rail, thereby preventing the seat being drawn too far forward; otherwise the weight of the sitter keeps the chair in its required position. Use stout back-flap hinges about 4 in. by 1¾ in. when opened out. The cushions are stitched at the edges where they meet and the back cushion could be tied to the top slat with tapes sewn to the back of the cushion.

CUTTING LIST

		Long		Wide	Thick
		ft.	in.	ft.	in.
A	2 Front legs	1	7	1½	1½
B	2 Back legs	1	5¼	1½	1½
C	1 Front rail	1	9½	2¼	⅞
D	1 Back rail .	1	9½	2¼	⅞
E	2 Side rails	1	11½	2¼	⅞
F	2 Arms .	2	3	2⅜	⅞
G	1 For braces		7	2	⅞
H	2 Seat rails	1	11	2	⅞
J	2 ,, ,, .	1	4½	2	⅞
K	2 Back Stiles	2	3	2	⅞
L	1 Back rail .	1	4½	2	⅞
M	1 Cross rail	1	9	2¼	¾
N	2 Stretchers	1	9½	1¼	¾
P	3 Back slats	1	4½	1¾	$\frac{7}{16}$
Q	5 Seat slats .	1	4½	1½	$\frac{7}{16}$
R	2 Side panels	1	9¾	9¾	¼

All sizes net. 1¼ in. long tenons allowed for. R in 4 mm. or 6 mm. plywood. E allows for tenoning.

(ELECTRIC TABLE LAMP.—*Continued from page 27*).

and cut, and the corners removed to form the octagonal shape. The facets around the edge are partly chiselled, partly planed. A hole for the flex is bored from one edge, the hole in the upright being continued right through the base to allow for threading through.

LADY'S WORK TABLE

A HEIGHT of 24 in. is convenient for working, but the legs of this table could be left several inches longer and cut off later. If oak or a similar hardwood is obtainable it would be preferable. Good straight hardwood should be used for the legs even if softwood

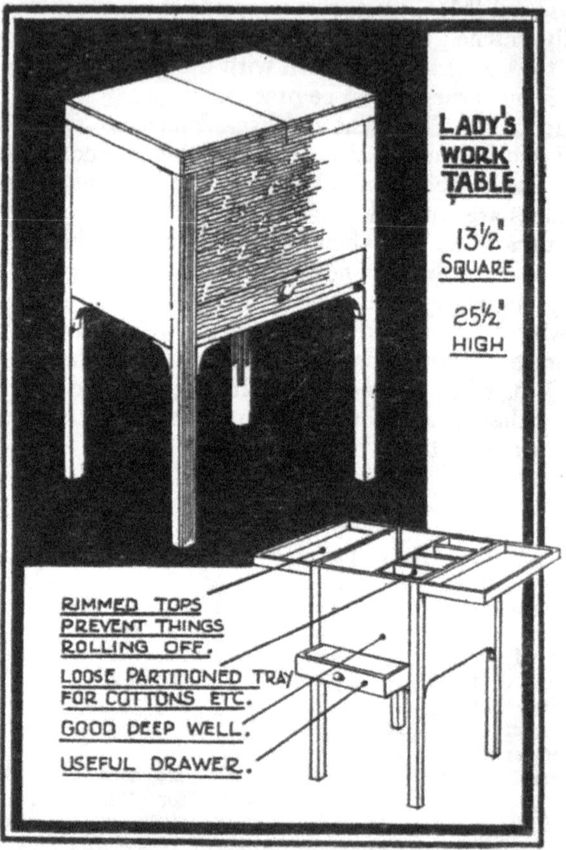

FIG. 1. TABLE WITH EXCELLENT ACCOMMODATION. A workbox is usually anything except convenient, being just a deep well from which everything has to be lifted to reach something at the bottom. Here the sliding tray and the drawer give invaluable extra space, and provide a definite place for items.

is used for the remainder. Oak-faced plywood, 6 mm. thick, would be best for the tops if obtainable; otherwise use ¼ in. thick dry solid wood. Where softwood or different kinds of wood are used an enamelled or lacquered finish is the only possible one.

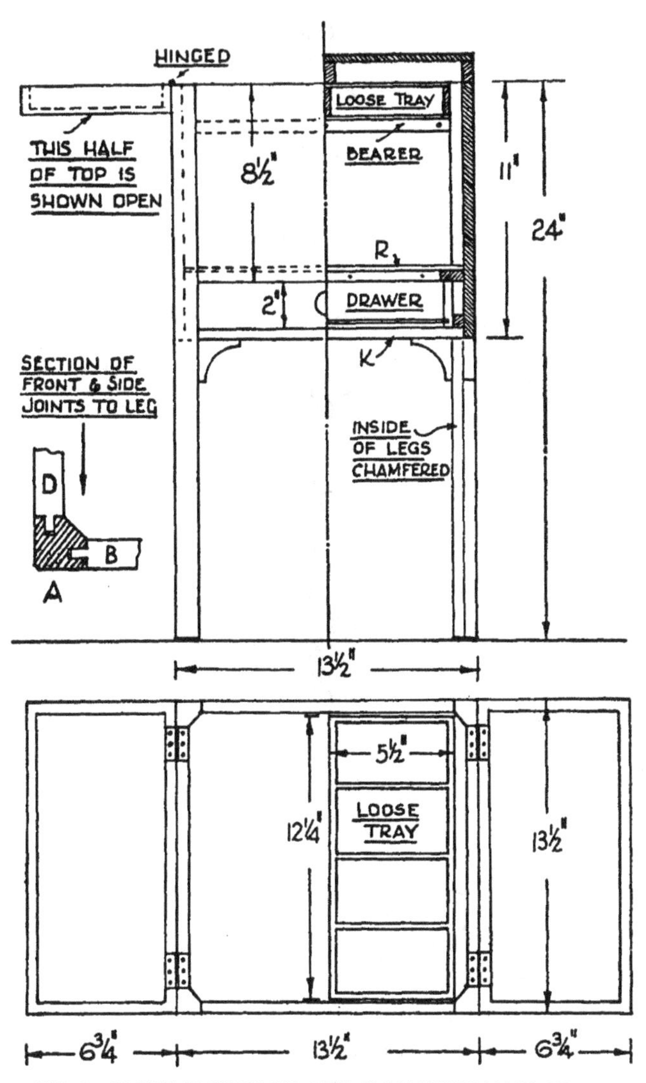

FIG. 2. FRONT ELEVATION AND PLAN WITH MAIN SIZES

Prepare the legs to finish 1⅛ in. square and groove the inner faces to take the tongued front, sides, and back.

Leg joints. It would be neater to stop the grooves about 1 in. from the top of the legs. Section through leg is given in Fig. 2. If grooving is awkward, try $\frac{5}{16}$-in. dowels spaced about 3 in. apart.

The thickness of the sides (say about $\frac{9}{16}$ in. or $\frac{5}{8}$ in.) will determine the amount of chamfering to be done to the inside corners of the legs. This can be stopped below the well bottom or carried right down the leg, Fig. 2.

Assembly. Assemble the sides (D) and legs first, then add front (B) and back (C). The bottom edge of the front should be trued to form a close joint with the drawer front. Behind this front and continued all round are blocks (F and G) screwed to the front, sides, and back to support the well bottom (R). The side blocks are

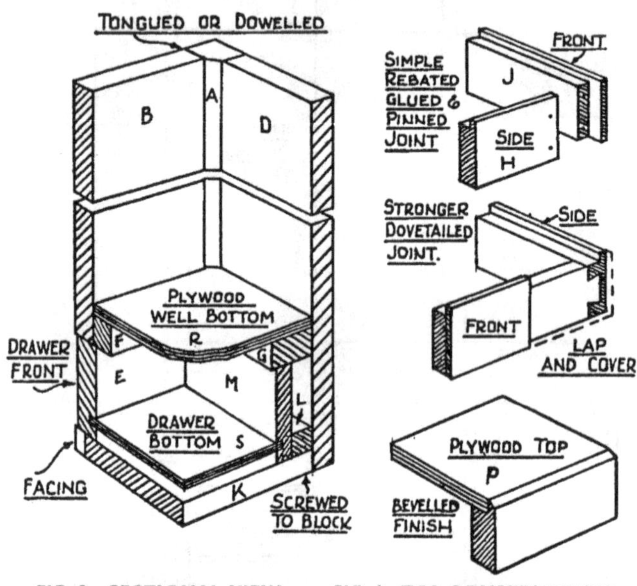

FIG. 3. SECTIONAL VIEW. This shows how the well bottom rests upon blocks F and G. The latter is extra wide to form a kicker for the drawer. Blocks L are guides.

FIG. 4. TOP CONSTRUCTION. Alternative construction is shown here. The best joint for those who have the time is the mitre dovetail.

wider to form kickers for the drawer, Fig. 3. The bottom (K) is a solid board of some inexpensive wood faced along the front edge that is seen with hardwood, Fig. 3. It is screwed to blocks (L) which are in turn screwed to sides and back, the side blocks forming guides for the drawer (Fig. 2, sectional elevation). The small corner brackets are glued and screwed on.

Top. The hinged top in two halves can be made in several ways. Alternative methods are shown in Fig. 4. First, rebate the top edges to receive the plywood (or solid tops), allowing about $\frac{3}{16}$ in. cover and working to the thickness for the depth of rebate. Notch away the fronts and backs and glue and pin the sides to them, or alternatively lap-dovetail the fronts and backs to rebated sides and add a $\frac{3}{16}$-in. thick facing to cover the dovetail, Fig. 4. When making the top frames try to secure a slight fullness in size over and above that of the lower portion to allow for fitting and levelling up with glasspaper.

The plywood (or solid tops) are glued into the rebates and pinned, punched in, and stopped with wood filling. The hinges should be good strong brass butts, $1\frac{1}{2}$ in. or $1\frac{3}{4}$ in., and the screws should be fairly long owing to the leverage.

Instead of grooving in the drawer bottom as Fig. 3, the drawer sides and back could be kept narrower than the front by the bottom thickness, which is glued and pinned underneath.

Tray. The loose tray is about half the size of the well opening. The sides are dovetailed or comb-jointed together, the divisions trenched in and the bottom glued and pinned on. The tray rests upon two bearers screwed to front and back respectively. The tray should fit easily inside.

CUTTING LIST

		Long		Wide	Thick
		ft.	in.	in.	in.
A	4 Legs .	2	0	$1\frac{1}{8}$	$1\frac{1}{8}$
B	1 Front .	1	0	$8\frac{1}{2}$	$\frac{5}{8}$
C	1 Back .	1	0	11	$\frac{5}{8}$
D	2 Sides .	1	0	11	$\frac{5}{8}$
E	1 Drawer front		$11\frac{1}{4}$	2	$\frac{5}{8}$
F	2 Blocks .	1	$0\frac{1}{4}$	$\frac{5}{8}$	$\frac{5}{8}$
G	2 ,, .		11	$1\frac{1}{8}$	$\frac{5}{8}$
H	4 Top frames	1	$1\frac{1}{2}$	$1\frac{1}{2}$	$\frac{5}{8}$
J	4 ,, ,, .		$6\frac{3}{4}$	$1\frac{1}{2}$	$\frac{5}{8}$
K	1 Carcase bottom .	1	$0\frac{1}{4}$	$12\frac{7}{8}$	$\frac{1}{2}$
L	3 Blocks .	1	0	$\frac{5}{8}$	$\frac{1}{2}$
M	2 Drawer sides	1	0	2	$\frac{3}{8}$
	1 Drawer back		$11\frac{1}{4}$	$1\frac{3}{4}$	$\frac{3}{8}$
	2 For tray .	1	$0\frac{1}{4}$	$1\frac{1}{4}$	$\frac{3}{8}$
	2 ,, ,, .		$5\frac{1}{2}$	$1\frac{1}{4}$	$\frac{3}{8}$
	3 ,, ,, .		5	$1\frac{1}{4}$	$\frac{1}{4}$
P	2 Tops .	1	$1\frac{1}{8}$	$13\frac{1}{8}$	$\frac{1}{4}$
R	1 Well bottom	1	$0\frac{1}{4}$	$12\frac{1}{4}$	$\frac{3}{16}$
S	1 Drawer bottom .		$11\frac{1}{4}$	12	$\frac{3}{16}$
T	1 Tray bottom	1	$0\frac{1}{4}$	$5\frac{1}{2}$	$\frac{3}{16}$

All sizes are net. P, R, S, and T in plywood if possible.

COT WITH DROP SIDE

AS cot mattresses are made to fixed sizes which are unalterable, it is essential that the mattress should be procured (or at least the exact measurements over all ascertained) before any timber is cut. The mattress rests on the battens (Q—see Fig. 3), and just a little clearance must be allowed in order to let it slip into position without binding. Different makes of mattress may vary slightly in length and width and allowance for this should be made.

FIG. I. IF FINISHED IN PAINT OR ENAMEL PRACTICALLY ANY WOOD CAN BE USED PROVIDING IT IS SOUND.

Although mattresses are made in stock sizes, it is advisable to obtain it before beginning the woodwork. The design as given is intended for a 4 ft. by 2 ft. mattress.

Construction. The two ends are first completed, splats (D and E) being fitted to rails (B and C) and the rails tenoned to posts (A). Note particularly that the post height from floor to under edge of lower rail must be not less than 13½ in., this to allow for the dropping front. Casters are extra.

The back of cot and the front are next prepared. Both are alike except for three points to note. In width, the rails (F and G) of back correspond with those of ends. Both rails, too, have tenons to enter the posts. The rails (L and M) of drop front have no tenons; the lower rail (L) is only 2 in. wide, and thus the front splats are a little longer than those of the ends and back. As the front is a detached piece it is desirable to carry the lower tenons of the end splats (N) right through the rail (L), also see that the upper tenons entering top rail (M) are as long as possible. The end splats (N) should allow ample clearance for the fall front rod and its fittings (see Fig. 2).

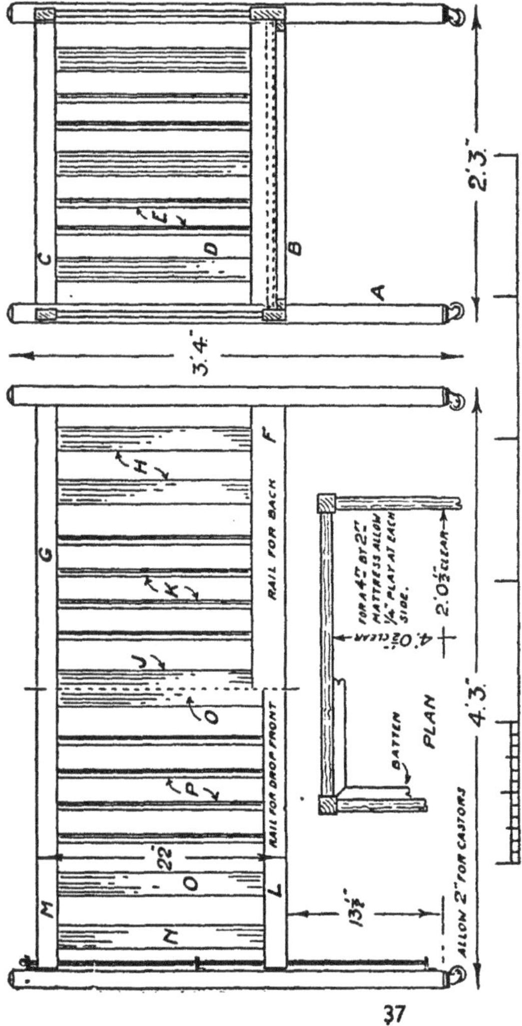

FIG. 2. ELEVATIONS OF SIDE AND END.

Drop front. The rails (L, M) of front are carefully bored for the rod, which is held to the posts by sockets (*a*, *b*, *c*), the two lower sockets acting as stops when the front drops. Complete sets of fittings are normally procurable for the purpose, these including a catch and release.

Cutting List appears on page 38.

(*See Fig.* 3 *on page* 38.)

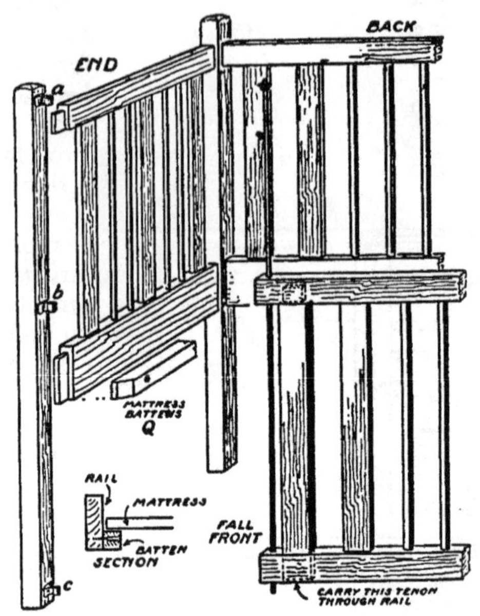

FIG. 3. HOW THE COT IS MADE.

CUTTING LIST

		Long ft.	Long in.	Wide in.	Thick in.
A	4 Posts	3	2	1½	1½
B	2 End rails	2	3	3	⅞
C	2 ,, (top)	2	3	1¾	⅞
D	6 Splats	1	7	2	⅜
E*	8 ,,	1	7	¾	⅜
F	Back rail	4	3	3	⅞
G	,, (top)	4	3	1¾	⅞
H	4 Splats	1	7	2	⅜
J	1 ,, (centre)	1	7	3	⅜
K*	8 ,,	1	7	¾	⅜
L	Drop front rail	4	0	2	⅞
M	,, (top)	4	0	1¾	⅞
N	2 Stiles	1	10	2	⅞
O	2 Splats	1	8	2	⅜
	1 ,, (centre)	1	8	3	⅜
P*	8 ,,	1	8	¾	⅜
Q	2 Battens	4	1	1	⅞
	2 ,,	2	1	1	⅞

* If preferred, ⅜ in. or ½ in. turned hardwood rod might be used instead of the ¾ in. by ⅜ in. intermediate splats. Lengths in all cases allow for joints and fitting, but widths and thicknesses are net.

LIGHT CANTEEN TABLE

A PIECE of this kind is useful in the home as well as in the canteen. Hardwood is advisable for hard wear. All rails are tenoned in, and (after testing for squareness) the carcase cramped up. Top rails are rounded over as shown, the top corners of legs being rounded to correspond. Under rails are rebated for the shelf and neatly chamfered on top edge. The shelf is screwed in, the top, if of plywood, being glued down and glue-blocked. Screw after blocking. If solid wood is used the top should be fixed with buttons.

FIG. I. USEFUL LIGHT TABLE.

CUTTING LIST

	Long ft.	Long in.	Wide in.	Thick in.
4 Legs	2	4½	1¼ (finished)	1¼
4 Rails	1	6	2⅝	1⅛
4 „	1	6	1⅜	1⅛
1 Top	1	6	18	½
1 Shelf	1	5½	17½	⅝

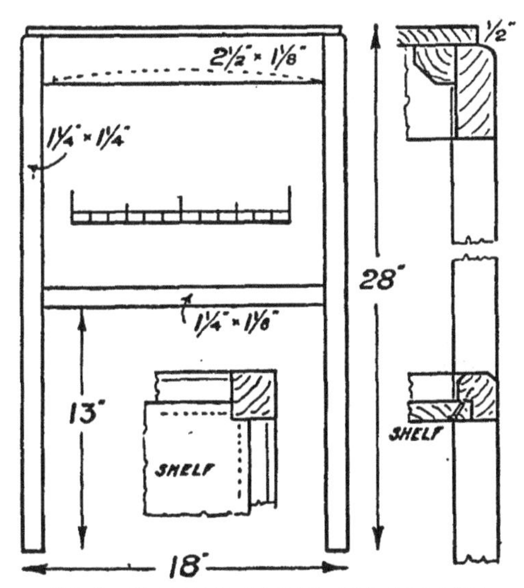

FIG. 2. SCALE ELEVATION AND SECTION.

Top and shelf may be jointed to width. Alternatively, both may be of stout ply, the edges of top being lipped. If casters are wanted, the length of legs will be adjusted accordingly. In the case of a light table the thickness of rails might, if desired, be kept to ⅞ in.

When assembling the framework of a piece of this kind it is advisable to glue up the two opposite sides independently first. Then when the glue has set the remaining rails can be added. The advantage is that it saves having to deal with a large number of joints in one operation. Furthermore fewer cramps are needed.

BED TABLE WITH BOOK REST

IN construction all can be made from oddments, and if to be stained, any light-weight softwood may be used.

The book-rest (G) may be cut from the top (F), thus saving timber. If the upper edging rails are added as shown, the end ones are 10 in. by $1\frac{1}{4}$ in. and the back one 24 in. by $1\frac{1}{4}$ in., all of $\frac{3}{8}$-in. (bare) stuff.

Construction. End rails (B) are tenoned to legs, the two larger top rails (C) being lap-dovetailed as shown. Cross rails (D) are tongued in, and the strut rail (E), notched as indicated to engage strut, screwed to *underside* of rails (C).

FIG. 1. A BLESSING TO THE INVALID.

This is equally useful for reading or for meals. The top measures 24 in. by 12 in. Legs are $8\frac{1}{2}$ in. long.

The top (F) may be pierced to take the book-rest, in which case a hole is used to enable the saw to be started. Alternatively it can be put together in separate parts. Since the whole is screwed to the lower framework it should be rigid.

The rails (C and D) form a rebate in which the book-rest lies when down (see Fig. 2 and also sectional view, Fig. 3). The book rest is hinged at front as shown, the strut (H) being hinged at back. The middle cross rail (E) is sunk so that the strut (when folded) will lie below the level of the top (F). As, however, the strut will be full in length, it will probably be necessary to pare away a little notch in front rail (C).

BED TABLE

FIG. 2. PLAN OF TOP AND FRAMEWORK, WITH SCALE.

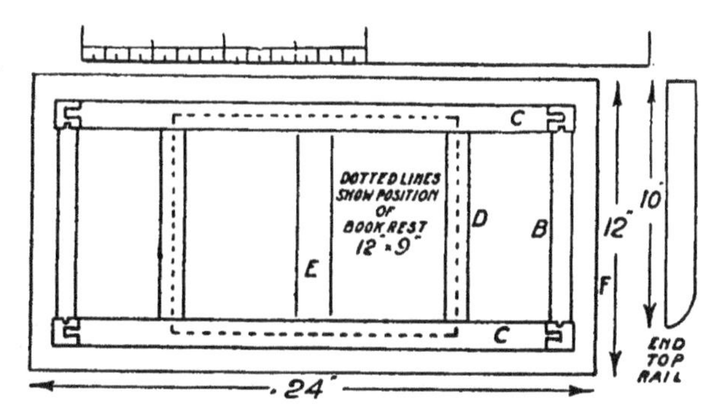

CUTTING LIST

	Long ft. in.	Wide in.	Thick in.
A 4 Legs .	8½	1¼	1¼
B 2 End rails .	10	1½	¾
C 2 Top rails .	1 10	1¼	¾
D 2 Cross rails	8½	1	¾
E Rail for strut	10	1½	½
F Top . .	2 0	12	½
G Book rest .	1 0	9	½
H Strut . .	8	3	⅜

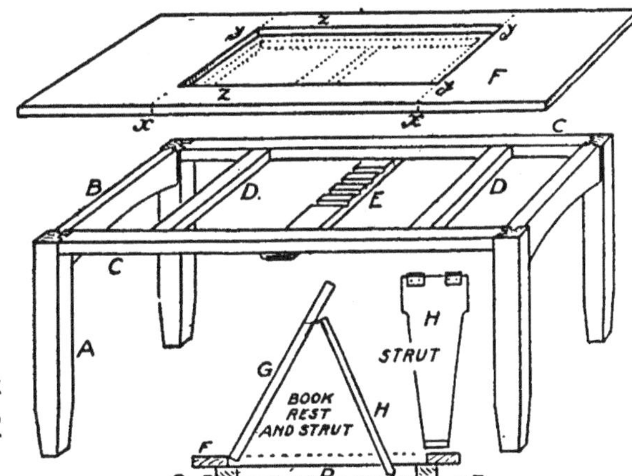

FIG. 3. FRAMEWORK CONSTRUCTION, AND BOOK REST DETAILS.

PICTURE OR MIRROR FRAME

ALTHOUGH of fair size and built on cabinet lines, this picture frame requires only a small quantity of timber. Nothing over 1¾ in. in width is necessary.

Oak is the natural choice, but any hardwood could be stained as desired. Whilst a definite size has to be given for guidance, it is understood that dimensions may be modified as required, always provided that the proportions are followed as closely as possible.

When marking out note two points. (1) The stiles (A) taper from 1¾ in. at base to 1¼ in. at top. Thus the width over *frame* at top is one inch narrower than at base. (2) The slabs (D) are vertical and they thus preserve the square form of the frame.

FIG. I. A FRAME OF CHARACTER.
This is suitable for either hanging or standing on a mantelshelf. Size as shown is 2 ft. 6 in. by 1 ft. 6 in., but dimensions may be altered to suit the mirror or picture to be framed.

In getting out the thicknesses, too, note the parts that are recessed. In this respect the thicknesses given in the cutting list should be followed. The slabs (D) and the pediment (G) are recessed ⅛ in. The plinth (E) is allowed 1 in. thick so that it may project ⅛ in. beyond frame. Below this the little drops (F) are recessed ⅛ in. The enlarged section will be a guide to the worker here.

Assembling. Stiles and rails (A, B, C) are rebated for the glass and picture, and mortised and tenoned together. Slabs (D) are tapered in width so that, when fitted to stiles, the under-edges remain vertical. They and the pediment (G) may be dowelled and glued. The little cappings at top of slabs are worked in the solid,

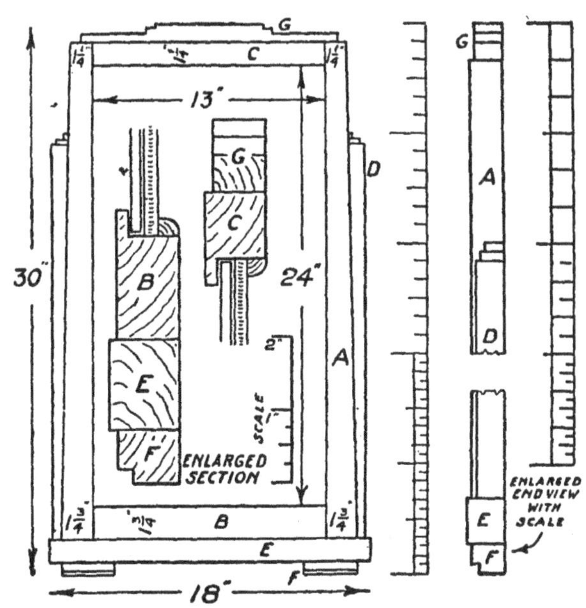

FIG. 2. ELEVATION AND ENLARGED DETAILS OF PARTS.

being recessed at front and side. Base (E) may be dowelled or pocket screwed to frame, and the drops (F) glued on and panel-pinned. Clean up the whole thoroughly with glasspaper before staining and waxing.

The picture is fitted in the usual way, preferably with a plywood backing. The lipping of the frame rebate should not exceed a full ⅛ in. If used for a mirror the rebate must be blacked, as otherwise it will be reflected in the mirror.

CUTTING LIST

	Long ft.	Long in.	Wide in.	Thick in.
A 2 Stiles	2	3½	1¾	⅞
B Bottom rail	1	4½	1¾	⅞
C Top rail	1	3½	1¼	⅞
D 2 Slabs	1	10½	1	¾
E Base	1	6	1¼	1
F 2 Drops		3	⅞	¾
G Pediment	1	2½	1	¾

FOLDING IRONING TABLE

FOR an ironing table top the usual size is 4 ft. long by from 9 in. to 11 in. wide, 3 ft. being regarded as a convenient height. The supporting legs consist of two frames pivoted together, the shorter frame being of a width that permits of its folding within the larger one. The difference in length of legs gives greater stability to the table when in actual use.

Leg frames. The larger frame (Fig. 2) is prepared first, following the sizes in the diagram. Ash is perhaps the best wood to use,

FIG. 1. A USEFUL ITEM INVALUABLE IN THE SMALL MODERN KITCHEN. This shows how the table folds flat and thus takes up little space. Length is 4 ft. and height 3 ft. The legs must be made from sound wood, free from knots.

but any straight-grained hardwood will do. The frame tapers from 15 in. at floor to 10 in. at top, the top ends of legs (A) being rounded so that they clear the top when hinged. The stiffening rail (C), 2 in. from top, may simply be screwed on. The X-pattern braces (D) are halved where they intersect, and screwed. Note that, whilst these braces are fixed to front of legs, the rail (C) is screwed at back, this to permit of the inner leg frame folding within the outer one.

The inner frame, shorter and narrower than the outer one, can be made to an exact fit by laying the legs (B) within the completed outer

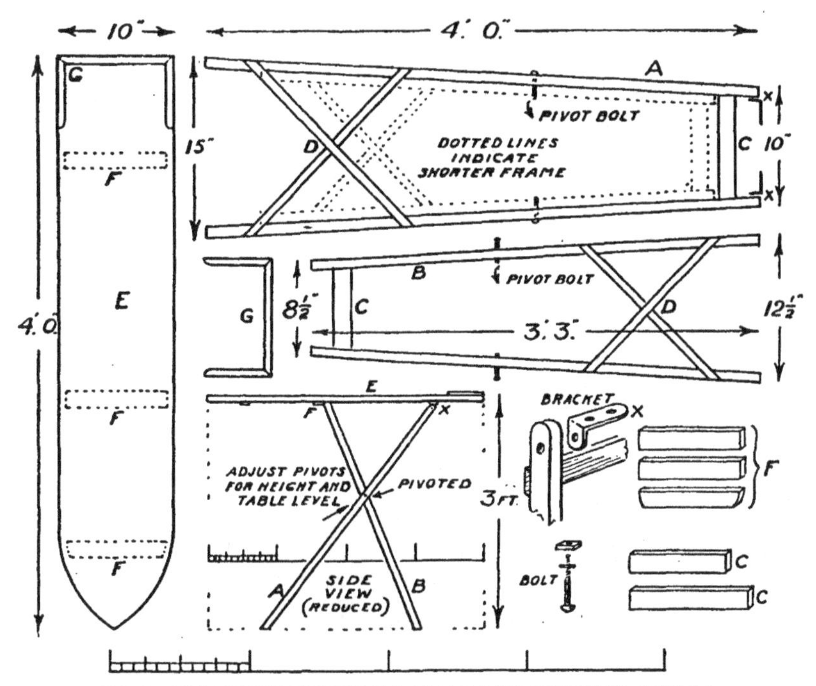

FIG. 2. THE PARTS DRAWN TO SCALE AND PIVOTING DETAILS.

frame, marking the pivot points, and then marking for the position of cross rail (C) and braces (D). The fit must be easy to avoid binding, but not too loose.

Top board (E). This may be in a single width of, say, 10 in., as three battens (F) are screwed to the underside. The board is covered first with a piece of thick blanket and then with a piece of calico. Strain the material to fold over the edges and tack with brass-head nails. At the far end, where the iron may rest, a sheet of asbestos is sometimes fitted.

Adjustment. This is not secured without care. The table has to stand firmly, the top must be horizontal at the height required, and the leg frames must fold so that the top lies flat against them: To make sure of a perfect job three points are of special importance: (1) the position of the battens (F) under the board; (2) the hingeing of the longer leg frame at the top (see X), and (3) the pivoting of the two frames. Thus, what is helpful is to set out a side elevation (see diagram at Fig. 2) to a scale of, say, 3 in. to the foot. Draw in the top at a height of 3 ft. from floor line; mark the position of the battens (F), then draw in the legs and thus find approximately the centres for the pivots.

By laying the shorter frame within the larger the pivot holes can be bored together. Each bolt should have thin brass or iron washers on each side. To the rear batten (F) the larger frame is hung by means of two iron brackets (X), the brackets being screwed to the batten and pivot screwed to each leg. In this way the legs will fold flat against the board (E).

Test here for the shorter frame. Its position when fixed depends on the placement of the *middle* batten (F) against which it butts (see side view diagram, Fig. 2). When the top (E) is approximately horizontal mark the position of batten and screw it on. Later the floor bevels of the legs are cut and any final adjustments made.

CUTTING LIST

	Long ft.	Long in.	Wide in.	Thick in.
A 2 Legs	4	0	1½	⅞
B 2 Legs	3	3	1½	⅞
C For 2 Rails	1	8	1½	¾
D For 4 X Strips	6	6	⅝	⅜
E Top	4	0	10	¾
F For 3 Battens	2	4	1½	⅞
G Stripwood for top	2	0	⅜	¼

Widths and thicknesses are net. Cut the legs (A or B) full in length to allow for adjustment later.

CLOTHES AIRER

FOR a small two-fold clothes airer the height may be from 3 ft. to 3 ft. 6 in. and the width from 21 in. to 24 in. It is essential to take straight-grained material, preferably hardwood, the lengths being of stuff either 1⅜ in. by 1⅛ in. or 1½ in. by ⅞ in. The stouter wood is easier to handle. For the article shown four lengths 3 ft. 6 in. and six lengths 2 ft. will be required.

After planing, lay the four posts together, side by side, and mark at one operation for the mortises. The same plan is adopted with the six rails, thus ensuring that all the shoulders are correctly

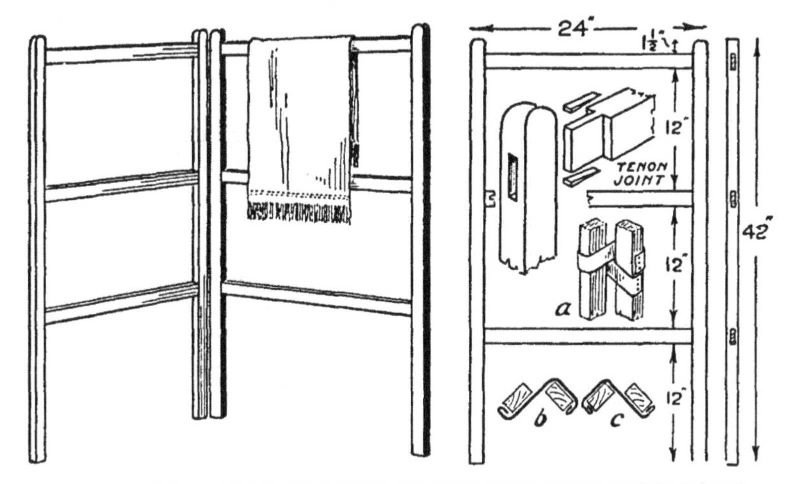

USEFUL KITCHEN ITEM, IT COULD BE ARRANGED WITH THREE FOLDS.
Height 3 ft. 6 in., folds 2 ft. wide each.

marked. From the detail shown it will be seen that the tenons pass through the rail, each being stiffened with two thin wedges glued in when assembling. The mortises can be cut by boring holes with a centre bit of suitable size and then paring with a ¼-in. and a ¾-in. chisel. In cutting the tenons allow a little full in length so that the raw ends may later be glasspapered flush.

In a simple way the folds are hinged with ordinary chair webbing 1½ in. or 2 in. wide. The usual method is as at *a*, a single tape being used. Another method is to use two tapes as at *b* and *c*. At the tacking ends the webbing is turned over to avoid fraying.

CUTTING LIST

	Long ft.	Long in.	Wide in.	Thick in.
4 Upright	3	6½	1½	1⅛
6 Rails	2	0½	1½	1⅛

DWARF STEPS FOR THE KITCHEN

THIS is a handy item in the kitchen to enable high shelves, etc., to be reached easily. An average size is shown here, three steps of 9 in. rise, giving a height of 27 in. Width over ends is 15 in. and the total spread 30 in. These dimensions give a thoroughly useful article which will serve all purposes where shelving, window fastenings, blinds, etc., are just out of reach. Whitewood of $\frac{7}{8}$-in. thickness will serve throughout.

The ends (A) are easily set out for the treads from Fig. 5. Line *a–a* is vertical (at right angles to floor line). On this line mark off the treads, allowing for the $\frac{7}{8}$-in. thicknesses. Lay the boards (planed to $5\frac{1}{2}$ in. wide) in position so that width across at floor is 30 in. and at top 10 in. The treads can then be marked as indicated. If a joiner's bevel is available the work is simplified.

Groove the inside faces of ends for the treads, this about $\frac{3}{16}$ in. deep. Each pair of ends is secured by screwing on the two battens (B) and (C), the former under the top and the latter immediately below the bottom tread.

In fitting, glue in the treads and pin through the ends with hardwood pegs. It is also wise to fit a cross-board (F) which may be half-lapped and screwed to battens (B) (see Fig. 4). The top is glued down and screwed from below through board (F). It may also be screwed direct to the ends, counter-sinking well for the screw-heads. A precaution which guards against the results of rough usage is to pass a $\frac{3}{8}$-in. iron rod with bolt and nut through each end just under the bottom tread (X, Fig. 1). This will keep the piece rigid.

Allow the top to overhang $\frac{1}{2}$ in. all round; also let the treads project the matter of $\frac{3}{8}$ in. or $\frac{1}{2}$ in. at front. In all cases round over as shown. Note also that the battens are cleaned off flush with the ends.

CUTTING LIST

	Long ft.	Long in.	Wide in.	Thick in.
A 4 Ends	2	$6\frac{1}{2}$	$5\frac{3}{4}$	$\frac{7}{8}$
B 2 Battens	1	1	$3\frac{1}{4}$	$\frac{7}{8}$
C 2 ,,	2	$2\frac{1}{2}$	$2\frac{1}{4}$	$\frac{7}{8}$
D 4 Treads	1	$2\frac{1}{4}$	$7\frac{1}{4}$	$\frac{7}{8}$
E Top	1	$4\frac{1}{2}$	$11\frac{1}{4}$	$\frac{7}{8}$

If the cross-top piece (F, Fig. 4) is added, allow for a board $15\frac{1}{2}$ in. by 4 in. or 5 in. wide.

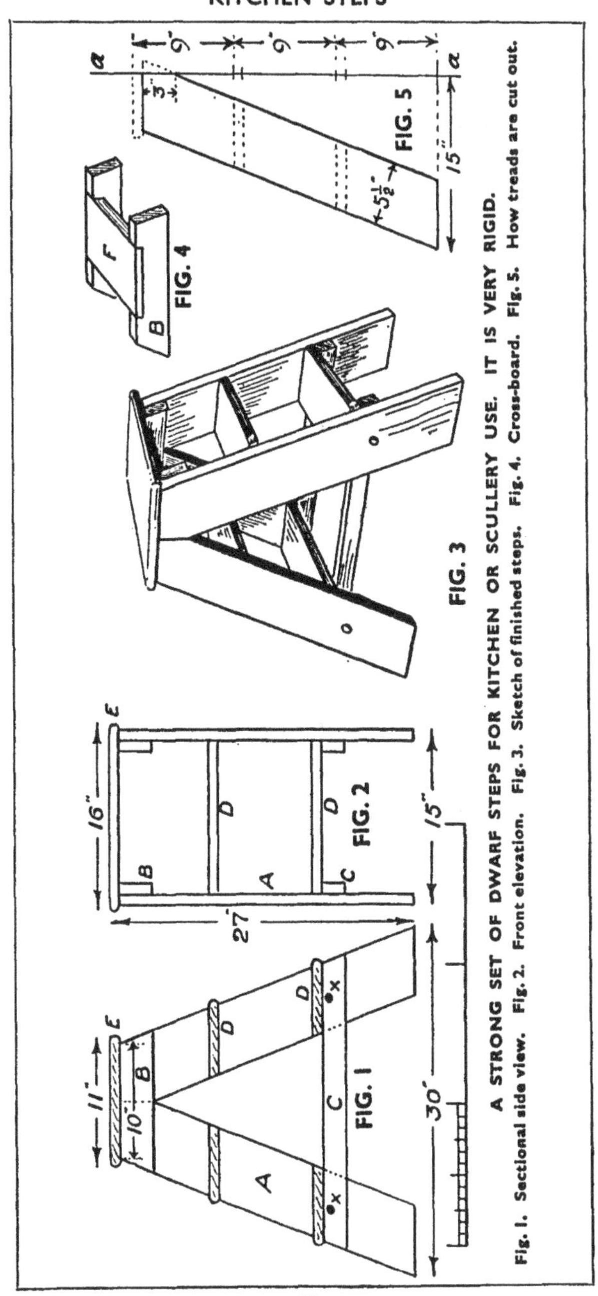

A STRONG SET OF DWARF STEPS FOR KITCHEN OR SCULLERY USE. IT IS VERY RIGID.

Fig. 1. Sectional side view. Fig. 2. Front elevation. Fig. 3. Sketch of finished steps. Fig. 4. Cross-board. Fig. 5. How treads are cut out.

FOLDING BED TABLE

CLEAN softwood free of knots or any minor hardwood (such as birch, plane, sycamore, beech, etc.) may be used.

Top. This should preferably be in multi-ply or laminboard. If solid wood is used it should be bone dry. It should have end clamps 2 in. wide tongued on. The size is 20 in. by 12 in. by $\frac{1}{2}$ in.

Leg frames. The legs are 7 in. long by $1\frac{1}{8}$ in. square, tapering to $\frac{3}{4}$ in. The rails are tenoned to the legs and shoulder size is $8\frac{1}{2}$ in.

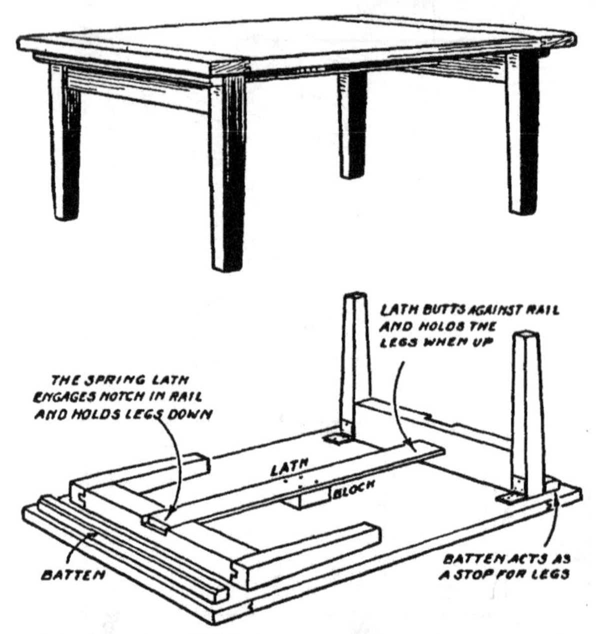

FIG. 1. USEFUL ITEM FOR AN INVALID. SIZE 20 in. BY 12 in.
A view of the underside is also given, showing how the legs are held in either position.

They are $1\frac{1}{2}$ in. by $1\frac{1}{8}$ in. or $\frac{7}{8}$ in. in section. Battens 11 in. long are $\frac{3}{4}$ in. by $\frac{5}{8}$ in. For the lath allow a strip 15 in. by 2 in. by $\frac{3}{16}$ in. thick. Each pair of legs is hinged with two stout back-flap hinges, the battens being screwed in position so that they will act as stops when the legs are up.

The lath is screwed to a 2-in. by 2-in. centre block which will have to be about 1 in. thick. When legs are folded the lath engages a notch ($\frac{3}{16}$ in. deep) cut in each rail (see Fig. 1). When legs are raised the lath is tilted up and, when free, springs back to its normal position, butting against the rails and thus preventing the legs from slipping. The exact height of block and length of lath are matters for simple adjustment when assembling.

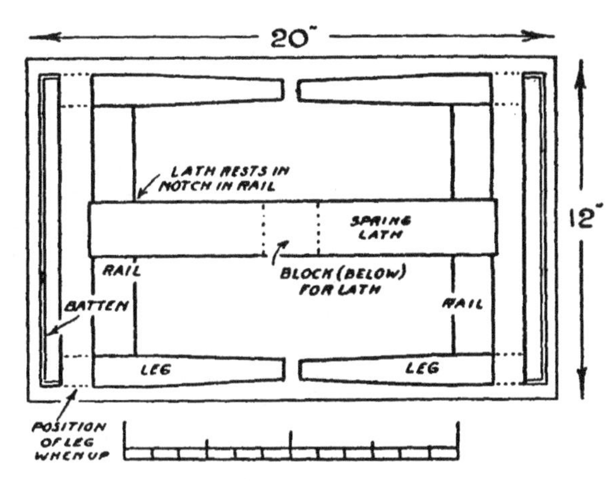

FIG. 2. SCALE PLAN OF THE UNDERSIDE.

LIGHT TABLE

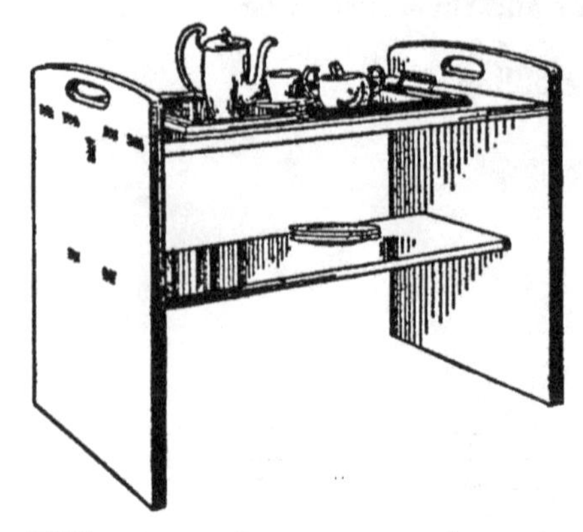

FIG. 1. NEAT TABLE FOR AFTERNOON TEA.

The plan size is 26 in. by 16 in., and height to main top 20 in.

IN construction one or other of two methods may be employed. One is by housing the top (B), rail (C), and shelf (D) to the ends. The housings for top and shelf would be stopped, and both parts would be glue-blocked underneath, the blocks later being screwed.

The other (and stronger) method is to cut tenons which pass through the ends and are wedged. This can be made a decorative feature, and is common in the case of oak. A dark wood is used for the wedges.

CUTTING LIST

		Long ft.	Long in.	Wide in.	Thick in.
A	Two ends	1	11	16	¾
B	Top	2	2	16	¾ bare
C	Rail	2	2	1½	¾
D	Shelf	2	2	10	½ bare

Sizes are net, so allowance should be made for trimming.

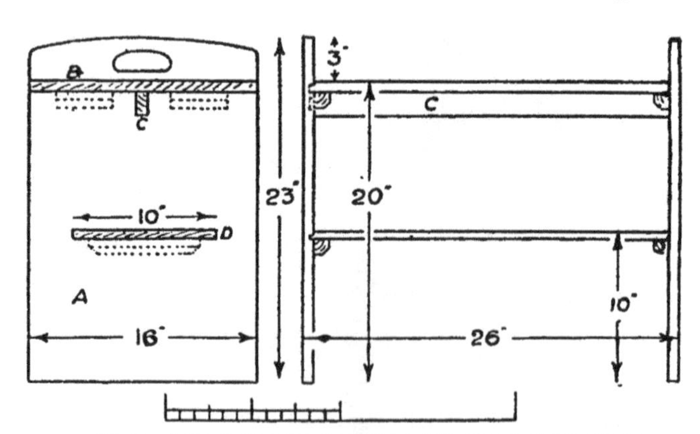

FIG. 2. END AND SIDE ELEVATIONS DRAWN TO SCALE.

CHILD'S STOOL

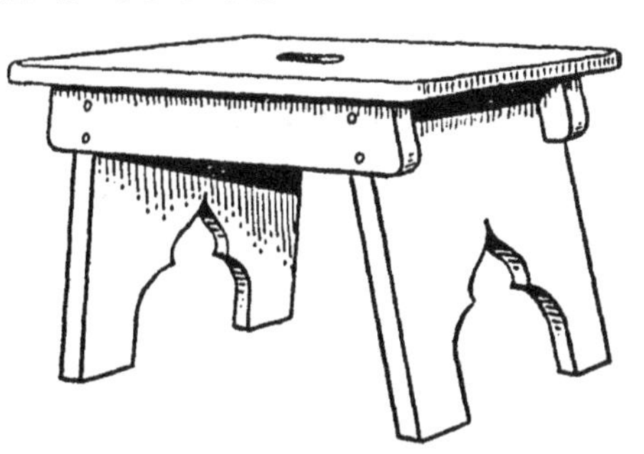

FIG. 1. HANDY ITEM IN LIVING ROOM OR KITCHEN.
Length 16 in., width 9 in., height 9 in. Sizes could be adjusted to suit age of the child.

THE parts for this will be:—(A) Two ends, 8¼ in. by 8 in.; (B) Two sides, 15 in. by 2 in.; (C) Top, 16 in. by 9 in. All may be ¾ in. or ⅞ in. thick according to the timber used. Clean sound softwood will serve.

The sides (B) are fixed to ends (A) with a simple grooved joint, the grooves in the former being cut slightly on the bevel to suit the splay of legs. If preferred the legs might be kept upright. The sides could be either glued and nailed, or glued and screwed. In the latter case the screw-heads are recessed and the holes plugged. The top (with or without fingerhold) is fixed either by thumb-slot screwing, or by glue-blocking underneath. In any case the blocks should be fixed at the top of ends (A) as they strengthen the last named which are necessarily weakened to an extent by the shaping. Round off the top corners and also the edges. The sharp arrises should be taken off all other edges.

CUTTING LIST

	Long ft.	Long in.	Wide in.	Thick in.
A 2 Ends .		8¼	8	⅞
B 2 Sides .	1	3	2	⅞
C 1 Top . .	1	4	9	⅞

Sizes are net so allowance should be made for trimming.

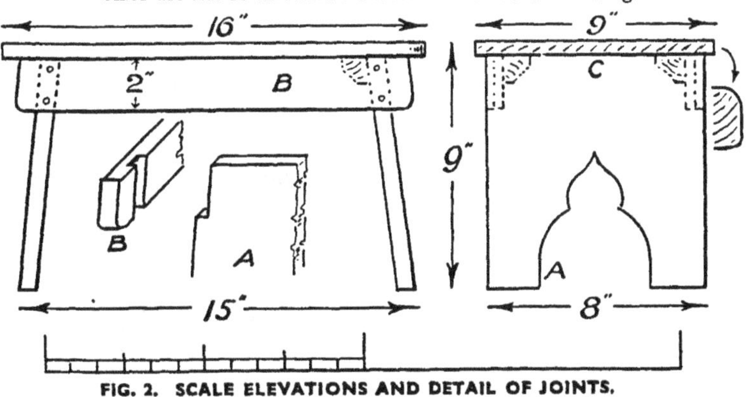

FIG. 2. SCALE ELEVATIONS AND DETAIL OF JOINTS.

3. TOOLS AND APPLIANCES

THE WORKSHOP BENCH

THE bench top should be as level as possible and the front board at least should be sufficiently thick to absorb blows—as, for instance, when mortising. The supporting frames should be sturdy, the legs and rails being properly jointed together. As a bench is subjected to considerable racking during planing operations, the front must be specially rigid.

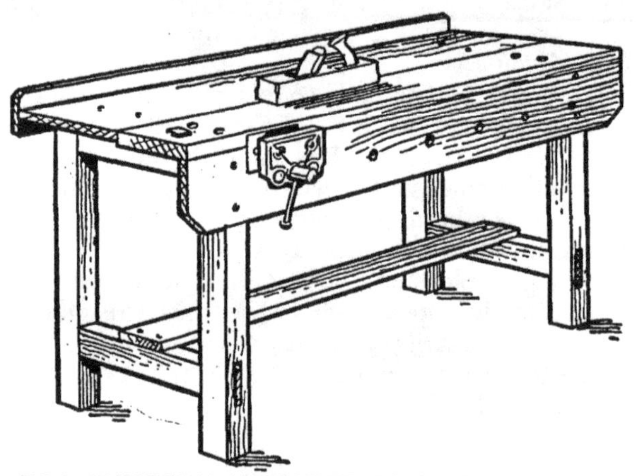

FIG. 1. SIMPLE BENCH SUITABLE FOR THE HOME CRAFTSMAN.
Suggested sizes are 6 ft. long by 2 ft. wide. A good average height is 2 ft. 11 in., though this could be adapted to suit the stature of the user. Length could be cut down if necessary.

Dimensions. A useful length for a bench is 6 ft. and the height should be in accordance with that of the worker. A rough guide is to make the surface of a bench level with the hip bone. For instance, if the height of the worker is 6 ft., that of the bench could be approximately 2 ft. 11 in.

Main framework. Labour can be saved by obtaining prepared stuff for the end frames, suitable sizes being 3 in. by 3 in. or 4 in. by 2 in. The lower rail of each frame, Fig. 2, should be about 6 in. from the floor. This member is tenoned into the legs, the tenons being glued and wedged. The top rails are secured with open mortise and tenon joints, the joints in this case being glued and dowelled. As it is imperative that the frames should be square, a careful test should be made across the diagonals before being finally set aside.

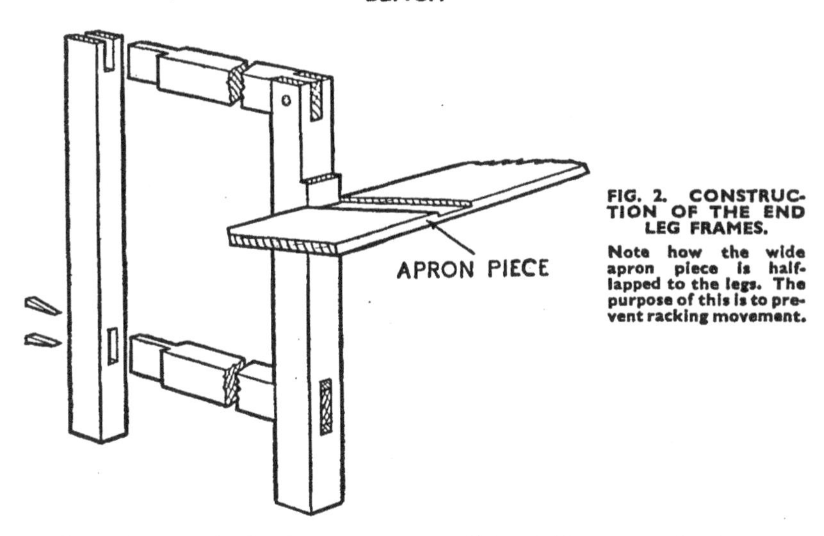

FIG. 2. CONSTRUCTION OF THE END LEG FRAMES.
Note how the wide apron piece is half-lapped to the legs. The purpose of this is to prevent racking movement.

In order to obtain the greatest possible rigidity towards the front of the bench, an apron piece is fitted, as shown in Figs. 2 and 3. This is half-lapped to the legs, as indicated in Fig. 2, and is screwed in position.

Top. As most of the heavy work is done towards the front of the bench, the front board can be thicker than those towards the back, thus effecting an economy in timber. For this front board, a deal 9 in. by 3 in. will do admirably, but if this cannot be obtained, a scaffold board 11 in. by 1½ in. will be found quite satisfactory. Obviously, care must be taken in the selection of the stuff to see that it is out of winding, not twisted.

It is as well to bolt the front board to the frames, as shown in Fig. 3,

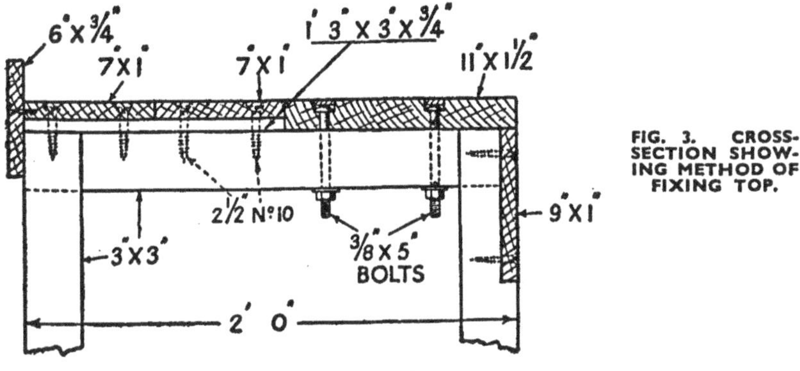

FIG. 3. CROSS-SECTION SHOWING METHOD OF FIXING TOP.

since this allows of the board being easily reversed when the surface becomes worn. It is, of course, important to recess deeply the heads of the bolts, and it improves the appearance of the bench if the recesses are plugged; 2 ft. represents about the minimum width for a bench, and if it can be made wider, so much the better.

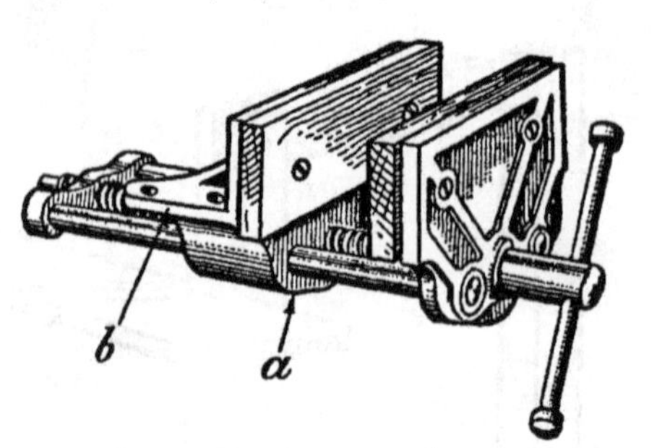

FIG. 4. SUITABLE METAL VICE.

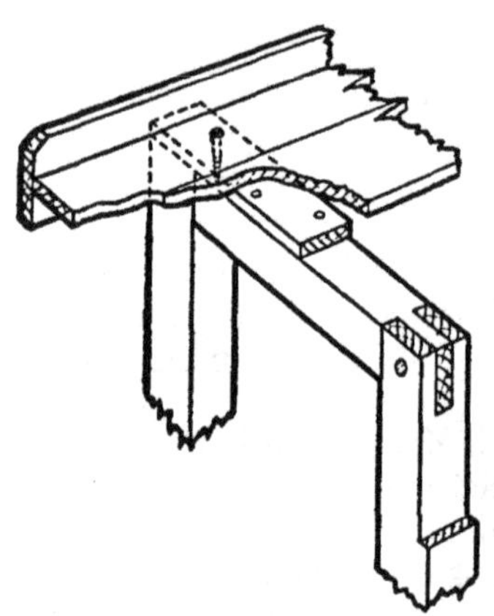

FIG. 5. HOW REAR BOARDS ARE PACKED UP.

Since the boards at the rear are thinner than the front board, it is necessary to provide packing pieces, Fig. 5, so that the top surface will be flush. The packing pieces are nailed to the frames and the boards screwed through the pieces and into the frames. The heads of the screws should be well countersunk.

Fixing the vice. A convenient size of vice is one having an opening of 7 in., and jaws 7 in. in width. A smaller size of vice is not recommended where serious work is concerned. Two types of vice are available to the worker, namely that having a plain screw action, illustrated in Fig. 4, and the kind having a quick-grip arrangement. The former type is probably the best for the home craftsman, since the saving of time in the manipulation of the vice afforded by the quick-grip action is not so important. Both types of vice are supplied fitted

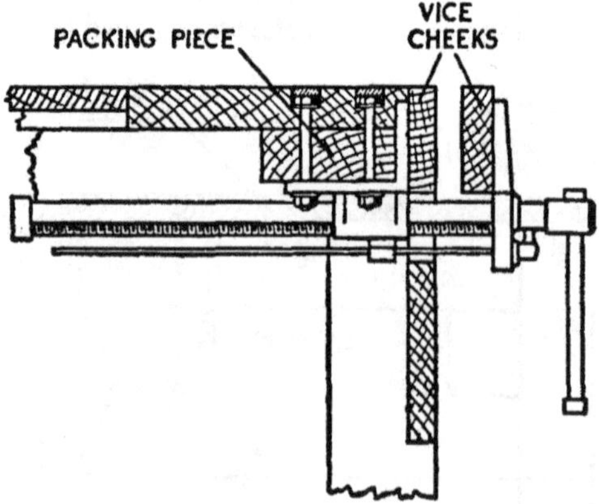

FIG. 6. SECTION SHOWING HOW VICE IS FIXED.

with hardwood cheeks and it is preferable that the back cheek should be flush with the edge of the bench and also the apron piece, Fig. 6.

As exposed metal parts are liable to cause damage to tools, it is as well to replace the existing wooden cheeks with others that project above the metal jaws, Fig. 7. That is, of course, if the existing cheeks do not satisfy these requirements. In fitting the vice it is therefore necessary to recess the edge of the bench to receive both the metal jaw and its wooden cheek so that when the vice is fitted both cheeks are level with the top of the bench and the back metal jaw is entirely recessed.

It is not necessary to cut away the apron piece to take the part *a* of the vice body, it being sufficient to make an opening to receive the flange *b* and the two guide bars and screw. In order to do this,

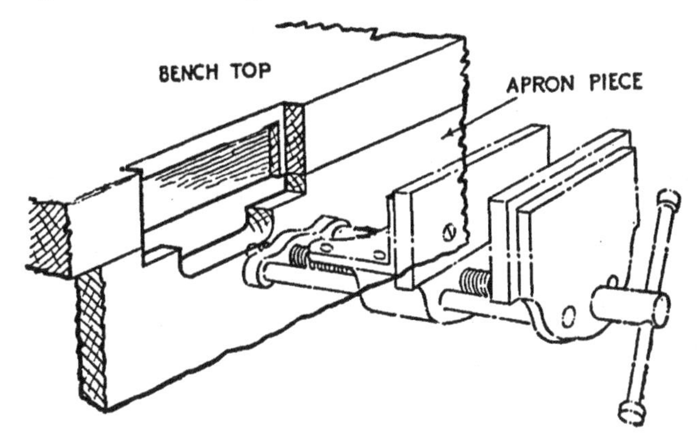

FIG. 7. BENCH TOP AND APRON PIECE RECESSED FOR VICE.

the vice must be fixed to the underside of the bench top, the apron being screwed in place after the vice is in position. It is advisable to secure the vice with bolts and nuts, Fig. 6, since, should the vice work loose, it can be readily tightened.

It may be that the worker will be unable to obtain stuff for the front board of the bench top that is equal in thickness to the depth of the back jaw, allowing for its recessing below the level of the bench top. In such circumstances it will be necessary to provide a packing piece, Fig. 6.

When a board is gripped in the vice for edge shooting, it is necessary to support the projecting end. This can be done by resting the end on a hardwood plug which is inserted in one of a series of holes made in the apron piece, Fig. 1, the holes being level with the vice screw.

Bench stop. This can comprise a piece of hardwood about 6 in. long and 1⅜ in. square. It should be a tight fit in a hole in the bench top so that it can be adjusted by blows from a hammer. Special metal stop devices, having adjustable means, can be obtained, but with a metal stop there is always the danger that damage will be done to planes by accidental contact with the stop.

(NEST OF DRAWERS.—*Continued from page* 61).

(inside) mark carefully for the positions, and test each fillet with its corresponding groove before screwing. The drawers should be allowed to run freely.

CUTTING LIST

	Long ft.	Long in.	Wide in.	Thick in.
2 Ends	1	3½	14¼	⅞
2 For top and bottom	1	6½	14¼	⅞
1 Back	1	6½	14	¾
1 For 4 toes	1	6	4¼	⅞
1 Drawer front	1	4½	2¼	⅞
1 " "	1	4½	2½	⅞
1 " "	1	4½	2¾	⅞
1 " "	1	4½	3¼	⅞
1 " "	1	4½	3¾	⅞
2 Drawer sides	1	1	2¼	⅝
2 " "	1	1	2½	⅝
2 Drawer sides	1	1	2¾	⅝
2 " "	1	1	3¼	⅝
2 " "	1	1	3¾	⅝
1 Drawer back	1	4½	1¾	½
1 " "	1	4½	2	½
1 " "	1	4½	2¼	½
1 " "	1	4½	2¾	½
1 " "	1	4½	3¼	½
5 Drawer bottoms	1	4	12½	¼

The five 6-in. drawer pulls may be cut from a length 2 ft. 7 in. by 1 in. by 1 in.

WORKSHOP TRESTLES

TRESTLES in the workshop are used for rip-sawing and cross-cutting, also for supporting work on hand and many other purposes. They are made in different sizes, and the height must be determined by the worker according to the uses for which he requires the trestle. For sawing the height may vary from 19 in. to 24 in., this depending not only on the height but on the preference of the carpenter himself.

Almost any odd lengths of timber will serve, the legs from stuff about 2¼ in. square, according to size. Top bar may be 4½ in. by 2½ in. or less, the struts (*a*) 2 in. by 1⅛ in., top rails (*b*) 3 in. by ⅞ in., and side rails (*c*) 1¾ in. by ⅞ in. These sizes are merely approximate for a stout trestle. The timber may be lighter if preferred, always remembering that a steady trestle is more convenient in use than one which is apt to slip.

For sawing purposes a flat-top board (*d*) is sometimes preferred to the upright bar. The joint for this is shown in the alternative detail sketch.

In assembling, the only joints to cut are the bridle notchings in the top bar and the dovetail slots for the half-lapped struts. The leg joint is as shown in detail, the top bar being allowed to overhang a couple of inches at each end. The parts are glued and screwed.

For a trestle 24 in. high the legs may splay out to 20 in. at ground. Splay for lower or higher trestles may be adjusted proportionately. Length of top bar varies from 24 in. upwards. On small trestles the stay rails (*c*) are sometimes omitted.

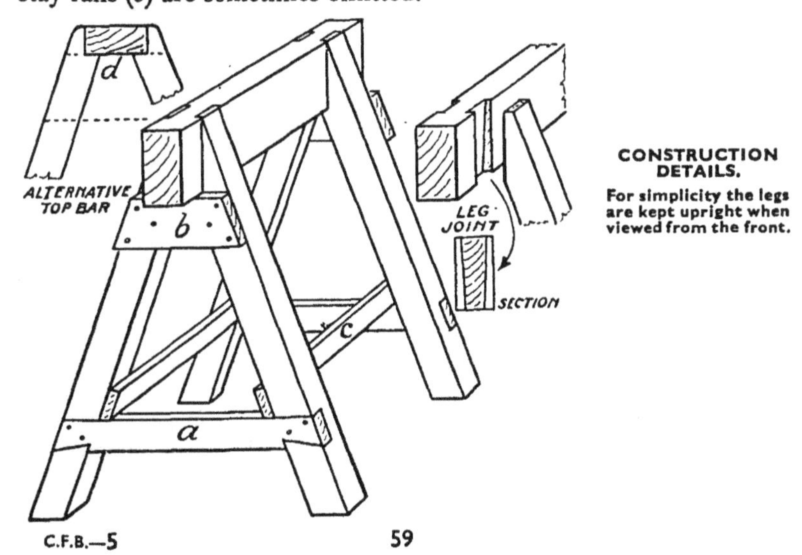

CONSTRUCTION DETAILS.
For simplicity the legs are kept upright when viewed from the front.

NEST OF DRAWERS

Suitable for small tools, nails, screws, etc.

WHILST for constructive purposes the dimensions of this nest of drawers is given, it will be understood that sizes can be adapted to suit individual requirements. The five drawers shown measure (inside) 15 in. by 11½ in., ranging in depth (inside) from 1½ in. to 3 in.

To save space no drawer rails are used. The drawers, by means of grooves channelled in their sides, slide on hardwood fillets after the manner of wardrobe trays. Birch, beech, ash, or oak may be used for the nest, a hardwood being essential for lasting wear.

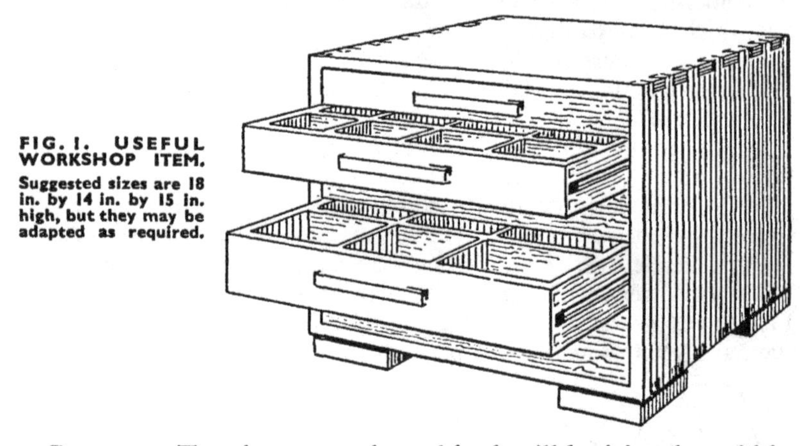

FIG. 1. USEFUL WORKSHOP ITEM. Suggested sizes are 18 in. by 14 in. by 15 in. high, but they may be adapted as required.

Carcase. Top, bottom, ends, and back will be jointed to width. Fig. 5 indicates that top and bottom are through-dovetailed to the ends, the back being screwed. The toes are screwed in, the screw-heads being well countersunk.

The drawers are lap-dovetailed at front and through-dovetailed at back, the ¼-in. plywood bottom being grooved in. Take care that the dovetail will clear the groove run in the sides (see Fig. 5). The grooves should be cut to take fillets ⅝ in. wide by ⅜ in. thick. They are stopped ⅞ in. at front, but run out at back.

The two (or three) shallower top drawers will be partitioned for various sizes of nails and screws, the lower ones for sundries such as hinges, screw eyes, screw and repair plates, locks, knobs, catches, and miscellaneous items. A division may be provided for glasspaper. For the partitions ¼ in. should be ample. They are halved where

Cutting List appears on page 58.

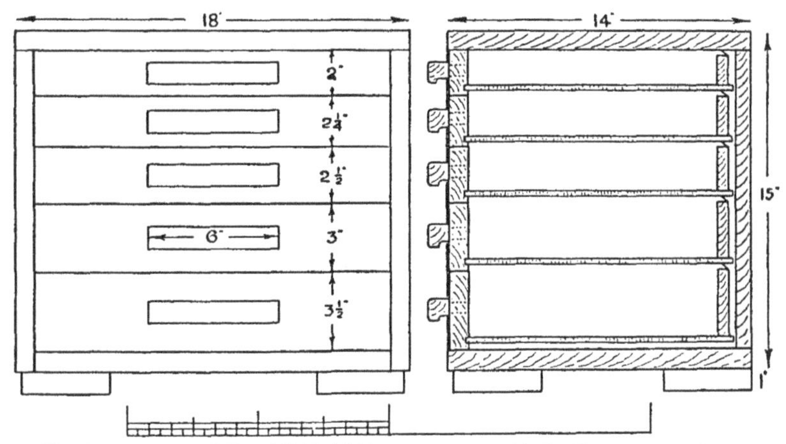

FIG. 2. SCALE FRONT ELEVATION.

FIG. 3. SIDE SECTION.

they intersect and are housed or V-grooved to sides, front, and back.

The drawer pulls, worked to the section shown, may be screwed from the inside. A single pull of a length of about 6 in. ensures smoother running of the drawer than a pair of smaller ones spaced apart.

For the fillet runners straight-grained oak is the best wood to use. On the ends

(*Continued on page* 58).

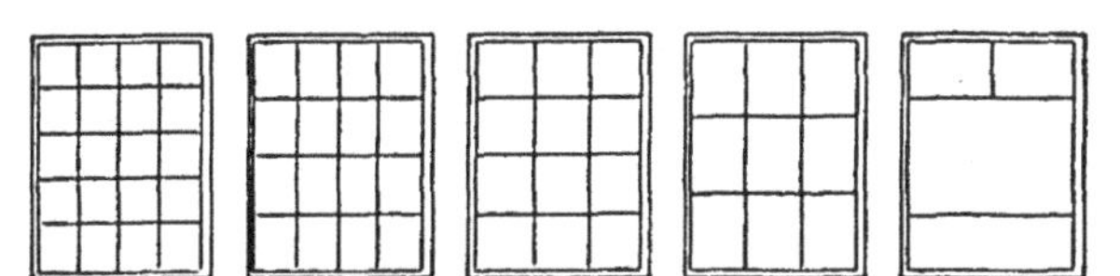

FIG. 4. PARTITIONING OF DRAWERS.

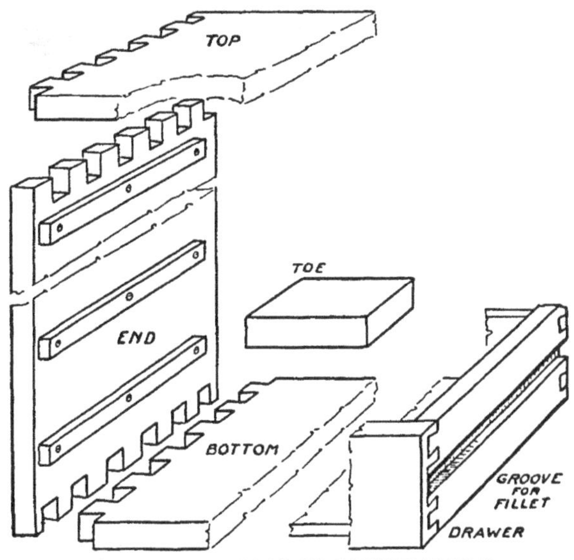

FIG. 5. MAIN DETAILS OF CONSTRUCTION.

TOOL CHEST

FOR the home worker a tool chest of the dimensions shown is a good average size. Much depends on the stock of saws and planes that a man may have. If, say, he has a 26-in. or a 28-in. rip-saw in addition to cross-cut and panel-saws, the length of chest will have to be at least 3 ft.; whilst, if he has a try and several moulding planes in addition to the jack and smoothing, he may have to increase the height to 22 in. or so. The chest shown will take a hand-saw or panel-saw up to 22 in., and otherwise provides amply for a moderate kit.

Carcase. The front, ends, back, and bottom of chest are jointed

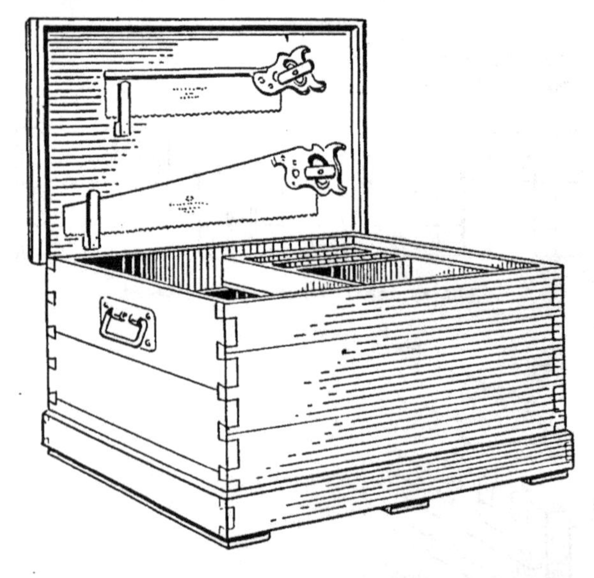

FIG. I. CHEST FOR MEDIUM SIZE KIT OF TOOLS.

Length 27 in., width 19 in., height 16 in. If the kit includes large saws the size of the chest should be increased accordingly.

to width and through-dovetailed at the corners. Here note that it is well to avoid letting the joints of the end boards coincide with those of the front and back. The bottom is boarded in the same way as the sides and is screwed on. To strengthen it and to take the wear, three battens (A) are screwed on underneath.

The skirtings (B) are chamfered on top and bottom edges. As the skirting binds the chest at the bottom it should (preferably) be dove-tailed at the corners. Failing this it will be mitred. It is screwed on, overlapping the battens ½ in. as indicated.

The lid, excluding its rim, is a trifle larger than the carcase and is made up of tongued-and-grooved boards. In the strongest way

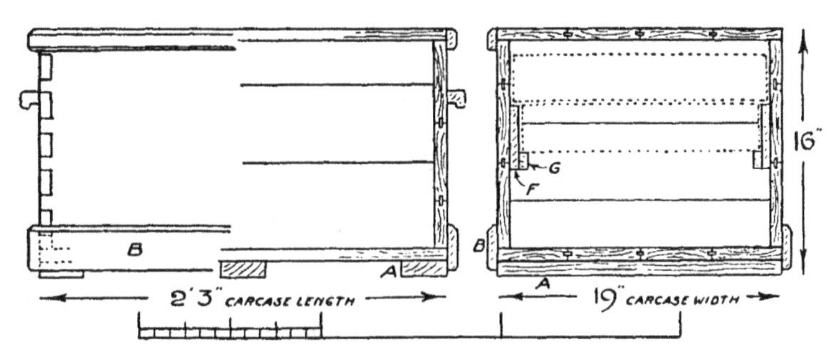

FIG. 2. FRONT ELEVATION IN PART SECTION, AND SECTIONAL END VIEW.

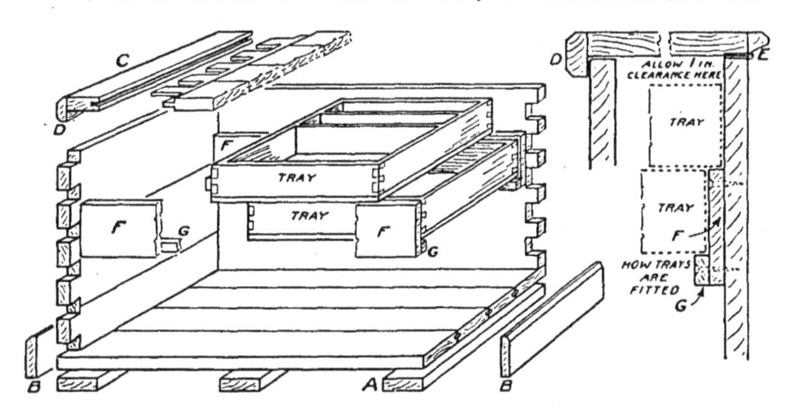

FIG. 3. GENERAL CONSTRUCTION AND ENLARGED SECTIONS.

it should be clamped at the ends with 2½-in. clamps (see C). If these clamps can be of hardwood (birch or ash), so much the better. In the best work the clamps have through mortises cut to take, say, five tenons. If tenons are *not* used, let the tongues be of hardwood. (A battened top is inconvenient as the battens interfere with the saws if these are fitted to inside of lid.)

The lid rim (D, Fig. 3) may be of 1½ in. by ¾ in. or ⅞ in. hardwood, slightly chamfered on both edges. As the rim engages the carcase sides the actual lid may be made about $\frac{1}{16}$ in. full in length and width to guard against binding. Fit the hinges before screwing on the rim, which is mitred at the corners. On account of the hingeing there can be no rim at the back. For finish, however, a rim slip (E, Fig. 3) may be glued on and pinned, the under-edge being bevelled so that the lid will open well back. Use a pair of 3-in. solid-drawn brass butt hinges, bedding both flanges and keeping the knuckle well out.

Handles. Wood, metal, or rope handles may be used. If of wood cut them at least 8 in. long from stuff 2⅛ in. wide by 1⅛ in. thick. They are screwed from inside.

Fittings. These may usually be left to the worker himself, as almost everything depends on the kit. Saws, however, may be schemed to fit on the lid, the blades slipping into racks whilst the handles are held by turnbuttons which pivot on circular blocks placed to come under the handholes.

For the body of the box at least two sliding trays should be provided. These hold chisels, screwdrivers, gauges, bradawls, and small tools which have to be handy. The upper tray will slide on two boards (F), the lower one on two battens (G) screwed to F. The under-tray is thus about 1½ in. shorter than the upper one. As both trays slide the full length of the chest access to either is immediate. Instead of the second tray some workers prefer a nest of, say, two shallow drawers.

The larger tray will come out at about 17 in. long, the lower one about 15½ in. Width should not exceed half the inside length of chest—that is (in this case) about 12½ in. Sides (dovetailed) may be of ⅝-in. stuff; bottoms, ⅜-in. plywood.

There is ample space for planes, brace, mallet and other items, and racks or other gadgets may be fitted according to inclination. The important thing is to make sure that cutting tools are so housed that their blades are protected.

Timber. Deal or other sound whitewood will be used. If 1-in. tongued-and-grooved stock stuff is procured the size of chest may be adapted so as to incur as little waste as possible. The following may be taken as a guide to thicknesses.

Boards (sides, bottom, and lid), ⅞ in. net.
Battens (A), ⅞ in. or 1 in. net.
Skirting (B), ¾ in. or ⅞ in. net, 3 in. wide.
Lid (C), ⅞ in. If it be clamped as shown, 1 in. is better.
Lid rim (D), 1½ in. or 1¾ in. wide by ¾ in. or ⅞ in. thick.
Tray guide (F), 4 in. by ¾ in.
Lower tray guide (G), 1 in. by ⅞ in.
Tray sides, ⅝ in.; bottoms, ⅜-in. plywood.

TRAY FOR NAILS AND SCREWS

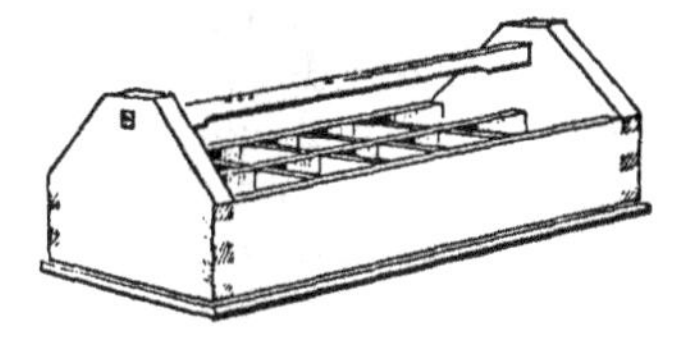

FIG. 1. PARTITIONED TRAY FOR NAILS AND SCREWS.
Size 16 in. by 7½ in.

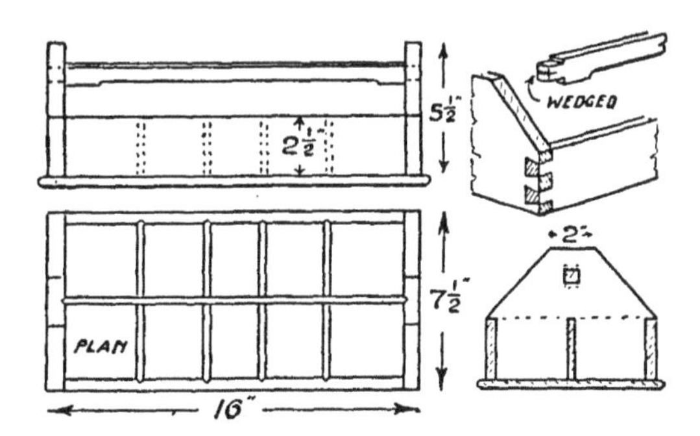

FIG. 2. ELEVATION, PLAN AND CONSTRUCTION DETAILS.

SIDES and ends are dovetailed and the bottom screwed on. Cross divisions are halved to main division, these parts being housed or V-grooved. Handle-bar is shaped to a comfortable hand hold and is through-tenoned and wedged to ends. (Bottom might be of $\frac{5}{16}$-in. ply and divisions of ¼-in. ply.) The dimension of tray may of course be adjusted to the worker's requirements.

CUTTING LIST

	Long in.	Wide in.	Thick in.		Long in.	Wide in.	Thick in.
2 Ends . .	5½	7½	⅜	Bottom . .	16¾	8¼	⅜
2 Sides . .	16	2½	½	Division . .	15¼	2½	$\frac{5}{16}$
Handle-bar .	16¼	1⅛	⅞	5 Cross-pieces .	6¾	2½	$\frac{5}{16}$

USEFUL TOOL CABINET

FOR the home workshop a tool cabinet is in many ways more convenient than a chest. In the cabinet shown in Figs. 1 and 2, the tools in frequent use are arranged so as to be close at hand. The heavy tools are accommodated in the cabinet proper, and the relatively light ones in the boxed-in-doors; thus, no undue strain is placed on the latter. The three drawers are intended for screws, nails and various small tools. As most workers prefer to use a combination plane instead of separate tools for such operations as ploughing, rebating, etc., a space is provided for the box in which the tool is usually kept. It will be noticed that the saws are placed edge-wise in the cabinet, so effecting considerable economy in space.

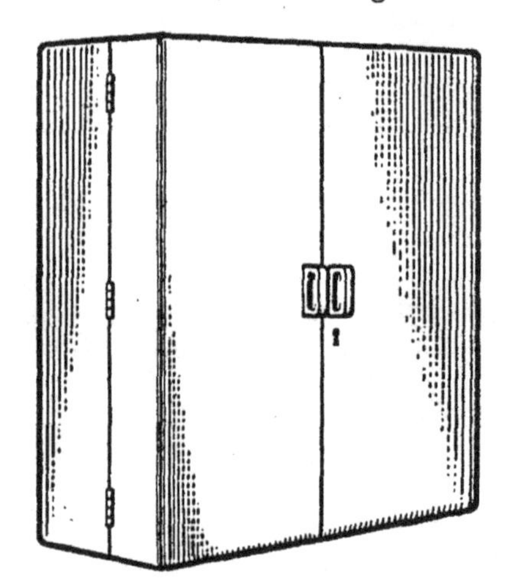

FIG. 1. CABINET WITH CLOSED DOORS.

With lightly rounded corners and a painted or lacquered finish, the cabinet makes a most attractive as well as useful item. The closed size is 2 ft. $9\frac{1}{2}$ in. wide, 3 ft. $7\frac{1}{2}$ in. high, and 11 in. deep. These dimensions can be varied to suit special tools.

As chisels are more in use than gouges, the former are placed on the right-hand side of the cabinet and the gouges to the left. It will be seen that the setting-out tools are together on the right-hand side, excepting the marking and mortise gauges.

Construction. The carcase, Fig. 5, can be made from $\frac{7}{8}$-in. stuff, finishing $\frac{3}{4}$ in. As the cabinet is divided by shelves and partitions, a good fixing for the back can be obtained; therefore this may be of $\frac{3}{16}$ in. ply. It is not possible to form the carcase and door-frames in one and separate one from the other, as would be done in making a box, since the two door-frames have to fit closely where they meet centrally. If they were made with the carcase, sufficient material would not be available for cleaning off, to obtain a good fit. If possible, it is advisable to true up the stuff for both door-frames together and rip the stuff down for the sides and ends for each frame. Rebated joints will suffice for the sides and ends of the carcase, and also for those of the door-frames. The parts, of course, could be dovetailed.

The partitions (*b*) and (*c*) are secured by stop housing; as also are the shelves (*d*), (*e*), (*f*), and (*g*). Although this may seem an unnecessary elaboration, it is well worth while, since if the grooves are set out accurately, the shelves will be found to be parallel and no trouble will be found in fitting the drawers. This might not be the case if

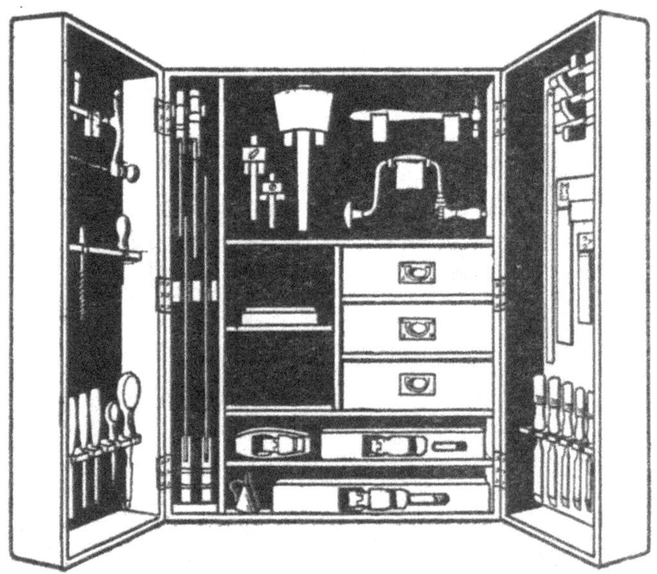

FIG. 2. DOORS OPENED SHOWING TOOL ARRANGEMENT.
When doors are opened back flat the position of every tool can be seen at a glance.

the parts were nailed together. The plywood back is fixed and pinned in a rebate, as shown in Fig. 6, and it will be necessary to reduce the width of the shelves and partition by an amount equal to the depth of the rebate. The drawer rails, which can be 1½ in. by ¾ in., are ploughed on their near edge, as shown in Fig. 7, the ends of the runners being tenoned into the grooves. The rails and runners are glued together and pinned to the side of the cabinet and the partition (*c*).

Drawers. The construction of the drawers is shown in Fig. 8. The fronts are made from ¾-in. stuff and the sides ⅜-in., the back being of similar thickness. For the bottom $\frac{3}{16}$-in. ply is suitable.

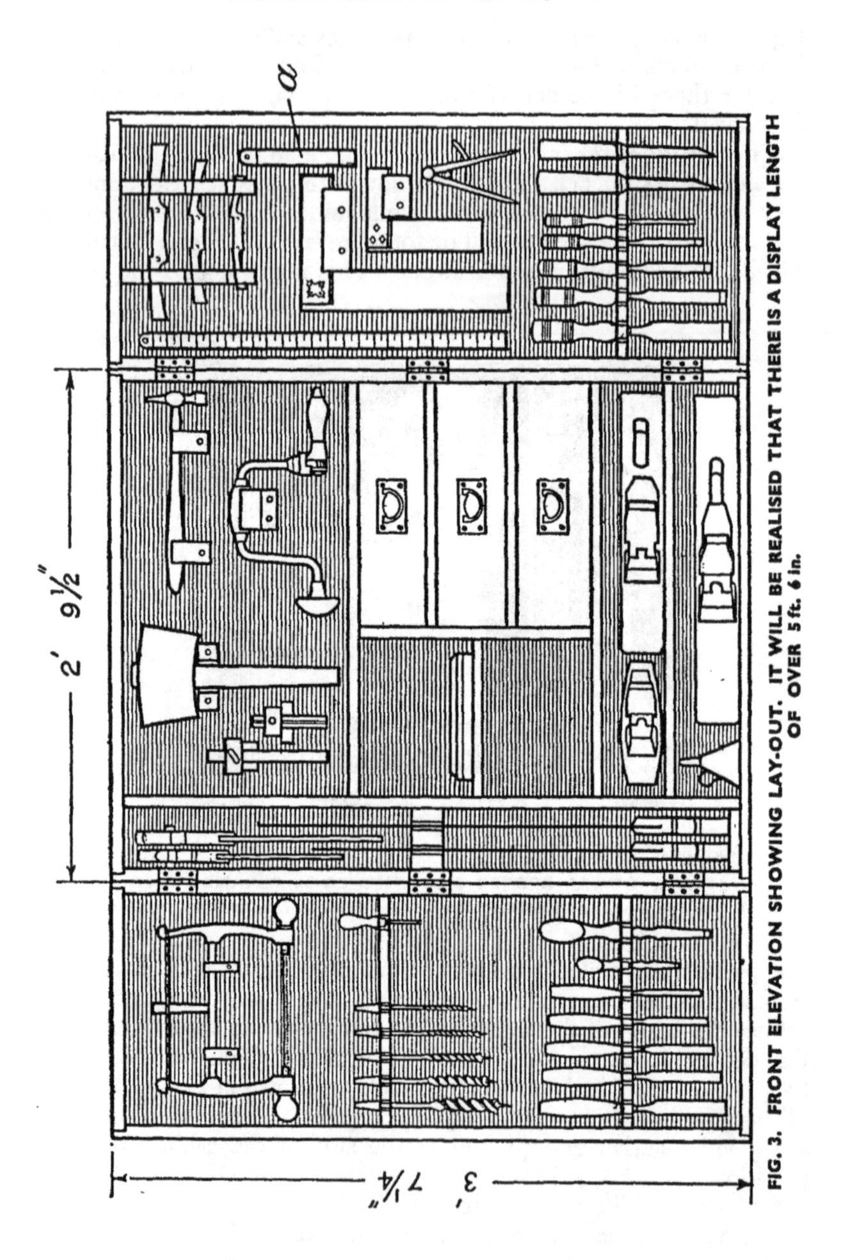

FIG. 3. FRONT ELEVATION SHOWING LAY-OUT. IT WILL BE REALISED THAT THERE IS A DISPLAY LENGTH OF OVER 5 ft. 6 in.

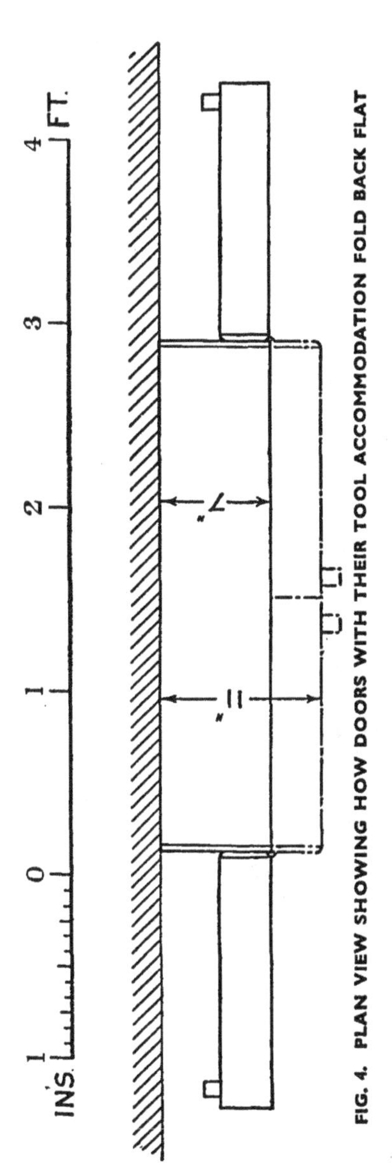

FIG. 4. PLAN VIEW SHOWING HOW DOORS WITH THEIR TOOL ACCOMMODATION FOLD BACK FLAT

This is ploughed into the front and sides and pinned from underneath to the back. If it is desired to have one or more partitions, it is best to stop house them into the front and back, as shown, rather than nail them in position.

If the worker is uncertain of making a success of the lapped dovetails, the fronts could be rebated at the ends and the sides secured in the rebates by gluing and nailing, using $1\frac{1}{2}$-in. oval nails. If possible, $\frac{3}{8}$-in. or $\frac{5}{16}$-in. ply should be used for the door panels, as ply of the thickness stated will enable the outside edges of the doors to be rounded, which will have the effect of improving the appearance of the cabinet.

Tool supports and racks. The profile of one of the spokeshave racks is shown in Fig. 9. In order to avoid short fibres, the grain should run lengthwise. The semicircular rests can be formed by boring with centre bits according to the size of the spokeshaves, and then cutting to shape with a bow-saw and finishing with scribing gouge and chisel. Fig. 10 shows one of the supports for the hammer. The two are made together by boring a central hole and then cross-cutting. In order to position the rip- and hand-saws in their pocket a block is positioned centrally, Fig. 3, the blades of the saws resting in saw cuts in the block. The block is shown in Fig. 11. The tenon- and dovetail-saws are hung on a wooden peg which should be slightly recessed on its upper surface in order to prevent the saws slipping off the end of the peg.

The formation of the other supports and racks will be clear from Figs. 3 and 5. As it will be difficult to obtain a good fixing for the supports and racks from the front, it is a good plan first to glue them

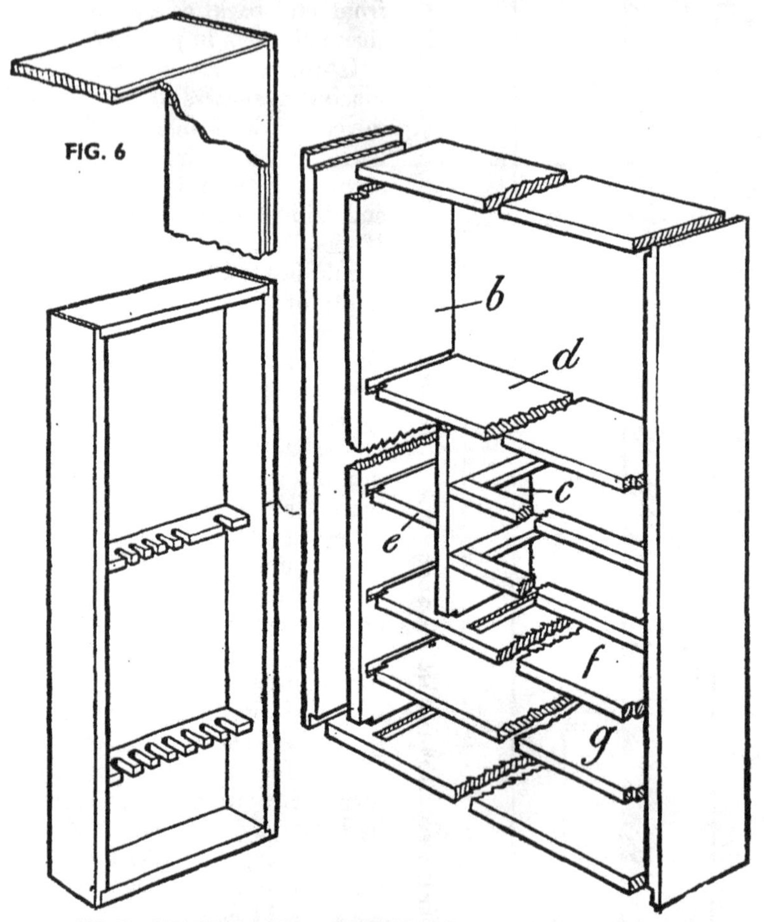

FIG. 5. GENERAL CONSTRUCTION AND (FIG. 6) BACK DETAIL.

in position and then when the glue is set pin or screw each from the back, taking careful measurement in order that the pins or screws will enter each part.

Finishing the cabinet. A pleasing form of handle for each of the doors is shown in Fig. 12. A recess is cut with a gouge on each side and the projecting edges of the handles are rounded. The handles are secured by gluing and screwing from the back. A satisfactory finish to the cabinet can be obtained by sizing and then

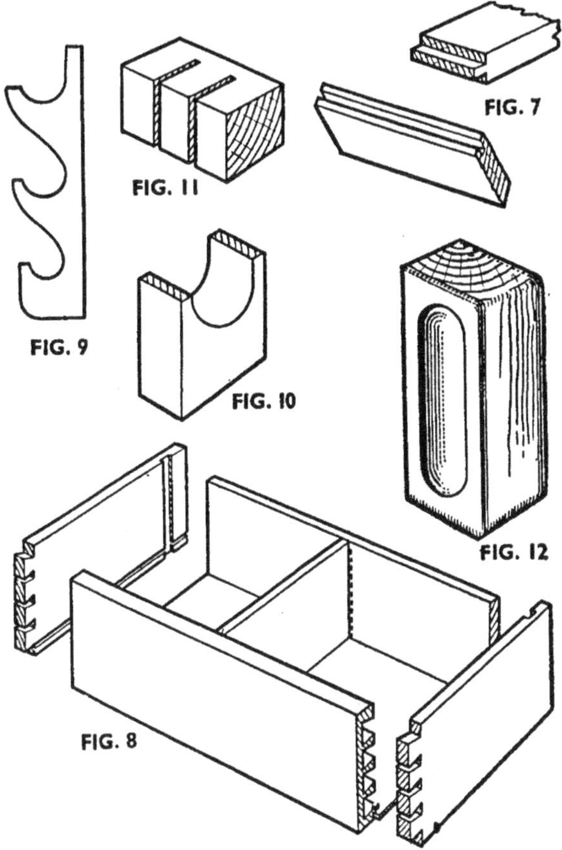

FIG. 7. RUNNER FIXING. FIG. 8. DRAWER CONSTRUCTION. FIG. 9. SPOKESHAVE RACKS. FIG. 10. HAMMER SUPPORT. FIG. 11. SAW-BLADE BLOCK. FIG. 12. HANDLE DETAIL.

applying two coats of knotting, or, alternatively, the cabinet can be painted according to the taste of the worker.

As the cabinet with its tools is of considerable weight, it would be as well to support it on two iron brackets, the attachment to the wall being effected by plates positioned towards the top of the cabinet.

SHOOTING-BOARDS

THESE workshop accessories are invariably constructed at home, the worker making them to his own sizes. Beech is the favourite wood to use, but birch, oak, and other heavy hardwood will serve. Deal is suitable for the shooting-board providing the

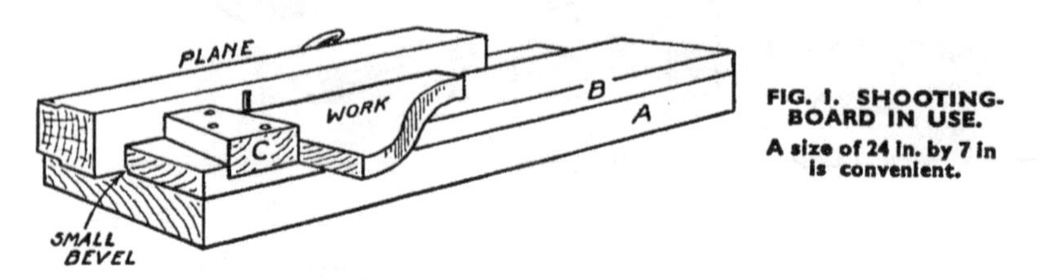

FIG. 1. SHOOTING-BOARD IN USE.
A size of 24 in. by 7 in is convenient.

stop is of hardwood. Experience will prove that a fair-sized shooting-board is more serviceable than a small one, because it takes in larger work. For a board 24 in. by 7 in. three pieces are required:

CUTTING LIST

	Long in.	Wide in.	Thick in.
A	24	7	$1\frac{1}{8}$
B	24	4	$\frac{3}{4}$
C	5	3	$1\frac{1}{4}$

Square pieces A and B, taking special care that the face edge of board (B) is absolutely straight. Before fixing, slightly chamfer the under-edge of this board so as to leave a little cavity which will absorb superfluous sawdust. Screw parts A and B from below, countersinking for the screw-heads.

For the stop (C, Fig. 2) take a thickness of $1\frac{1}{4}$ in. and taper the

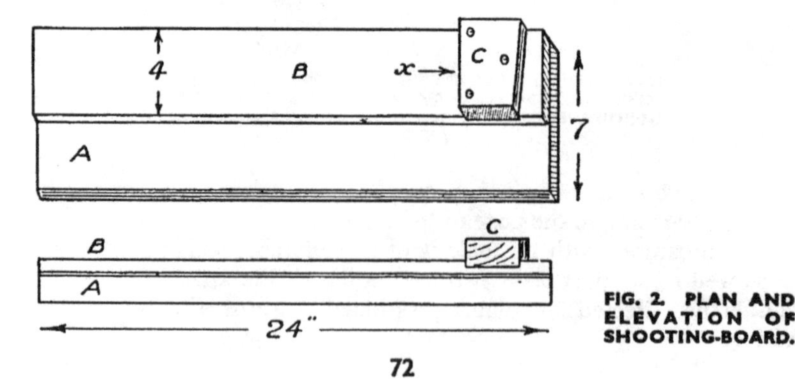

FIG. 2. PLAN AND ELEVATION OF SHOOTING-BOARD.

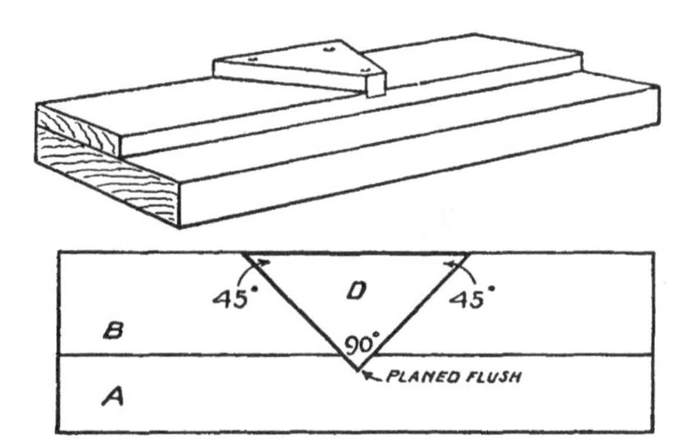

FIG. 3. MITRE SHOOTING-BOARD.
Completed board and plan with main uses.

piece from 3 in. wide at the outside end to 2½ in. at front. Allow a length of 5 in. At least an inch from the end of board (B) cut a channel ¼ in. deep, tapered, to take the piece (C). Note that the line *x* must be at right angles to B—that is, square; this because the work, which rests on (B), butts against (C) whilst shooting. Glue the channel and drive in the wedge-shaped block (C). Screw from above and afterwards cut and true the waste ends so that the block is in alignment, front and back, with (B).

The board is used as indicated in Fig. 1, the plane resting (sidewise) on the lower board (A) whilst the cutting iron faces the work.

A mitre shooting-board (Fig. 3) is made on similar lines. The pieces A and B may be as before, but the block (D) must be truly shaped to a right-angled triangle with the two base angles each 45 degs. In other words, it represents a 45-deg. set-square (see page 74).

Cut the block from 1¼-in. beech with a base line about 8 in. or 9 in. long. Mark and cut with the greatest accuracy, and on the upper board (B) mark the 45-deg. angles to correspond. Cut a recess about ¼ in. deep. When gluing down allow the apex of the block to overhang about an inch. After screwing, the overhanging apex is planed off flush with edge of board (B). Mitre boards are required for shooting the ends of mouldings and other mitred work.

MITRE BOX AND MITRE BLOCK

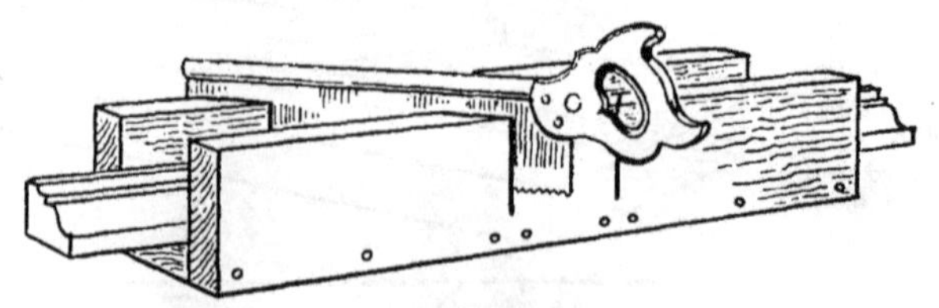

FIG. 1. MITRE BOX TO TAKE MOULDINGS UP TO 3 in. WIDE. In the case of a larger box it is advisable to nail three strips to the top to join the sides and to strengthen them.

MITRE BOX. For sawing wide mouldings or other parts that have to be mitred a mitre box is more convenient than the small mitre block, which offers only one guide to the saw. Its advantage is that the saw is accurately guided at both sides of the moulding.

The box may be any length from 16 in. to 24 in., the heavier the better to ensure stability. For the size shown two sides 18 in. by 3½ in. are required, the bottom being 18 in. by 3 in. Use beech, if possible, finishing ⅞ in. thick, but any seasoned hardwood will serve. Glue and screw the sides to the bottom.

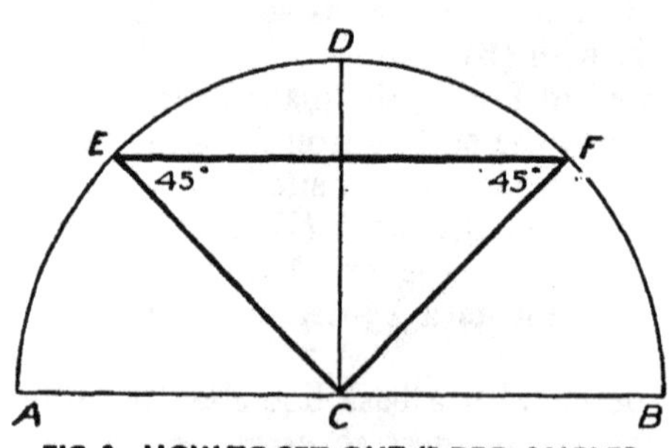

FIG. 2. HOW TO SET OUT 45 DEG. ANGLES.

The marking of the guide lines is the next task. These have to be at an angle of 45 degs. and accurate setting out is essential. On a sheet of card or (better) a board of thin plywood, draw a line AB about 17 in. long, halve it at C and draw the

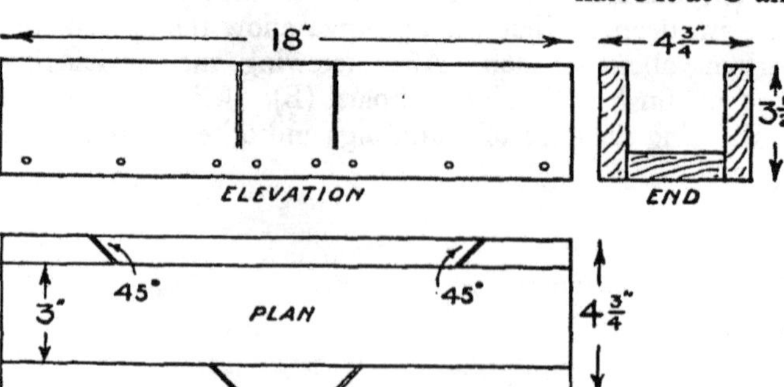

FIG. 3. SIDE ELEVATION, END SECTION, AND PLAN.

perpendicular CD. With the compasses at a radius of 8½ in. draw the semi-circle shown. Halve the arc AD at E and BD at F. Join EF and then join CE and CF. The triangle CEF gives an apex angle (C) of 90 degs., the angles at E and F both being 45 degs. Cut the triangle with a sharp penknife and straight-edge after testing every side carefully.

Lay the template on the top of box keeping the long edge (EF) flush with the outside edge. Mark on both top edges for the saw cuts. Also, with the try-square, mark the two vertical lines on each outer side. When cutting the guide lines it is wise to drop the saw handle so that it cuts mostly on the near side. The whole is then reversed and cut completed. In this way the line being sawn is always visible.

Mitre block. For small section work this is the preferable appliance. The main base is rebated along the back edge to receive the block. Fix the latter with glue and screws, making sure that the last named do not foul the saw kerfs. The front edge

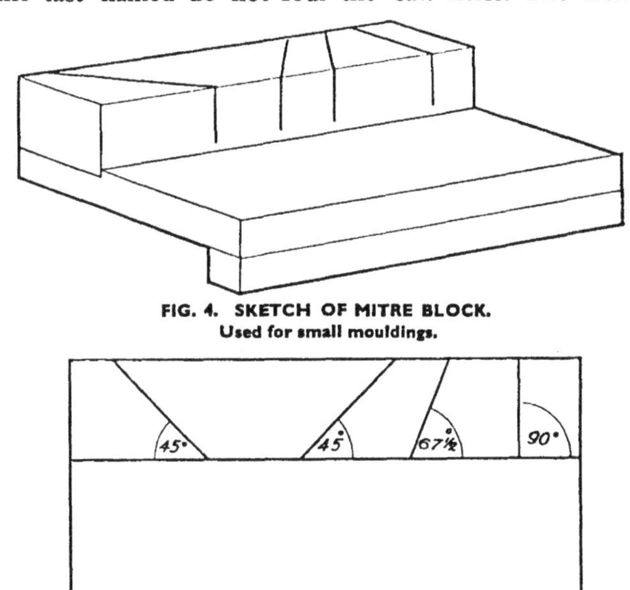

FIG. 4. SKETCH OF MITRE BLOCK.
Used for small mouldings.

FIG. 5. SCALE PLAN WITH SIZES.

piece is best dowelled on ; otherwise with continuous wear screws or nails may become bared. Extra saw kerfs at 90 degs. and 67½ degs. are an advantage, the latter being the correct mitreing angle for 135 degs. (a right-angle plus 45 degs.).

LARGE TRY-SQUARE

A WOODEN try-square of large size is useful for testing the squareness of frames, boxes, cabinet carcases, and similar work. It is not difficult to make. Blades of 12 in., 15 in. or 18 in. are common, and may be larger if required, up to, say, 30 in.

For the stock a piece of hard mahogany, $\frac{7}{8}$ in. thick, is desirable. The blade may be of sycamore or maple, although either mahogany or birch will do as a substitute. For an 18-in. blade allow a width of $2\frac{1}{2}$ in. or 3 in. and thickness of $\frac{1}{4}$ in. The stock will be $11\frac{1}{2}$ in. long from stuff $2\frac{1}{2}$ in. or 3 in. by $\frac{7}{8}$ in. At the head the blade may project from $\frac{1}{4}$ in. to $\frac{1}{2}$ in., as shown, or may be left flush.

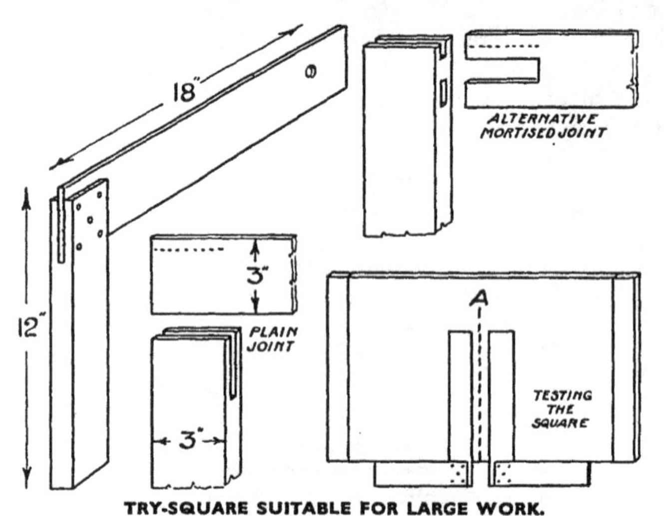

TRY-SQUARE SUITABLE FOR LARGE WORK.

Size is 12 in. with 18 in. blade. Note that the inner edge of the blade should be tested, as it is difficult to correct this after gluing up.

Plane both parts perfectly true and gauge for the joint. This may be either a plain open-slot mortise or a double mortise as in the alternative sketch. In the former case it is simply a matter of careful sawing; in the latter the stock must be gauged on both edges for the small mortise, then bored and the opening chopped out with a $\frac{3}{16}$-in. or $\frac{1}{4}$-in. chisel. The fit must be glove-tight.

The parts are glued and screwed. When glued, however, but before screwing, the blade must be tested for squareness. To do this, place the square on a drawing board (see sketch), or on any fairly wide board with the edge perfectly true and draw or score a vertical line along the inner edge. Reverse the square and draw a second line on or near the first. If the lines coincide, or are absolutely parallel, the square is correct—that is, a right angle. If there is the slightest divergence adjust the blade and test repeatedly till both lines exactly correspond. Unless the angle is a perfectly true right angle the square is useless. Note that the inner edge should be tested because it is difficult to make any correction in this after the glue has set, whereas a shaving can easily be taken from the outer edge.

Allow the glue to set before screwing. Use five brass screws, spaced as indicated. To preserve the edge of the square let it hang on the wall when not in use. For this purpose bore a $\frac{3}{8}$-in. hole in the blade.

BENCH HOOK

THE saw-cutting board (Fig. 1) can be squared from a $\frac{7}{8}$-in. piece of beech 12 in. by 6 in. The short lengths are squared to 5 in. by $1\frac{1}{2}$ in. and are also $\frac{7}{8}$ in. thick. These are screwed on.

The board (or hook) supports work whilst cutting and protects the face of the bench. The under-block engages the edge of board or table, thus giving it stability, and the work is held against the upper block when cutting. The board will also be found useful when chiselling.

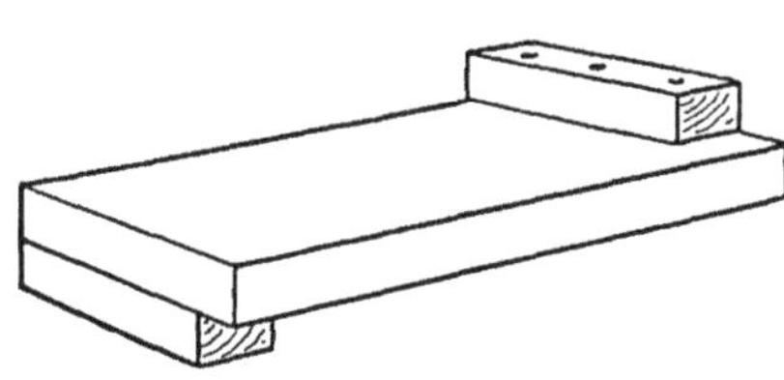

FIG. 1. BENCH HOOK, 12 ins. by 6 ins.

CARPENTER'S MALLET

CARPENTER'S mallets are not costly, but they are interesting to make if a sound piece of beechwood is available for the block, or head. For an average size of fair weight the block may be 5½ in. by 4 in. and 3 in. thick. The handle will require a piece 14 in. by 1½ in. and 1⅛ in. thick.

Beech is the first choice in timber, but hickory (if procurable) or ash is sometimes used for the handle. Failing beech for the block, ash, oak, or any strong hardwood with a close end grain may be used. The chief point is that the end grain must be hard to withstand wear, and that the piece is near the heartwood.

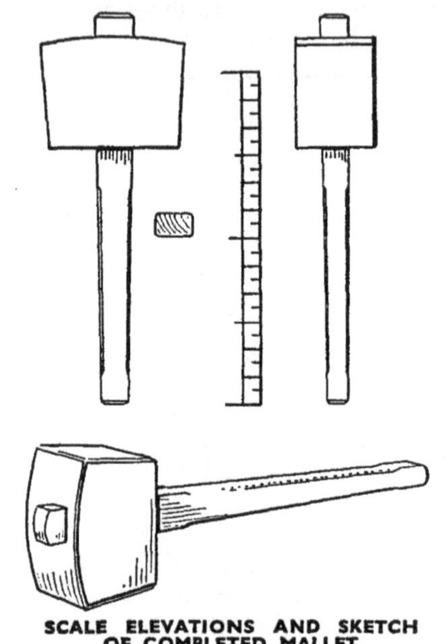

SCALE ELEVATIONS AND SKETCH OF COMPLETED MALLET.

Square the block, gauge for the slightly convex top and for the taper at ends; also mark the centre for the mortise which takes the handle. Gauge for mortise on both sides, noting that, on account of the taper on handle, the mortise is a shade smaller on the under-side. With a twist bit bore holes from each side and finish by chopping with the chisel. The ends of the mortise must be perfectly flat.

On its front faces the handle tapers from 1½ in. to 1⅛ in.; on its side faces the taper is from 1⅛ in. to ¾ in. Work the handle to this taper and round off the hard edges for a convenient hold. Try the handle in the block and plane as necessary to fit. By dropping the thick end of handle on the bench the concussion will help the block to its place.

SMALL SCREW AND NAIL BOX

WHEN no large case for holding nails and screws is required a small box of stout build will serve the home workroom. Sides need not exceed 2 in. in width. If a deeper box is preferred, add ¼ in. or so to the width. The sides have a single dovetailed corner joint (see detail). Before assembling, mark and cut the shallow housings which are to take the partitions. The bottom is

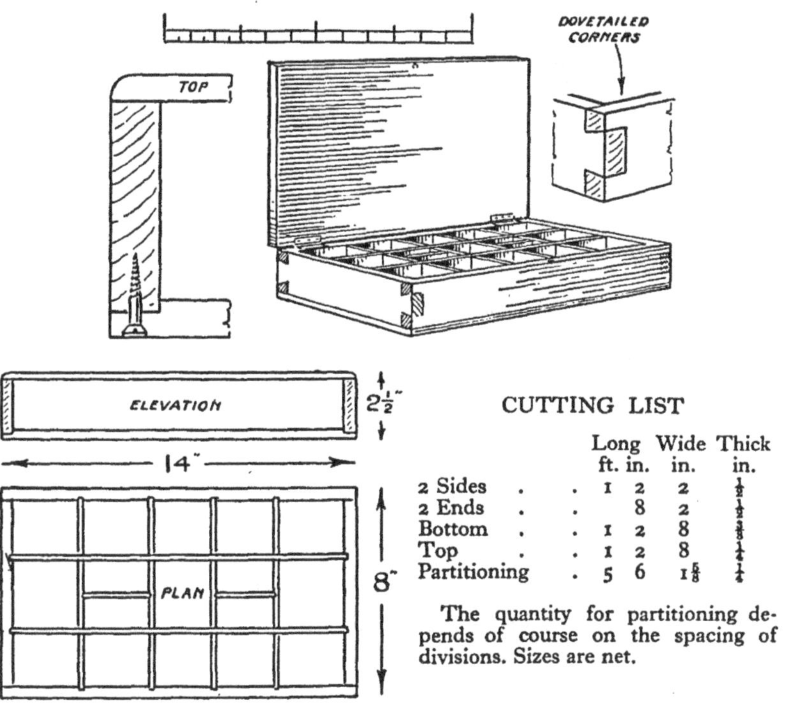

CUTTING LIST

	Long ft.	Long in.	Wide in.	Thick in.
2 Sides . .	1	2	2	½
2 Ends . .		8	2	½
Bottom . .	1	2	8	⅜
Top . .	1	2	8	¼
Partitioning .	5	6	1⅝	¼

The quantity for partitioning depends of course on the spacing of divisions. Sizes are net.

A USEFUL WORKSHOP ITEM. SIZE 14 in. by 8 in.
Partition arrangement can be adapted.

rebated and screwed on. Countersink for the screws so that all are driven well home.

For the partitioning ¼ in. bare will be adequate, and plywood is suitable. Accurate marking is essential for a good fit, the spacing being arranged according to the worker's own requirements. The strips are halved where they intersect and are housed and glued to the sides. The under edges should be planed true so that they bed down to the bottom.

4. OUTDOOR WOODWORK

GARDEN FRAME

IT is customary to speak of garden frames as " lights," the actual light being the sliding glazed frame, shown in Fig. 2. For these lights there are two recognized standard sizes, 4 ft. by 3 ft. and 6 ft. by 4 ft. Larger and smaller sizes are not uncommon, but the 4 ft. by 3 ft. is a convenient frame for the average cottage garden.

The under-framing may be built to hold one, two, or three lights (two are seen in Fig. 1). In nurseries the number may be increased, but the householder rarely goes beyond three lights. Complete frames are referred to as 1-light, 2-light, 3-light, etc.

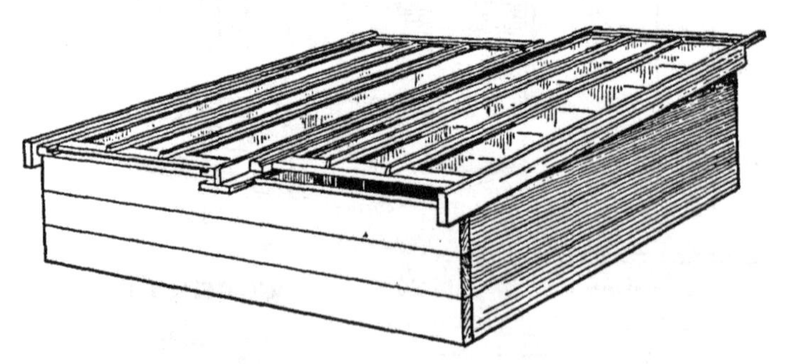

FIG. 1. USEFUL FRAME WITH SLIDING LIGHTS. 4 ft. by 3 ft.
This may be made with one, two, or three lights as required.

Light. The construction of this may be followed from Fig. 3, the outside dimensions being 4 ft. by 3 ft. Stiles (A) and top rail (B) may be of 3 in. by 2 in., rebated ⅝ in. on upper edge for the glass. Bottom rail (C), over which the glass overlaps, is of 4 in. by 1⅜ in., kept flush with rebate in stiles. For durability rails are through-tenoned and wedged, fitting being by paint. Under-edges of stiles and rails are usually chamfered and a throating is run on underside of bottom rail (C) to drain off water.

Sashes (D) may finish only 1½ in. wide, but should correspond with stiles in thickness (that is, 2 in.). They can be either rebated for the glass, or built up in two pieces as at (E). At both ends they are tenoned to rails. The projecting parts of the sashes run out over the bottom rail (see Figs. 2 and 3).

As lights have to slide and are exposed to extremes of weather it is desirable—on sizes of 4 ft. by 3 ft.—to fit a ⅜-in. or ½-in. diameter tie rod across as indicated at (*x*). This helps rigidity and protects the glass from fracture through vibration. Larger lights of 6 ft. by 4 ft. and over will require two tie rods.

Lower Frame. The posts (F) are of 2 in. by 2 in., tongued and grooved stuff of 1⅛ in. being used for the boarding (H). Fig. 1 shows a frame some 18 in. at front and 24 in. at back.

Frames are provided with two guide boards (J), say, 4½ in. by 1⅛ in., these being the same length as the lights. Between them the light glides freely, but not loosely. The actual front-to-back length of frame is partly determined by the angle of slope. Two-light frames have an intermediate slide constructed as (K, L). Stuff for the parts will be 2 in. by 1⅛ in. and 3 in. by 1⅛ in. respectively. The slide is let into the front and back boarding and screwed, battens (G) being screwed as below to afford extra support. The slide (L) is usually grooved to drain off surplus water. Top edges of end boarding (H) may also be grooved.

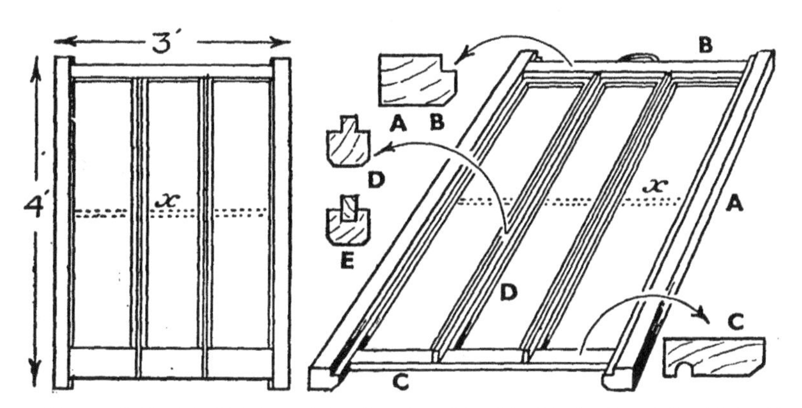

FIG. 2. SIZES OF LIGHT. FIG. 3. CONSTRUCTION OF LIGHT AND SECTIONS.

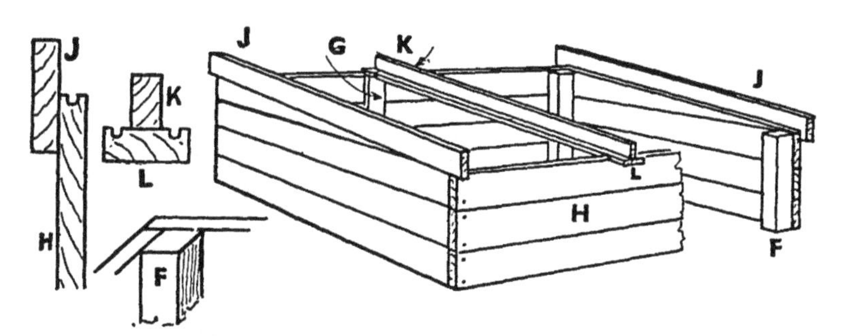

FIG. 4. HOW THE UNDER-FRAME IS MADE, AND SECTIONS.

RABBIT HUTCH

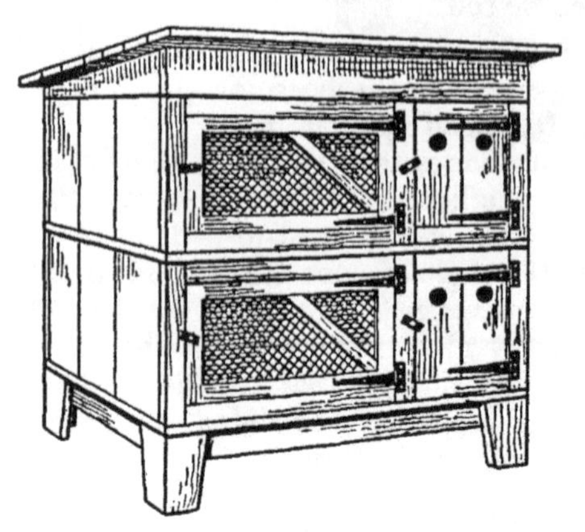

FIG. 1. RABBIT HUTCH OF THE UNIT TYPE.

Two units are shown here, each with day and sleeping compartments. Over-all size is 4 ft. wide, 1 ft. 8 in. deep, 4 ft. high. A third hutch could be added if desired.

A RABBIT HUTCH is an inexpensive item to make, as so much scrap material can be utilized in the construction. The "unit" type of hutch is shown here, this being the most convenient for the home keeper of rabbits. Two units only are shown in Fig. 1, but a third section could be added without unduly adding to the height. Softwood may be employed throughout, and it is assumed that $\frac{7}{8}$-in. stuff will be used unless otherwise suggested.

Hutch. Fig. 2 shows how the structure is built in sections—base, hutch (or hutches), and roof. Dealing first with the hutch—the actual living compartment—the floor (A, 4 ft. by 1 ft. 8 in.) is of three or four boards tongued together. As the front and back are nailed over the ends, these latter (B) will be boarded to a width of about 18¼ in., each secured by 2-in. battens top and botton. Back (C) is boarded. The partition (D) which separates the sleeping from the day room is similar to the ends, but to provide for a passageway, only two upright

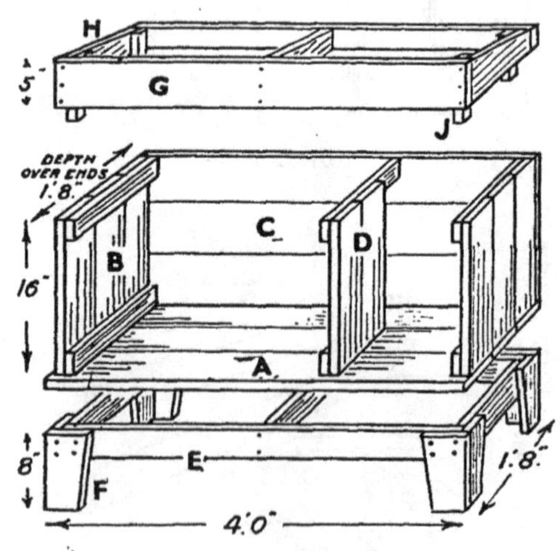

FIG. 2. THE THREE SECTIONS: BASE, ROOF, AND HUTCH.

boards are used. The whole is strongly nailed together, the size when finished being 4 ft. by 1 ft. 8 in. by 1 ft. 5 in. high (including floor).

The front of hutch is a frame (K, Fig. 3) made of stuff 2 in. by $\frac{7}{8}$ in. half-lapped and screwed. Two doors have to be provided. That at L will be of $1\frac{3}{4}$-in. or 2-in. stuff half-lapped and screwed. At the hanging end, however, notch in a strut as indicated, this to prevent the risk of sagging. Line inside with close-mesh wire netting. The smaller door (M—back view) may be solid or boarded, with two battens nailed across inside. A couple of ventilation holes are bored as shown. Hang both doors with tee hinges and provide strong turn-buttons, which should be kept tight.

Base. This is kept in alignment with the hutch. A framework (E, Fig. 2) of 3 in. by $\frac{7}{8}$ in. is nailed together, the size being adjusted so that the over-all dimensions are uniform with those of the hutch.

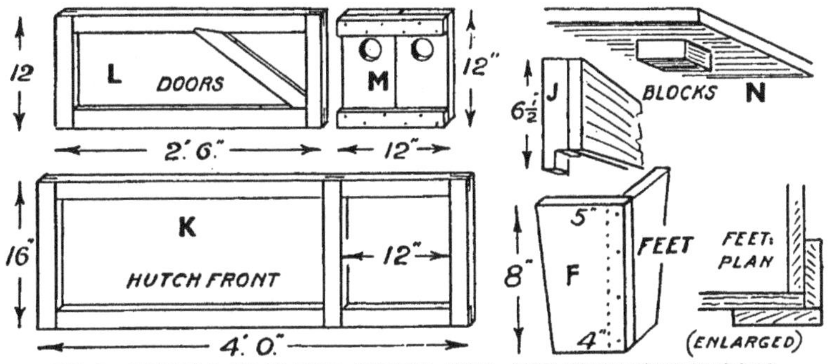

FIG. 3. DETAILS OF FRONT, DOORS, FEET, AND ENGAGING BLOCKS.

It is wise to add a centre stiffening rail. The leg pieces (F) are butted and nailed together and then screwed to the frame (E). The hutch is later screwed down to the frame.

Roof. This again is in line with the hutch, the front board (G, Fig. 2) being 4 ft. by 5 in., back board 4 ft. by 2 in. The ends (H) slope from 5 in. in front to 2 in. at back. Again fit a rail. The parts are nailed as before. The boarded roof may overhang about $1\frac{1}{2}$ in. on all four sides. Tongued matchboarding of $\frac{3}{4}$ in. will be sufficient if the roof is to be covered with a waterproof felt. Weatherboard may be used if preferred.

To secure the hutch to the base, blocks about 2 in. square (N) are screwed to underside of floor, so adjusted in position to drop within the corners of the frame (E). In the same way blocks about $6\frac{1}{2}$ in. long (J) are screwed to the inside corners of the roof frame to engage the hutch. These, obviously, will be cut in (as diagram at Fig. 3) to clear the top of the hutch ends (B).

POULTRY PEN

THIS poultry pen is suitable for the garden or back-yard poultry keeper, or even the man who keeps poultry in a large way. It is one of the most economically made pens hitherto designed, and is just as suitable for its purpose as the more usual type of house.

Fig. 1 shows a pen approximately 8 ft. long by 4 ft. 6 in. wide and 4 ft. 3 in. high. The enclosed portion of the pen occupies 3 ft. 6 in. of the length, the remainder being fitted up as an open run. A nest-box is provided in the end of the enclosed portion, two perches run lengthways, and one side of this portion is made so that it may be detached. The whole is enclosed with wire netting, with the

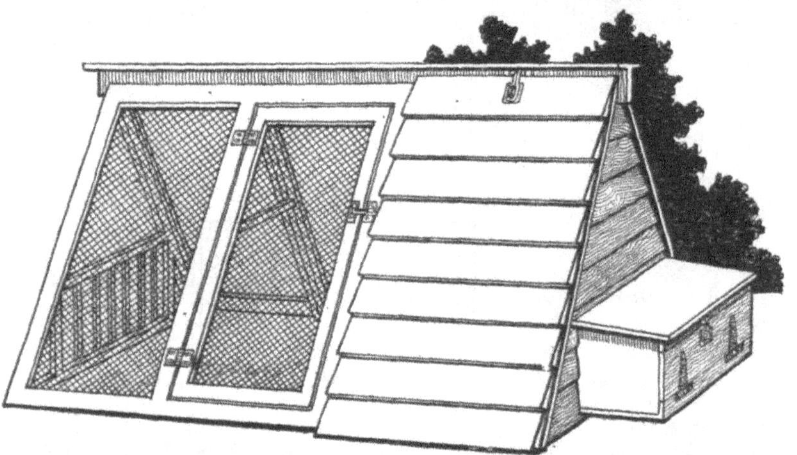

FIG. 1. IDEAL PEN TO HOLD HALF-A-DOZEN BIRDS IN THE GARDEN. This occupies a ground space of just over 8 ft. by 4 ft. 6 in., and the height is 4 ft.

exception of a small portion at the front where fairly widely placed slats are fixed to enable the birds to feed, the feeding and drinking vessels being placed outside. An entrance hole with a semi-circular head connects the run with the enclosed portion of the pen.

Frames. The framework of the pen is arranged with four triangular-shaped frames, three being similar to that shown in Fig. 2, and one as shown in Fig. 3, the stuff for a small pen being 1½ in. square. For the three frames (Fig. 2) the side and bottom rails are half-lapped and screwed together at the corners as in Fig. 4, the horizontal rail is notched in and nailed as in Fig. 5, while in two of the frames short uprights are notched into the bottom rail, fitted under the horizontal rail and against the side rails and nailed. For the frame (Fig. 3) the two side rails are half-lapped and screwed together at the top, and a strut is fitted across some little way down to regulate the width at the bottom.

Assembling. To make the pen (see Fig. 6 for details) the two end frames are spaced at a distance of 8 ft. and joined together by two bottom rails 8 ft. 2 in. long by 3 in. wide and 1 in. thick, nailed in place with their ends projecting 1 in. beyond the frames. The inner frame of the enclosed portion is placed 3 ft. 3 in. from the

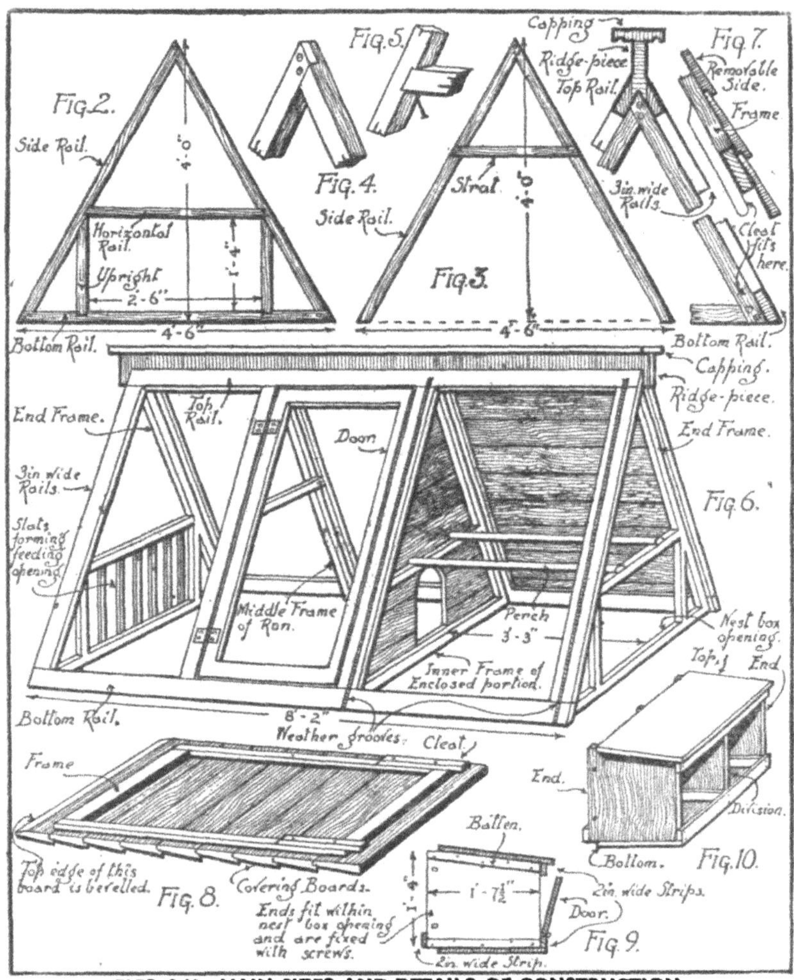

FIGS. 2-10. MAIN SIZES AND DETAILS OF CONSTRUCTION.

outer end, and the middle frame of the run is placed across midway, both frames being nailed through the bottom rails.

A ridge-piece 8 ft. 6 in. long by 5 in. deep and 1 in. thick is notched down over the apex of the frames, as shown in Fig. 7. Two top rails 8 ft. 2 in. long by 3 in. wide and 1 in. thick, with their inner edges appropriately bevelled, are nailed to the frames on each side of the ridge, while a capping with two weather grooves run on the underside is fixed above the ridge-piece. To complete the main framework, rails 3 in. wide are fixed over the side rails of the triangular frames on each side of the pen. Those at the ends are allowed to overhang the end frames 1 in. on the outside to finish level with the ends of the top and bottom rails, while those fixed to the two inner frames overhang an equal distance at each side.

Boarding. Weathered, grooved and tongued, or any boards available could be used for covering the enclosed portion of the pen. The boards are nailed on one side, across the division between the enclosed portion and the run, leaving an entrance roughly 1 ft. 4 in. by 10 in. wide, and across the end, leaving the opening where the nest-box is to be fitted. For the portable side, a frame is made up to fit the opening in the main framework, and boards are nailed to it as shown in Fig. 8. This removable side may be secured by nailing two cleats at the bottom end of the frame in such a way that they will drop inside the bottom rail of the main framework. The edge of the top covering board is bevelled where it fits against the ridge-piece.

Door. The door which is fitted in the side of the run should have stiles about 2 in. wide and top and bottom rail 3 in. wide by 1 in. thick, half-lapped and screwed together, the frame being hinged at one side, and fitted with a lock on the other. If six slats about 1 in. wide by ½ in. thick are nailed across the oblong opening in the front of the run the spaces between them will enable the birds to feed.

The sliding shutter which covers the entrance hole needs no special description as it is simply a board, or boards battened together, running in grooves at each side. The two perches fitted across the interior of the pen should be substantial, say 2 in. wide by 1 in. thick, worked to an oval section, and fixed as in Fig. 6.

Nest Box. The nest box is made with two ends and a division 1 ft. 7½ in. wide by 1 ft. 4 in. high, sloping 1 in. on top towards the back, battens being nailed at the top and bottom, as shown in Fig. 9. Boards are nailed across the top and bottom edges, a width of 1½ in. being allowed at the front edge for fitting into the nest box opening. Strips 2 in. wide are nailed across at the bottom of the front, and at the top and bottom of the back. A door, hinged at the bottom, and provided with a lock at the top, is fitted at the back.

GARDEN WORKSHOP

FIG. I. INEXPENSIVE SHED SUITABLE FOR WORKSHOP OR GARDEN.
Suggested sizes are about 8 ft. long by 5 ft. 3 in. deep, but these could be adapted if desired. Positions of door and window too could be altered to suit any particular site.

MADE as shown in the sketch, Fig. 1, the workshop requires four sections—a front, back, and two ends, framed from 2 in. square stuff, the outer members being half-lapped and screwed together, and the inner members notched ¼ in. into the outer members and nailed, as shown in Fig. 5.

Front. The front section (Fig. 2) requires two uprights, and top and bottom rails, half-lapped and screwed together. A door upright is notched into the top and bottom rails 2 ft. from the end upright at either of the sides as may be the more convenient. A lower rail is carried between the door upright and the other end upright, while the lower portion of the framework is completed by fitting a short inner upright and carrying two braces across to stiffen the framework. The window opening is arranged by fitting two uprights between the top and lower rails.

Back and Ends. The back (Fig. 3) consists of two uprights half-lapped to top and bottom rails, with an inner upright and braces fitted as shown. The ends (Fig. 4) are also made with two uprights half-lapped to top and bottom rails, with an inner upright and braces arranged as shown.

Foundation. A concrete foundation should be prepared on the

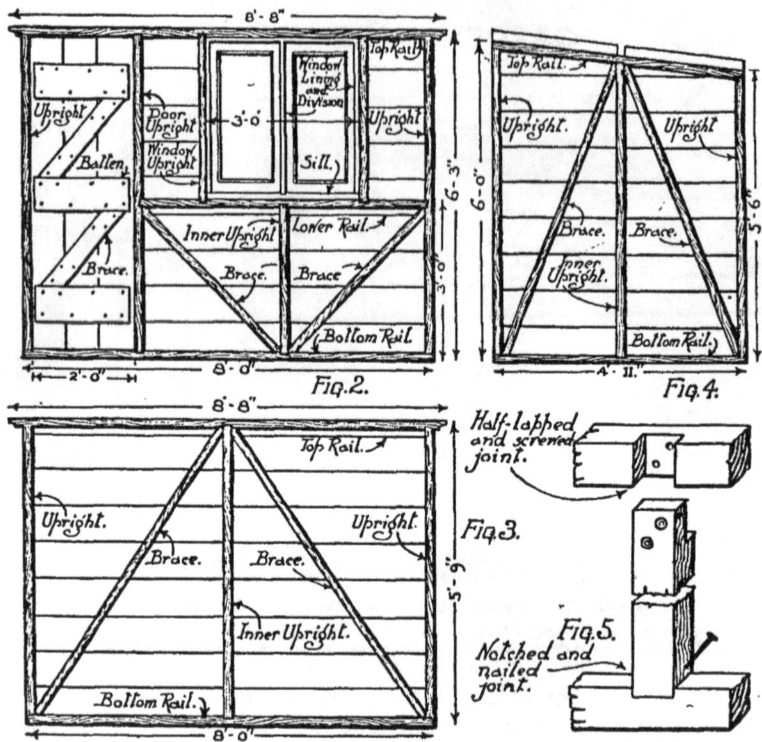

FIG. 2. FRONT ELEVATION. FIG. 3. BACK ELEVATION. FIG. 4. END FRAMING FIG. 5. JOINTS.

spot where the building is to stand, the soil being taken out for a depth of about 8 in., and for the sake of dryness it is a good plan to bring the concrete a couple of inches above ground level, slats of wood being pegged down to the ground to form a mould whilst the concrete sets. If thought desirable, and it may be in an exposed position, the building could be bolted to the ground. The four sections are assembled as shown in Fig. 6, and fixed by passing ⅜-in. bolts through the uprights at the corners, as shown in Fig. 7. If the sections are to be bolted to the foundation the bolts with holding plates under their heads must be embedded in the concrete, as shown in Figs. 6 and 8.

It will have been noticed that the front and back sections are 3 in. higher than the end sections. This allows a 3 in. deep purlin to be fixed across above the end sections as shown in Fig. 6 to give additional support to the corrugated asbestos cement sheets forming the roof. These sheets should overhang about 4 in. all around the

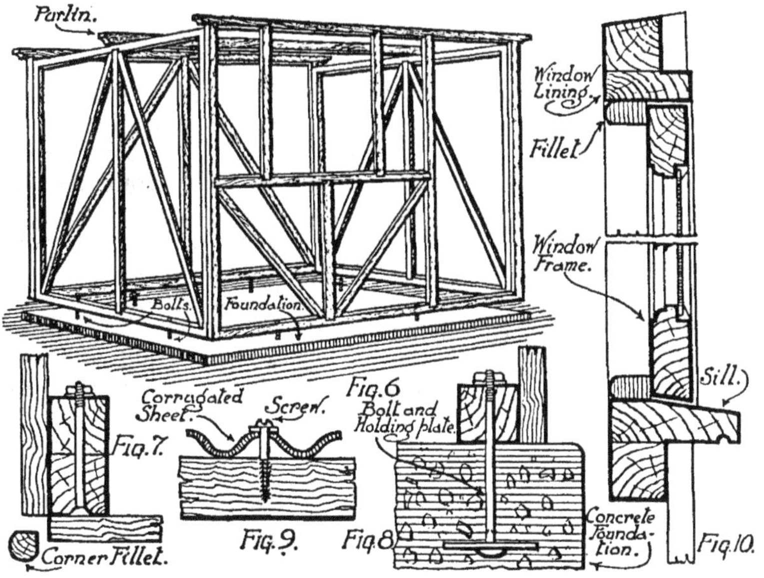

FIG. 6. MAIN FRAMEWORK. FIG. 7. CORNER SECTION. FIG. 8. BASE SECTION. FIG. 9. ROOF FIXING. FIG. 10. WINDOW SECTION.

building, and are fixed down to the top rails of the front and back sections and to the purlin with screws, as shown in Fig. 9.

Covering Frames. Covering the front, back, and ends should next be proceeded with. If grooved-and-tongued or weather boarding can be secured it is nailed on in the usual way, leaving the openings for the door and window. The edges could be finished level with the framing at the corners, and small rounded fillets nailed in the angles, as shown in Fig. 7, will give a neat finish. Failing other material plain asbestos cement sheets could be used, these being secured by screwing wood slips around the edges. In any case the door should be of wood, battened and braced, as shown in Fig. 2, hinged in the usual way and fitted with a lock and key.

Window. In fitting up the window a 4½ in. by 1½ in. sill, with the top edge bevelled and with a weather groove cut on the underside, is first arranged across the bottom of the window opening, the ends of the sill being allowed to project an inch or so. A 3 in. by 1 in. lining is then carried around the sides and top of the opening. If the window is to have a pair of casement frames, a division must be carried from the top lining to the sill. The window frames are made with two stiles and a top rail 2 in. wide, and a bottom rail 3 in. wide by 1½ in. thick, moulded or chamfered, and rebated for the glass. Mortise and tenon joints are used for framing.

TOY WHEELBARROW

As a toy is invariably painted, practically any kind of wood can be used, providing that it is reasonably free from knots. Using 1-in. square stuff, make a frame as shown in Fig. 2. Draw the shape in full size so that the adjustable bevel can be set to the required angle. This will enable the ends of the cross-rails to be marked; also the shallow notches in which they fit. The ends forming the handles can either be left straight and rounded over, or pieces can be glued on beneath, as in Fig. 4, to enable the shape to be worked.

Put the parts together with glue and nails and bore holes at the front to take the axle. Judge it as closely as possible and bore right through the one piece. Repeat on the other rail, and then allow the

FIG. 1. HAVING A PAINTED FINISH MIXED WOODS CAN BE USED.

Care in marking and planing the bevelled edges is essential, but otherwise this is a quite simple piece of work. Sizes are 24 in. long over the frame by about 12 in. wide.

bit to pass right across to correct any inaccuracy. Fig. 5 shows how the wheel is made from two ½-in. thicknesses, the grain at right angles. Bore a hole half-way in from each side to take a tightly-fitting iron axle rod, and add a ½-in. circular block at each side, as in Fig. 5, to stiffen it. Fig. 5 also shows how the ends of the frame rails are cut away to enable the axle to be fitted afterwards. If a metal wheel is available by all means use it.

For the body use wood about ½ in. thick. Prepare the bottom to the sizes in Fig. 3 to fit on the framework, standing in a trifle. All edges will have to be bevelled, but this is best done after the sides have been added. The angles at which the ends of the long sides are planed are not important. Since the bottom edges are a trifle over 12 in. long, the top edges might be about 18 in. Cut to shape, and

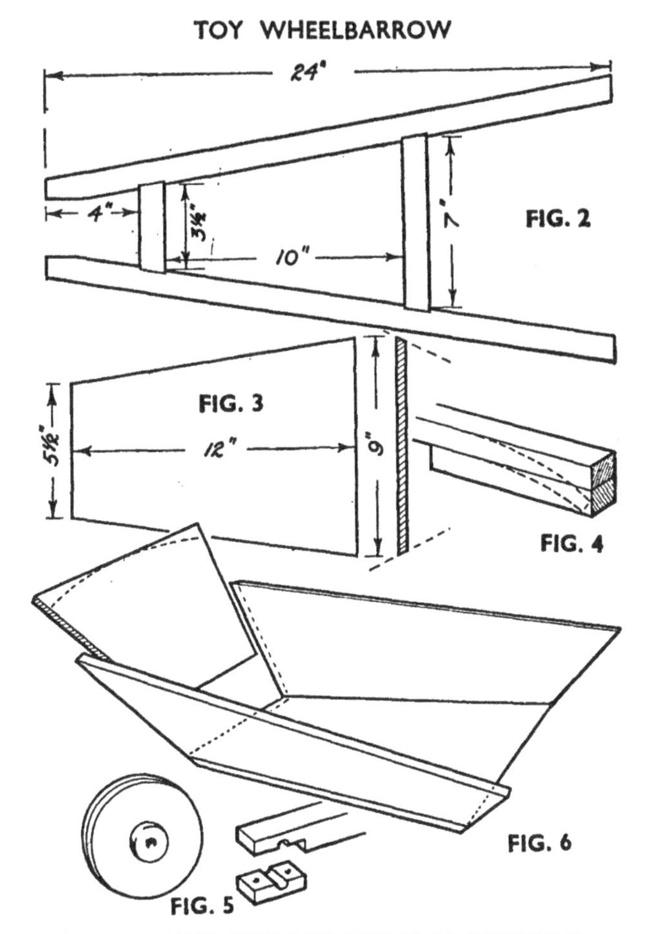

FIGS. 2—6. MAIN SIZES AND DETAILS OF CONSTRUCTION.

bevel the bottom edges of both to give the required slope. They must be alike.

Fix to the bottom with glue and nails, and fit the front end as in Fig. 6, noting the edges must be at an angle. Cut the top to a curve and fix, again with glue and nails. Follow with the rear end. Level the edges and either nail or screw to the frame.

The legs are notched to fit over the rails, and are taken off at an angle to line up with the slope of the sides. Fix with a screw through each rail, and nail through the body at the top.

USING THE TOOLS

I. SAWING

YOU will most likely buy your wood in boards which you will have to cut up to form the various parts of the things you make, and it is for this work that you mostly require the hand-saw. From the list facing page 1 you will note that the cross-cut type is recommended, the reason being that you can use it for cutting both across and along the grain.

Sawing on trestles. For the greater part the wood is supported on trestles or boxes, as shown in Fig. 3, and these are moved about to clear the saw as occasion requires (compare Figs. 3 and 4). To start the cut hold the saw at a low angle at the end of the wood, as

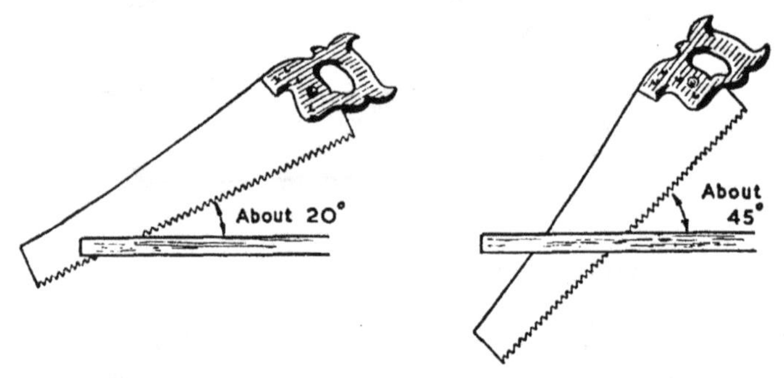

FIG. I. ANGLE FOR STARTING CUT. FIG. 2. NORMAL SAWING ANGLE.
Holding the saw low for the first few strokes enables its direction to be more easily judged.

shown in Fig. 1, and make a few short strokes. The advantage of holding the saw low at the beginning is that it enables you to judge better whether the blade is in alignment with the line to be sawn, a really important point, because the accuracy of the cut depends largely upon making a good start. It so often happens that the saw is badly started, and in trying to correct it the blade is twisted so that it begins to cut the other way, and this continues to the end, the result being a long undulating line instead of a straight cut. Once a reasonable start has been made, the handle can be raised so that the teeth are at about 45 degs. with the wood, as in Fig. 2.

Control of the saw. To steady the saw at the start, hold the left hand at the far end of the wood and raise the thumb so that the blade

RIPPING ON TRESTLES OR BOXES

FIG. 3. STARTING THE CUT WITH WOOD SUPPORTED ON BOXES.
Pressure from the knee keeps the wood steady.

FIG. 4. CONTINUING THE CUT ALONG THE WOOD.
If the wood is long or is thin the boxes should be moved more closely together as otherwise it will bend.

bears against it. This enables you to start the cut in the exact position, and it prevents an accident in the event of the saw jumping out of the kerf. Without this precaution the teeth might jar across

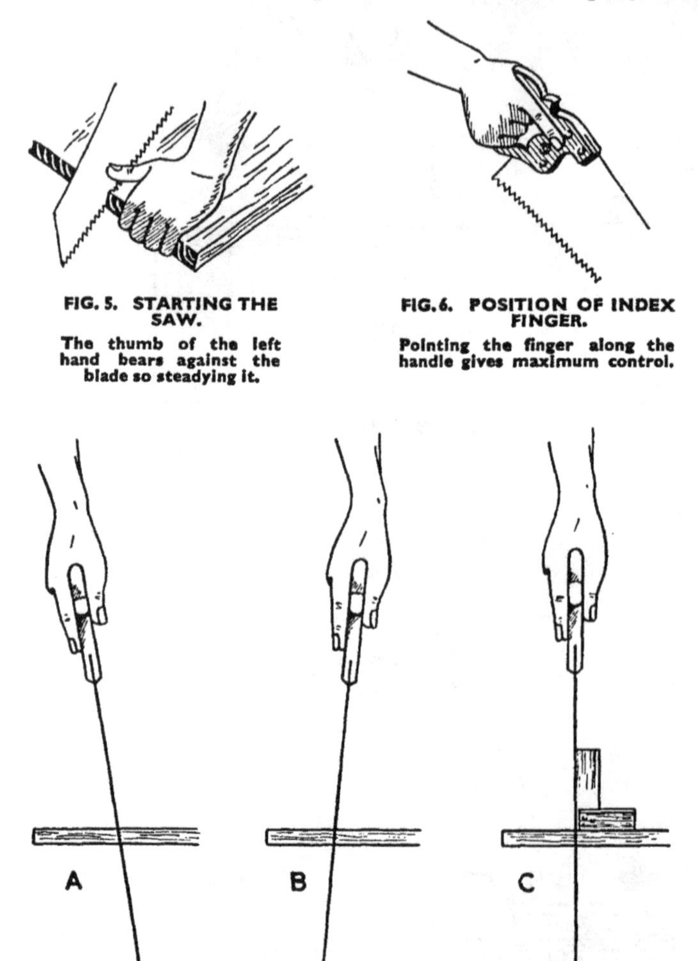

FIG. 5. STARTING THE SAW.
The thumb of the left hand bears against the blade so steadying it.

FIG. 6. POSITION OF INDEX FINGER.
Pointing the finger along the handle gives maximum control.

FIG. 7. FRONT VIEW OF SAW IN ACTION.
Obvious faults are shown at A and B. The try-square in C is a useful guide to the beginner.

the left hand. Fig. 5 shows the idea. After the few preliminary short strokes, work the saw with full, even strokes, stopping it on the down stroke just short of the handle. Do not force it. Just keep it moving up and down, the latter with just enough pressure to ensure control and to keep the teeth well up to their work. If the saw is sharp it will cut perfectly well.

Speaking of control brings us to the function of the index finger of the right hand. This should point down the blade as shown in Fig. 6. It is a tremendous help in accurate cutting, and is a rule that applies to almost all saws.

Upright cutting. Clearly it is desirable to hold the saw as upright as possible, and until you are used to it this is a little difficult. You don't know when you are leaning over. One of the commonest faults is that at B, Fig. 7, in which the saw slopes towards the shoulder. Some beginners become aware of this fault, and in trying to correct it, slope it the other way as at A. A good plan is to stand a try-square on the wood just next to the line as at C. It then becomes obvious whether the blade is upright. Try to memorize the stance when the blade is upright and it will soon be unnecessary to use a square at all.

Cross-cutting. Cross-cutting a board can be done either on the trestles or the bench. The process is similar, but there are one or two precautions to be taken to prevent the grain from splitting, especially at the completion of the cut. Fig. 8 shows how the wood is held on a box or trestle when a short piece is being cut from the end.

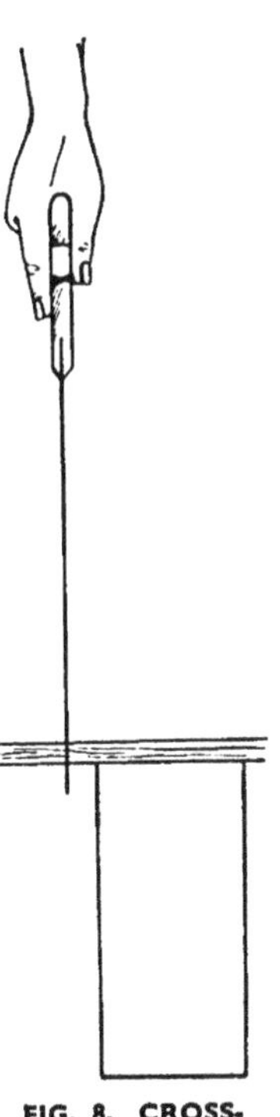

FIG. 8. CROSS-CUTTING.
The wood is supported so that the piece to be sawn overhangs.

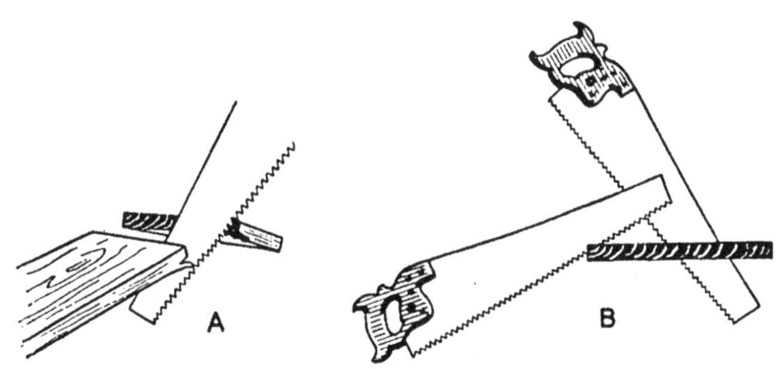

FIG. 9. POINTS TO NOTE WHEN CROSS-CUTTING A BOARD.
A shows the danger of the edge splintering out. The best way is to finish the cut with the saw pointing upwards as at B.

As the saw approaches the near edge, it is worked as lightly as possible so that the lower corner is not splintered out. The latter happens easily as shown at A, Fig. 9. To minimize the risk the saw can be pointed upwards for the final strokes as at B, Fig. 9, at any rate when the wood is resting on the bench. It is rather awkward when on trestles as it is too low.

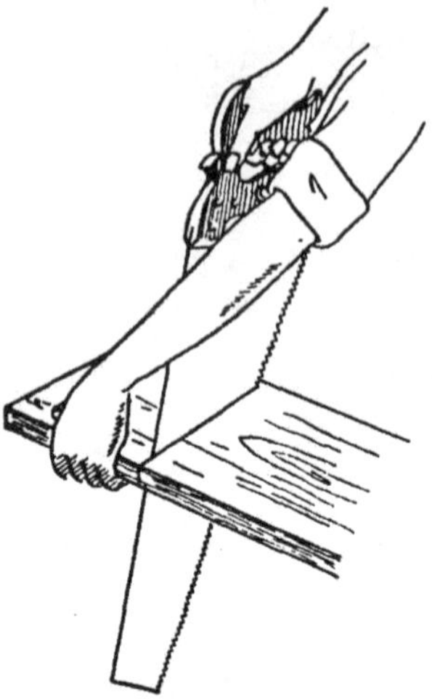

When there is a fair overhang on the piece being cut off, the left hand should be brought over to support it when the cut is nearly through, as in Fig. 10. Otherwise a splintered corner is probable. If there is a really large overhang it is better to ask someone to support the end as in Fig. 11 or to rest it on a trestle of the same height. It is still necessary to bring over the left hand as shown. Never adopt the method in Fig. 12, in which the cut occurs midway between the trestles. It means that you have two pieces of wood to support and a splintered edge is almost inevitable.

FIG. 10. CROSS-CUTTING.
The left hand supports the overhanging end so preventing the edge from splitting.

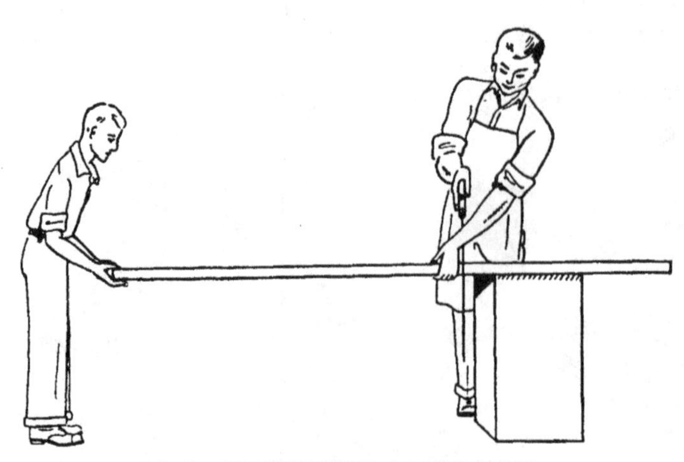

FIG. 11. CROSS-CUTTING A LONG PIECE.
An assistant holds the end and when the cut is nearly completed the left hand of the sawyer supports the wood next to the saw.

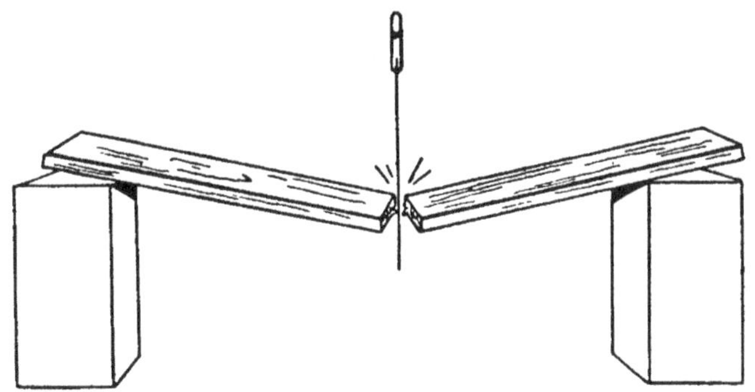

FIG. 12. SOMETHING TO AVOID WHEN CROSS-CUTTING.
One box should be as close to the saw as possible and the projecting end supported on a box or by a helper as in Fig. 11.

Clearly the wood must be held down securely when being sawn, and when cutting on trestles pressure from the knee is enough. On the bench, however, it is necessary to use a cramp or holdfast as in Fig. 13. Otherwise there is constant annoyance due to the wood shifting and the risk of a buckled blade. The same thing applies to overarm sawing on the bench, except that two cramps are desirable.

Overarm sawing. This latter method of sawing is sometimes adopted as being less back-aching. Cramp the wood down so that the line to be sawn overhangs, and, pointing the saw upwards, make

FIG. 13. CROSS-CUTTING ON THE BENCH.
The hand-screw holds the wood steady.

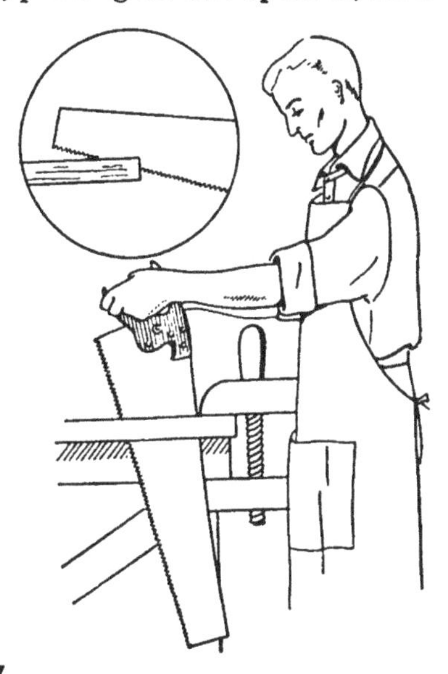

FIG. 14 (*right*). OVERARM RIPPING.
The cut is started as shown inset. Two cramps should be used to hold the wood down.

a few short strokes as shown inset in Fig. 14. Having made a start, grip the saw in both hands as in Fig. 14 and work with full strokes. You cannot cross-cut wood in this way.

Sawing in the vice. In some cases it may be an advantage to

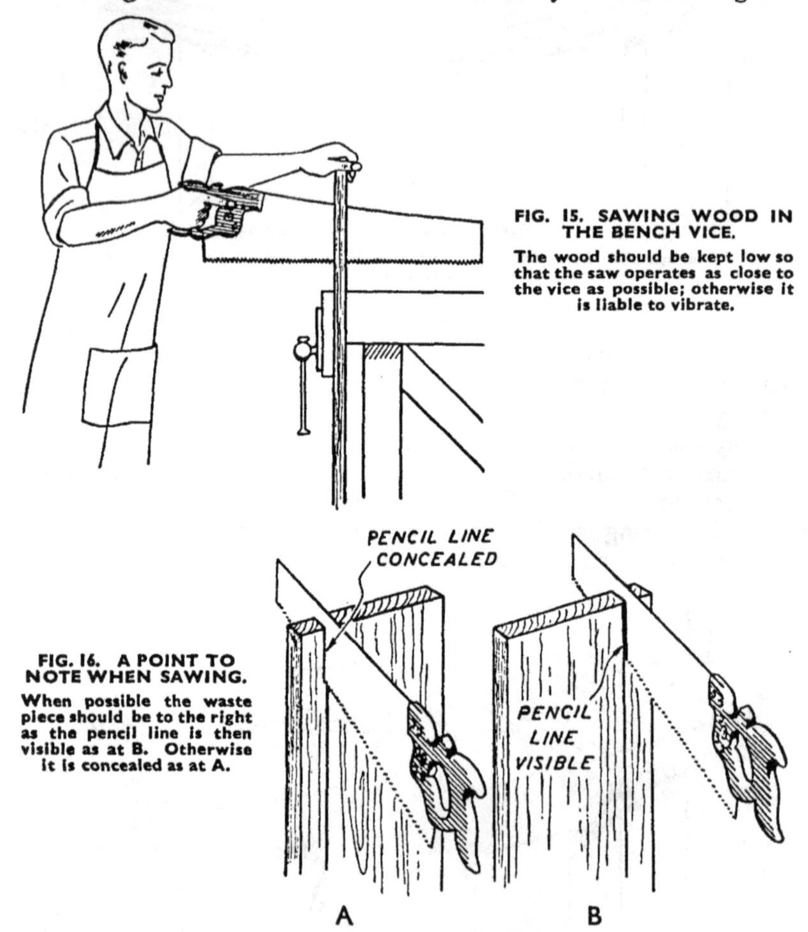

FIG. 15. SAWING WOOD IN THE BENCH VICE.
The wood should be kept low so that the saw operates as close to the vice as possible; otherwise it is liable to vibrate.

FIG. 16. A POINT TO NOTE WHEN SAWING.
When possible the waste piece should be to the right as the pencil line is then visible as at B. Otherwise it is concealed as at A.

hold the wood in the bench vice whilst sawing, as in Fig. 15. The only point to watch here is that there is a clear space on the bench so that the blade will not foul any tools on the top; also that there is ample space at the back—otherwise the end of the saw may strike the wall.

Most cutting is done to one side of the line rather than right on it, the reason being that allowance has to be made for trimming afterwards with the plane. It is always an advantage to be able to keep the line in sight, and this means that the waste piece should be to the right when practicable. Fig. 16 shows the idea. At A the saw-blade conceals the pencil line, whereas at B it is clearly visible. This may not always be practicable, but it should be attempted when feasible.

Use of the back-saw. The back-saw is used mostly for cutting up the smaller pieces of wood on the bench and for cutting joints. It should be held similarly to the hand-saw with the index finger

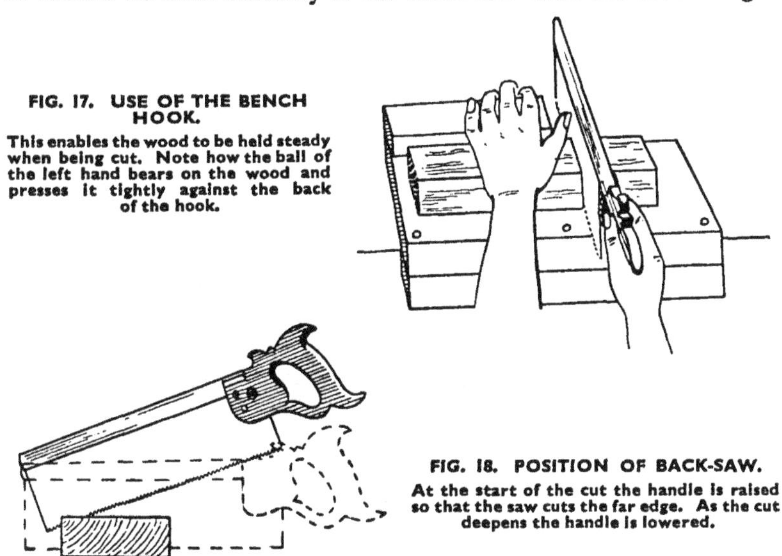

FIG. 17. USE OF THE BENCH HOOK.

This enables the wood to be held steady when being cut. Note how the ball of the left hand bears on the wood and presses it tightly against the back of the hook.

FIG. 18. POSITION OF BACK-SAW.

At the start of the cut the handle is raised so that the saw cuts the far edge. As the cut deepens the handle is lowered.

pointing along the blade and the thumb of the left hand should act as a guide for the blade when starting the cut (see Fig. 17). This illustration shows the hands as you would actually see them when sawing. Note that the wood is held on the bench hook, a simple device specially made to hold the wood steady when sawing (see details on page 77). The left hand serves to keep the wood tightly up against the back of the hook.

Cutting on the bench hook. To start the cut, hold the saw at an angle as in Fig. 18 so that the teeth touch the far corner only. Make a few short strokes and then gradually lower the hand so that the saw becomes horizontal (see dotted lines in Fig. 18). Accurate upright sawing is clearly essential, and the sooner you can do this automatically the better. For a start it is a good plan to square a pencil line across both width and thickness as a guide even on thin

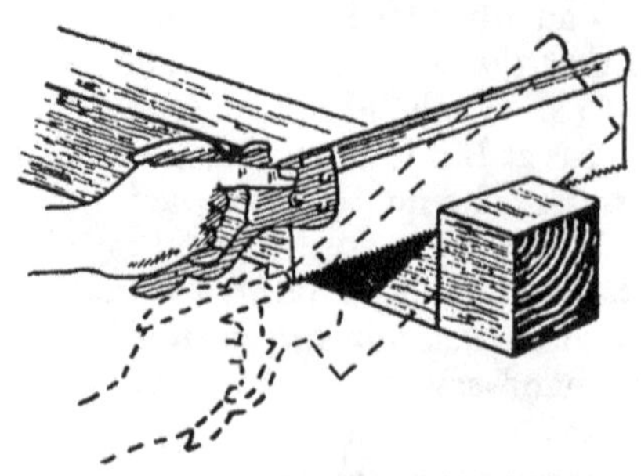

FIG. 19. SAWING THICK WOOD.
Gradually lower the hand as the cut deepens so that the saw follows the squared line.

wood. Test the edge with a square afterwards, and note over a number of tests whether you tend to saw one way or the other.

When the wood is thick you can follow a more definite plan as a guide to upright sawing. Square the line round on to all four sides, and, holding the wood on the bench hook, begin a cut on one of the faces as shown in Fig. 19. Gradually lower the hand until the saw slopes down, as shown by the dotted line, and cuts about halfway through. Give the wood one turn away from you and repeat the process. Do the same again until all four sides have been sawn. It will be found that the saw tends to run in the kerfs already made, and it will prove a great help. It all depends, however, on how you start the cut, especially the first one. You won't need to adopt this method eventually for *every* cut you make, but it will help you to develop a sense of when you are cutting square.

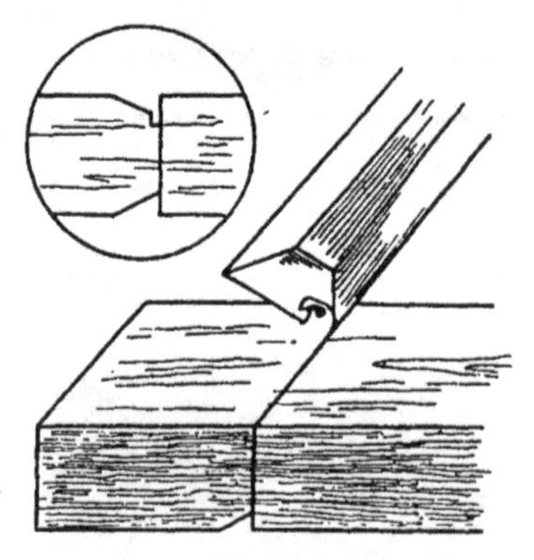

FIG. 20. CUTTING A SHOULDER.
A sloping groove chiselled against the line provides a channel for the saw.

FIG. 21. SAWING A TENON.
Note angle at which wood is held in the vice.

Sometimes square sawing is specially vital, and the line should then be put in with chisel and square (if possible). An example is the shoulder of a tenon, a halving joint, or a plain butt joint. On the waste side of each line a sloping groove is chiselled as in Fig. 20, and this forms a channel in which the saw can run.

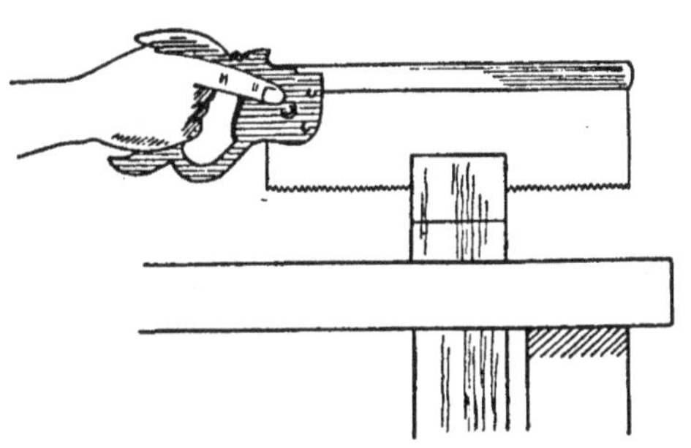

FIG. 22. COMPLETING THE TENON.
The wood is reversed in the vice, this time upright.

Tenoning. When a deep cut has to be made at the ends of the wood, as in tenoning, it is an advantage to hold the wood in the vice at an angle as in Fig. 21. A cut is made down to the extent of the diagonal, the wood reversed, this time upright, and the cut completed, as in Fig. 22. The advantage of holding the wood at an angle is that you can see two faces and it is thus easier to keep to the line.

The bow-saw. You need this saw when you have to cut curves in wood, its narrow blade enabling it to negotiate reasonably quick shapes. It is given in Fig. 23, and the tourniquet for holding the blade rigid is shown clearly. This should be slackened after use. A point to note is that the handles are free to revolve so that the blade, which is attached to them, can be set to cut in any direction which will give clearance for the frame. It can thus cut a line of almost unlimited length providing that it is not more distant from the edge than the blade from the centre cross bar. Interior cuts can be made by knocking out one of the rivets holding the blade. It can then be removed, passed through a hole bored through the wood, and fixed afresh.

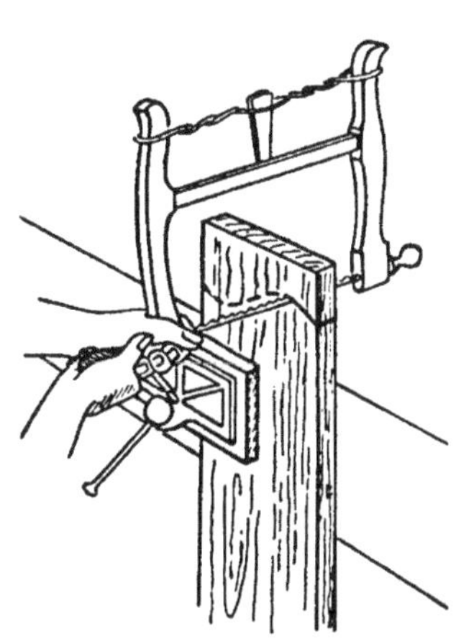

FIG. 23. USE OF BOW-SAW.
The wood should be held low in the vice to prevent vibration.

Square cutting is clearly necessary, because otherwise there is so much work left to the subsequent cleaning up—in a bad case the edge may be undercut, a fault which cannot be put right. This means that the saw must be held square in all directions, a thing which comes only with practice. It is not practicable to use a square to test the blade, and the only plan is carefully to examine the edge afterwards and to note whether there is any bias in the cut and endeavour to correct it. Even cutting, free from lumps, is another ideal to strive for. Watch the line closely and try to turn the saw slightly with each stroke. One slight difficulty is that the saw generally tends to follow the grain, so that when cutting on a part of the line which curves away from the grain it is usually necessary to overdo the turning movement of the saw.

Use two hands as in Fig. 23 when practicable, and fix the wood as

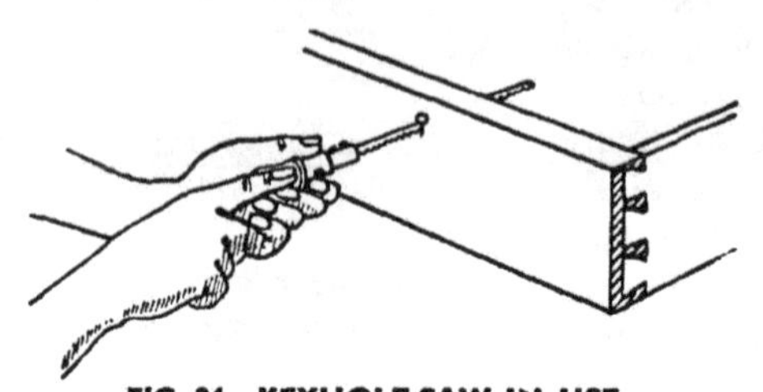

FIG. 24. KEYHOLE-SAW IN USE.
The blade should have the minimum projection consistent with a reasonable stroke. It is also known as the padsaw.

low as possible in the vice. Otherwise there will be undue vibration.

Keyhole-saw. This is occasionally needed for interior cuts which are too far in from the edge to be reached with the bow-saw, and for small cuts for which it would not be worth while to set up the latter—for instance, the sides of a keyhole. It is not so satisfactory a tool, however, because it has to rely upon the stiffness of its narrow blade for rigidity. It is thus easily buckled, and the rule is to give the blade the minimum projection consistent with a reasonable stroke.

2. PLANING

CHIEF amongst the uses to which you put a plane is that of making wood straight and flat, and it is because of this that a jack plane is suggested as the best with which to start off. A shorter plane than this is liable to follow any hollows or inaccuracies in the wood, whereas the jack plane will ride on the high parts only and so reduce them.

FIG. 1. PLANING A SURFACE USING THE JACK PLANE.
The left hand is held astride the plane.

Planing a surface. When planing a surface hold the plane as shown in Fig. 1, with the left hand astride the tool where it is capable of exerting a strong downward pressure. This is especially important at the start of the stroke because it helps to avoid that failing which so many beginners have, that of making the wood round instead of

FIG. 2. WHERE TO APPLY PRESSURE WHEN USING THE PLANE.

FIG. 3. ENDS DUBBED OVER. A COMMON FAULT OF THE BEGINNER.

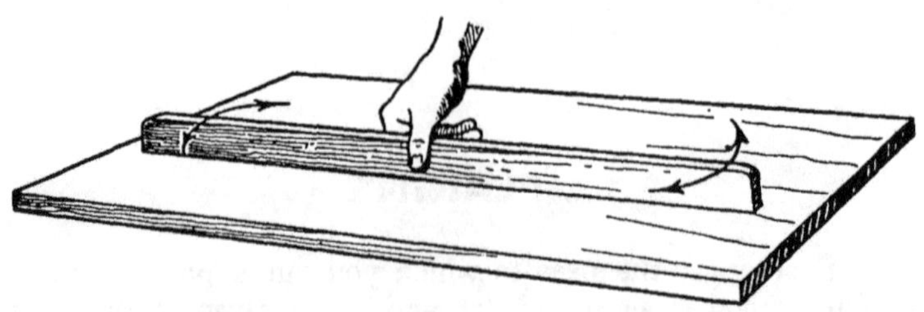

FIG. 4. USE OF STRAIGHT-EDGE TO TEST TRUTH OF WOOD.

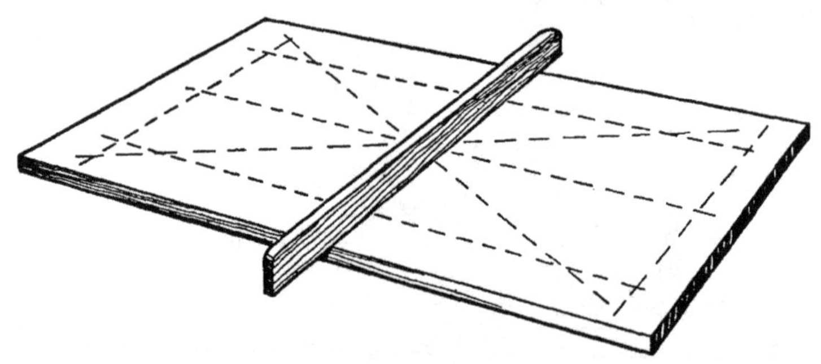

FIG. 5. STRAIGHT-EDGE SHOULD BE HELD IN POSITIONS SHOWN BY DOTTED LINES.

FIG. 6. A. BOARD IN WINDING. B. TRUE BOARD FREE OF TWIST

FIG. 7. SIGHTING BOARD TO SEE IF FREE OF WINDING.

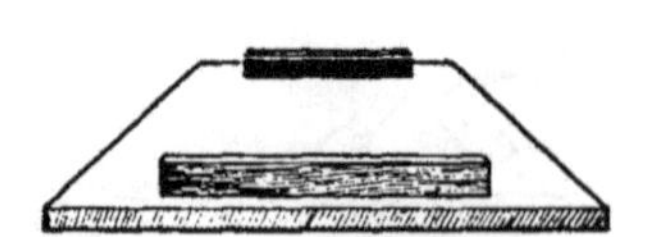

FIG. 8. USE OF PARALLEL OR WINDING STRIPS FOR WINDING TEST.

flat. Put the front of the plane flat on the wood, press strongly down as at A, Fig. 2, and push forward with the right hand. As the far end is reached decrease the pressure and transfer it to the right hand (B). Unless this is done the plane will tend to take the curved path shown in exaggeration in Fig. 3, resulting in the wood becoming rounded.

Testing. To test the flatness of the wood use a straight-edge as in Fig. 4. The high parts will be obvious to the sight, but a quick test is to hold it in the middle and endeavour to swivel it as shown by the arrows. If it pivots easily the wood is certainly round. There should be definite friction at the ends. Use it along the length, across the width and diagonally, as shown in Fig. 5.

Bound up with straightness is the question of *winding*. Look at the board at A, Fig. 6. Clearly the diagonally opposite corners are high, so that if you placed it on a flat bench it would rock. It is said to be "in winding." A rough test for this is to hold the wood up level with the eye and look across it as in Fig. 7, when any major inaccuracy will be obvious.

For a closer test, however, the winding strips must be used. These are two straight and parallel strips, generally with a line inlaid in one of them. They are placed across the wood as in Fig. 8, the inlaid one at the far end. If the wood is true the top edge of the near strip will appear parallel with the inlaid line in the far strip. To correct the winding the plane should be worked diagonally across the high corners. If the plane itself is true it will automatically take shavings from the high corners without touching the middle.

Thicknessing. Most wood nowadays is bought machine-planed. Consequently it is already straight and is of an even thickness. This means that subsequent hand planing is reduced to a minimum. If, however, you buy it in the rough you will have to make one side flat and then thickness it. To do this set a gauge to the thickness required or to the thinnest part and mark all round the edge, working from the side already made true. (The latter is known as the face side, and a pencil mark should be made upon it.) It is then just a case of planing down to this line. If much wood has to be removed the work is lightened by working diagonally across the grain. There is less resistance and it enables a thicker shaving to be taken. Stop the plane short of the far edge, however, as otherwise the corner may splinter off. Finish off *with* the grain.

Edge planing. In the case of an edge the plane should be held as in Fig. 9. Note how the fingers of the left hand pass beneath the sole, where they bear against the side of the wood. In this way they act as a sort of fence, keeping the plane in the same position in

FIG. 9. HOW PLANE IS HELD WHEN PLANING AN EDGE.

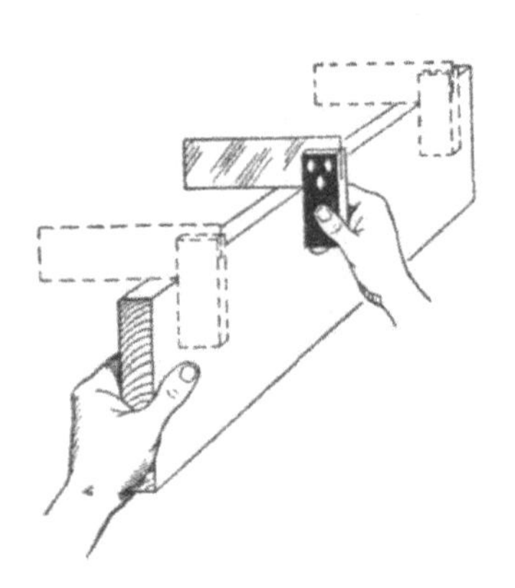

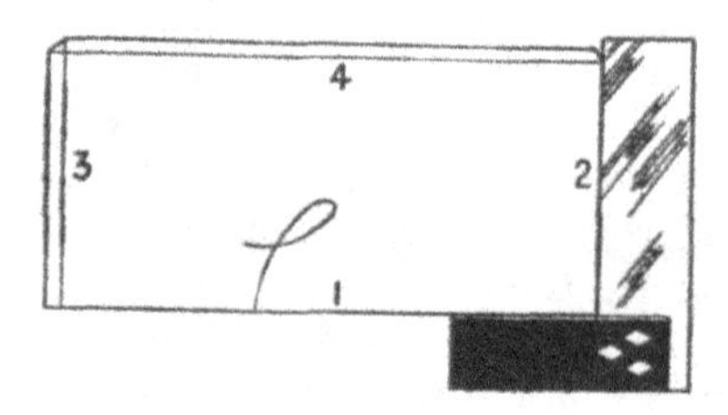

FIG. 11 (*above*). ORDER IN WHICH EDGES ARE PLANED.

FIG. 10 (*left*). TESTING EDGE WITH TRY-SQUARE.

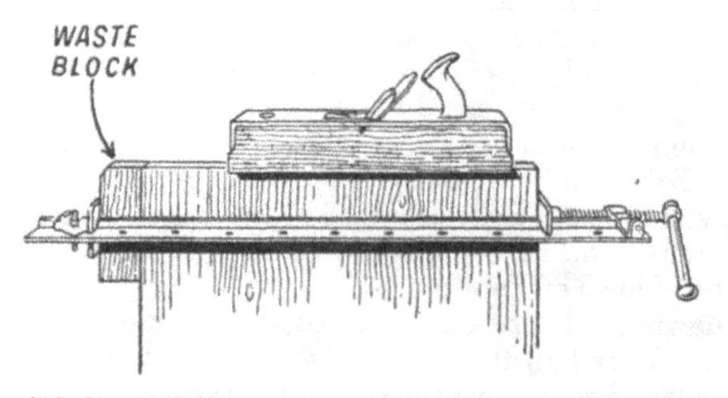

FIG. 12. AVOIDING SPLIT WHEN PLANING END GRAIN.
The waste block supports the corner and prevents a split.

relation to the wood. This steadies the plane and enables the shaving to be thicker at one side if required. Fig. 9 makes this clear. The cutter is slightly rounded so that the shaving is thicker at the middle, tapering to nothing at the edges. The advantage of this, of course, is that if an edge is out of square it can be corrected by passing the plane over towards the high side.

So far as straightness is concerned, the rule about pressing with the left hand at the start of the stroke and with the right hand at the end applies. You can get a good approximation of a straight edge by removing shavings from the middle only until the plane ceases to cut, then taking a couple of shavings straight through. However, a straight-edge should be used to test it. As before, see whether it appears to swivel about the middle.

Fig. 10 shows how the try-square is used to test the squareness of an edge. Try it in several positions along the length. Remember, however, that the surface from which it is used must be free of winding. Otherwise the test will be merely misleading.

Order of planing. There is a definite order to be followed when planing the edges of a panel. One edge is planed true and a pencil mark made upon it so that it is easily recognisable in subsequent operations. This is known as the face edge (see 1, Fig. 11). One end is now planed perfectly square with it as at 2. Note that the back corner is chiselled off to eliminate danger of the grain splitting out when the plane is taken right through. The required length is next marked as at 3, and the waste wood planed away, the back corner again being taken off. Finally the width is gauged, 4, and the panel trimmed to this. In this way the last operation is *with* the grain and it takes out the chiselled corners at the back. If it should so happen that this is not sufficient width to enable the corners to be chiselled, it will be necessary to cramp on a waste block of wood as in Fig. 12. The corner of this is taken off, enabling the plane to go right through without any splitting taking place.

Shooting-board. Wood of some ⅜ in. or more in thickness can be planed easily in the bench vice, or, if it is narrow, standing on edge against the bench stop. Thinner wood is difficult, however, owing to the liability of the plane to wobble. It is therefore necessary to adopt a different method, and this brings us to the shooting-board. This invaluable appliance is shown in detail in Fig. 2, page 72, and its use in planing an edge is given in Fig. 13. The wood is placed upon the upper platform, and the plane, lying on its side, is worked along its edge on the lower platform. Thus, providing that the side of the plane is square with the sole, the edge is bound to be square. For this particular piece of work there is no need for the plane to bear against the edge of the upper platform—in fact there is an advantage in allowing the edge of the wood to overhang slightly. You then plane the edge true by virtue of the truth of the plane.

One of the commonest applications of its use is in making a simple

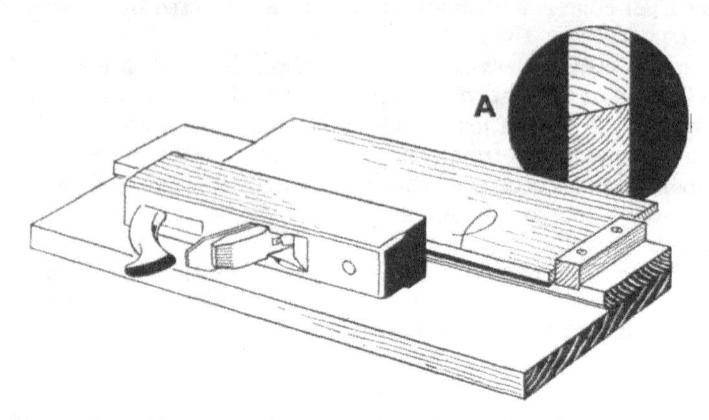

FIG. 13. JOINT BEING PLANED ON THE SHOOTING-BOARD.
One piece has face side upwards, and the other downwards. If edge is out of truth the angles will cancel out as at A. This is purposely exaggerated for clearness.

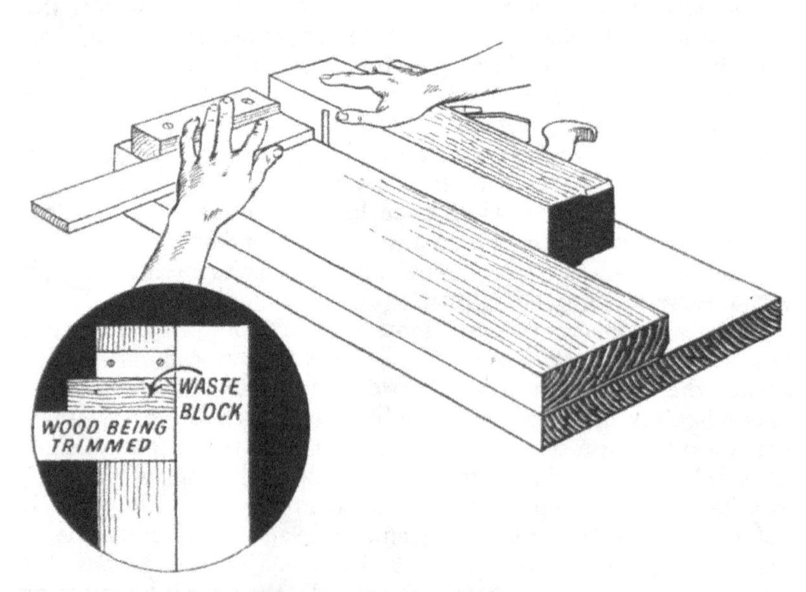

FIG. 14. TRIMMING END OF WOOD ON THE SHOOTING-BOARD.
The wood is pressed tightly against the stop.

butt joint between two pieces of wood. In this case, since it is essential that the two go together in perfect alignment, the one piece should be planed with the face side uppermost and the other the reverse way. Then, if the edge should be slightly out of square it will not matter because the two angles cancel out, so to speak, as shown at A, Fig. 13.

A second application of the shooting-board is in trimming the end of a piece of wood as in Fig. 14. Here it is necessary to keep the sole of the plane well up to the edge of the upper platform because it is essential that it is square with the stop of the shooting-board. Note how the far corner is chiselled off when end grain is trimmed. If there is not sufficient width of wood to do this a waste piece, the

FIG. 15. USE OF REBATE PLANE.
Note how fingers curl beneath the sole to act as a fence.

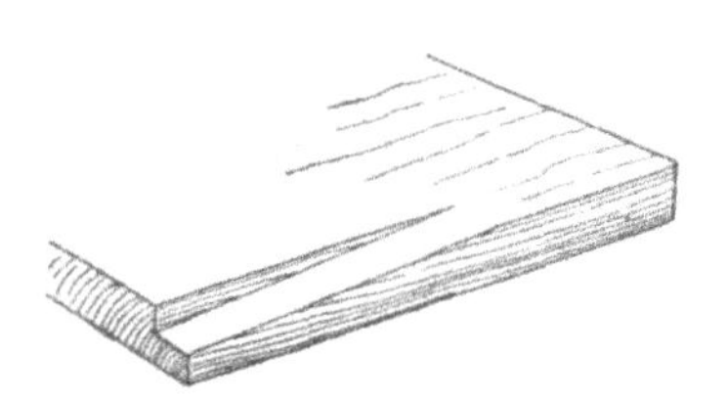

FIG. 16. WORKING REBATE.
Rebate should be started at the end farthest from the worker.

edges of which are parallel, should be placed between the stop and the wood being planed (see inset, Fig. 14).

Rebate plane. Amongst the tools for which you will soon find the need once you get down seriously to woodwork is the rebate plane. You probably know that a rebate is a sort of step formed at the edge of a piece of wood, and when it is of any length the rebate plane becomes a necessity. It can be of either wood or metal, the latter having the advantage of being fitted with a fence which ensures its working equidistantly from the edge. There is also a spur or side cutter which is useful when working across the grain. This metal type costs more, but is worth it.

The usual way of holding the wood rebate plane is shown in Fig. 15, in which the fingers of the left hand form a sort of fence. It is a little hard on the fingers if the wood is rough, but generally it has already been planed smooth. Start a trifle short of the line so that a final cut can be made with the plane on its side. Begin at the far end of the wood, taking a few short shavings, and gradually increase the stroke so that shavings are at last taken right through. In this

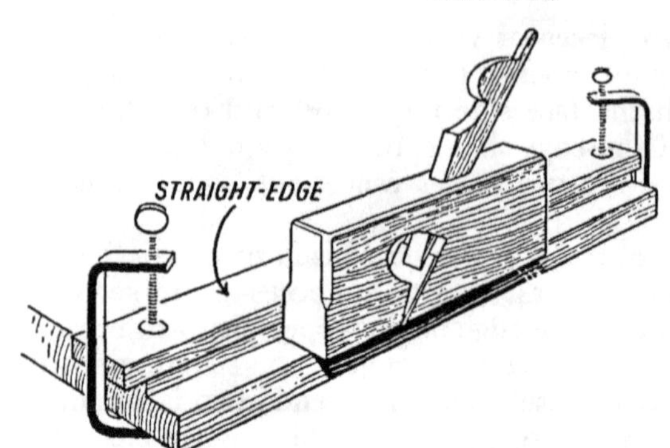

FIG. 17. REBATE PLANE WORKING AGAINST STRAIGHT-EDGE.

The plane should be pressed tightly against straight-edge.

way the plane is less liable to wander, since it runs into the rebate it has already formed. Fig. 16 shows the idea. An alternative method is to fix a straight-edge along the line as in Fig. 17 and work the plane along this. In some work a couple of nails can be used to hold the straight-edge.

Grooving plane. A grooving plane is a necessity for some work. For instance, a panelled framework such as a door with grooved-in panel. You can have the full-sized plough (wood or metal) with its range of seven or eight cutters, or you can get a small metal plough plane with three cutters, $\frac{1}{8}$-in., $\frac{3}{16}$-in. and $\frac{1}{4}$-in. The latter is ample for most requirements. The required cutter is fitted and adjusted to give a medium shaving; the fence is set so that the cutter works at the required distance from the edge; and the depth stop fixed at a distance from the sole of the plane equal to the depth the groove has to be.

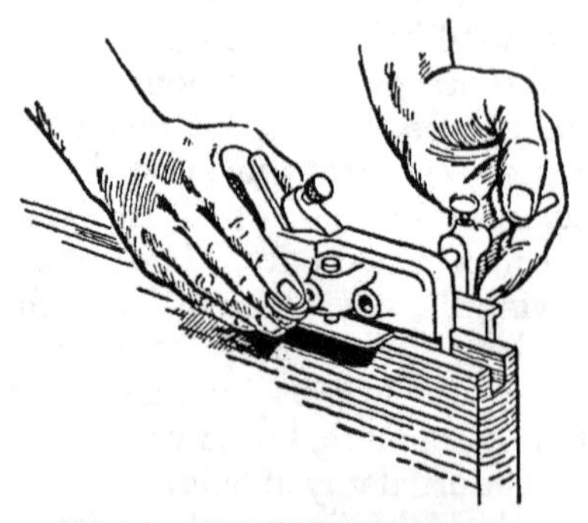

FIG. 18. GROOVING PLANE.

Note fence and depth stop.

As with the rebate plane, start at the far end of the wood and maintain a constant inward pressure to counter the tendency of the plane to drift from the edge. Clearly it is necessary to hold the plane upright, as otherwise, apart from the groove sloping, the plane will rapidly bind. When several pieces have to be grooved in the same relative position, work from the face side in every case. In this way the grooves will always be in alignment if they are jointed together.

3. CHISELLING AND BORING

YOU need a chisel for comparatively heavy work, such as chopping out dovetails, notches, and so on, and also for light paring. The former needs a robust sort of chisel which will withstand heavy mallet blows, whilst a more delicate chisel is desirable for light work. The man in the trade generally keeps special chisels for each purpose, firmer chisels for chopping and bevelled-edge chisels for paring, but you can manage quite well using a firmer chisel only. Do not

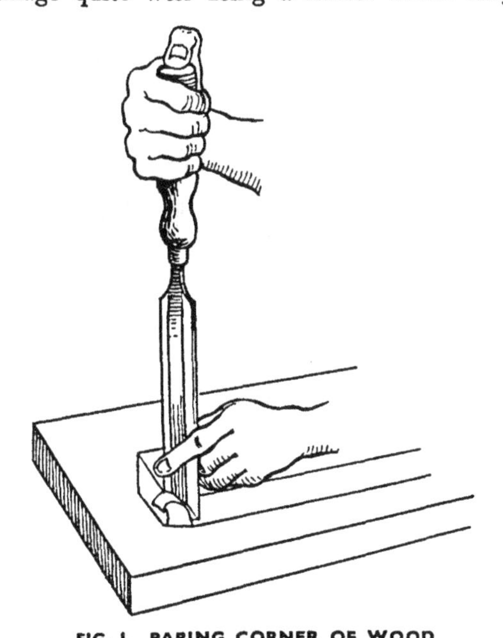

FIG. 1. PARING CORNER OF WOOD WITH CHISEL

The wood rests on a flat surface. Finger of left hand curls around blade to guide it.

attempt heavy chopping with a bevelled-edge chisel, however. It is liable to snap.

Paring. This may be done either vertically or horizontally, according to the nature of the work. Fig. 1 shows a corner being pared, the wood held on a flat block. The latter is important, because if there are any indentations on the surface beneath, the wood is liable to splinter out on the underside. Note how the left

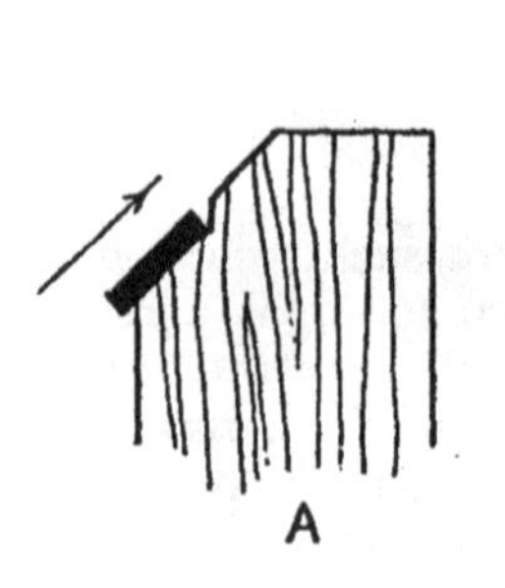

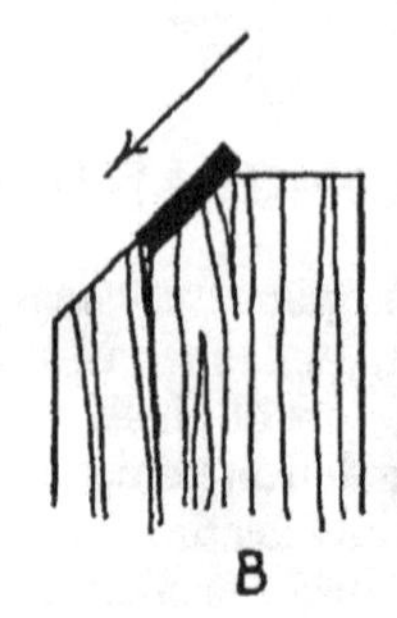

FIG. 2. VERTICAL PARING WITH CHISEL.

This is a plan view, the black rectangle representing the chisel. Work as at A rather than at B.

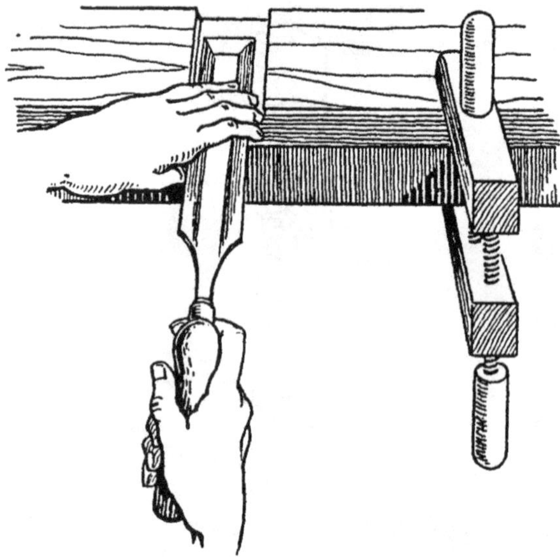

FIG. 3. HORIZONTAL PARING WITH CHISEL.

The chisel should be used with a slicing movement. The sides of the groove are sawn first of course.

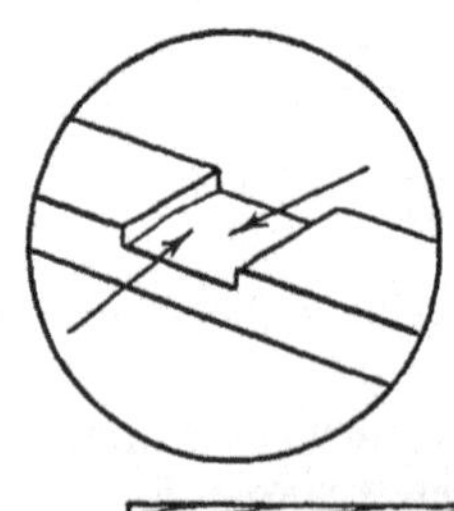

FIG. 4. CUTTING A GROOVE.

Work inwards from each side, removing the wood gradually as shown by the lines in the lower diagram.

hand bears down on the wood to steady it, the index finger passing around the blade to act as a guide. When a corner has to be taken off and the chisel is not so wide as the wood, work inwards from the side as at A, Fig. 2. Working outwards is liable to cause a split as at B.

It is generally more convenient to pare a groove or notch horizontally. The wood can be either fixed in the vice or cramped down on the bench as in Fig. 3. When there is the width it is generally an advantage to take a slicing cut. This not only eases the work

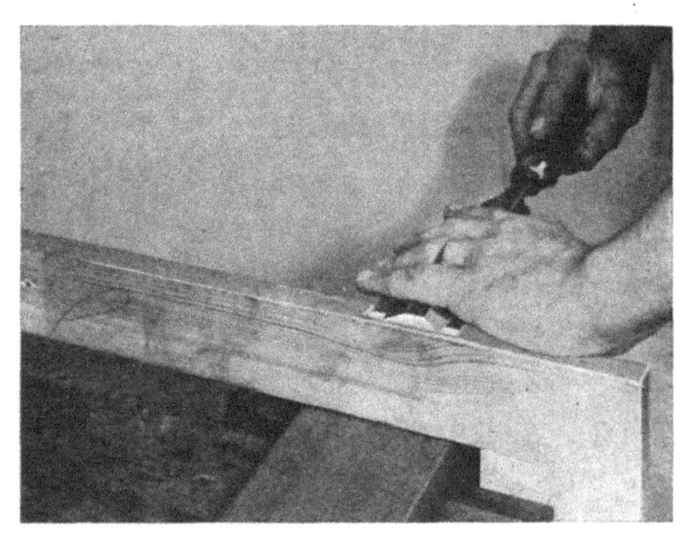

FIG. 4a. CUTTING HINGE RECESS WITH BEVELLED-EDGE CHISEL. The door is held in the vice, but a block of wood is placed beneath the frame to support it.

but it enables you to detect more easily where the high parts are. To do this pass the tool sideways as it is pressed forwards, when it will automatically cut the high parts.

Cutting a groove of this kind really involves two types of chiselling, the preliminary removal of the bulk of the waste, followed by the fine finishing-off cuts. Make a saw cut at each side down to practically the finished depth, and if the groove is wide make an extra cut or two in between. Hold the chisel in the left hand, the blade pointing slightly upwards, and tap the handle with either the hand or a mallet. This will remove the near corner of the wood, and you can continue as shown by the lines in Fig. 4 until the back corner is reached. Do not continue beyond this as the wood may splinter

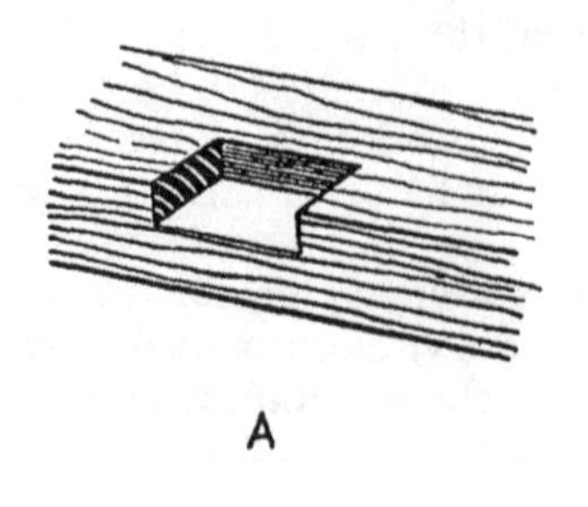
A

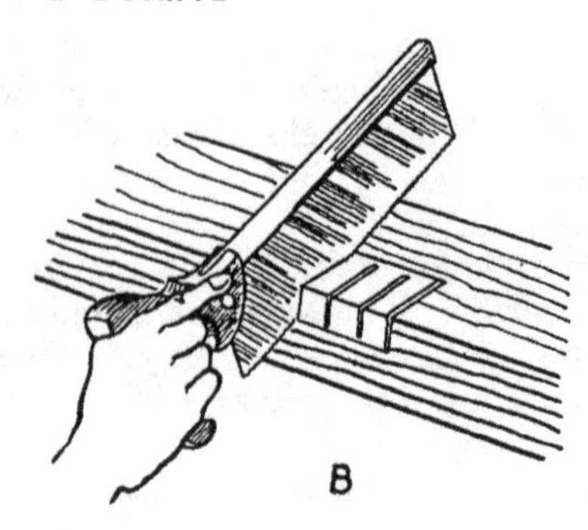
B

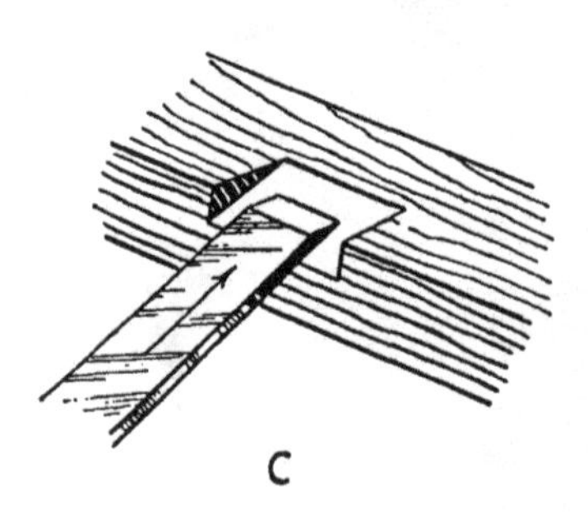
C

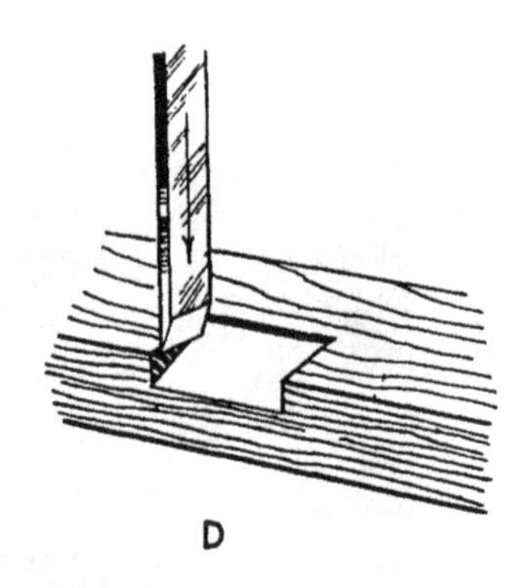
D

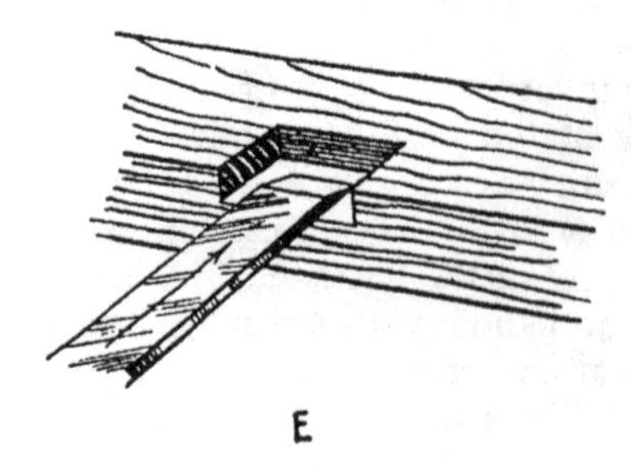
E

FIG. 5. STAGES IN CUTTING NOTCH AS WHEN RECESSING A HINGE.

A. Completed notch.
B. Preliminary cuts with the saw.
C. Chiselling away waste as far as diagonal.
D. Chopping down sides.
E. Paring bottom flat.

out, but reverse the wood and work from the other side. It is in the final cuts that the slicing movement is adopted. It often happens that wood cuts more smoothly in one direction than the other, and the best plan then is to arrange it so that the final cuts are made in the smooth-cutting direction.

Cutting a notch. An example of a job calling for both chopping and paring is that of a notch closed at one side as at A, Fig. 5. The sides are sawn in to the extent of the diagonal and a couple of cuts made in between to just short of the finished depth (see B). These cuts serve to break up the grain and help to prevent splitting. The point is that if a split should develop it could not run beyond the next saw cut. The first chiselling operation is to remove the waste down to as far as the saw cuts, that is, just short of the gauge line, as at C. Downward chopping with chisel and mallet follows as at D. Do not attempt to cut right down to the finished depth in one cut, but ease away the waste wood first and then cut down a second time. This is specially important when cutting the back which runs *with* the grain, as a split may result from chopping too severely. Another point in this connection is that it is better to start the chisel short of the gauge line, and shift right on to the line for the final cut only. Otherwise the wedge shape of the chisel may cause it to be forced beyond the line. E shows the final paring.

Note that in all these operations both hands are kept behind the cutting edge. If you follow this rule there will be little risk of your having an accident.

Mortising. Cutting a mortise is essentially a job for the chisel, and, as it involves some rather heavy chopping, a specially heavily built chisel is generally used for the purpose. This is either the mortise chisel or the sash mortise chisel, the latter being the lighter of the two and generally handier. However, the ordinary firmer chisel can be used providing that too heavy blows and undue levering are avoided.

The work of mortising is lightened considerably if a series of holes is bored first. It enables the chisel to enter the wood more easily, as the grain crumbles into the holes as the chisel is knocked in. Clearly it is important that the holes are upright, and to ensure this you should stand at the end of the wood, because it is easy to tell whether the brace leans to right or left, but takes considerably more judgment to decide whether it leans away from or towards you. Use a twist bit slightly smaller than the mortise width. As the commonest wood for framing is $\frac{7}{8}$ in. thick, a $\frac{5}{16}$-in. chisel is used, because this is the nearest to one-third the thickness of the wood.

This means that a $\frac{1}{4}$-in. bit is the best size to use. Bore the holes as close together as practicable.

For the same reason as when boring, stand at the end of the work when using the mortise chisel. Place the wood over a solid part of the bench (as over a leg), and fix it down with a cramp or hand-

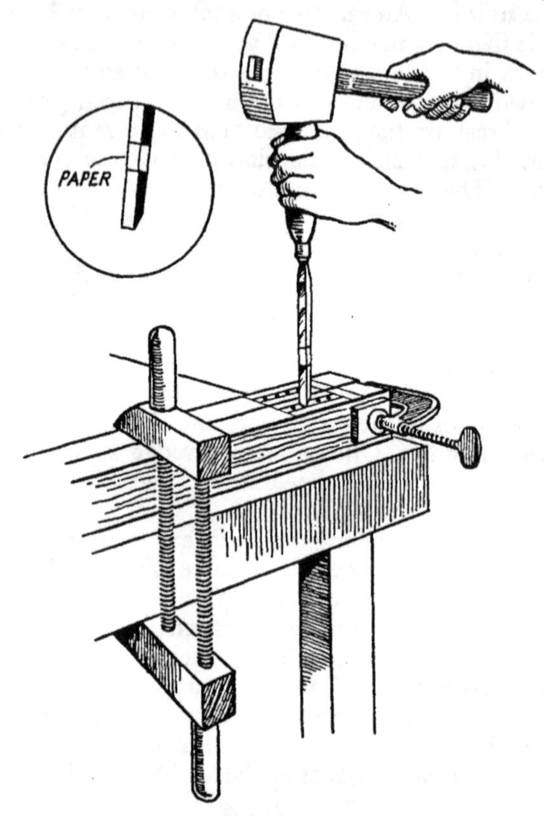

FIG. 6. HOW MORTISES ARE CHOPPED.
The wood is cramped over a solid part of the bench. The end cramp prevents splitting. Paper glued to chisel indicates depth.

screw. A second cramp is also fixed sideways at the end as in Fig. 6, as this, by the support it affords, prevents the wood from splitting. A piece of paper glued to the chisel is useful as a depth gauge.

Start at the middle of the mortise and chop down. The chisel is then levered backwards slightly and withdrawn. It is again started slightly in advance and a second cut made. This is repeated until the mortise reaches up to within about $\frac{1}{16}$ in. of the finished length. The chisel is reversed and the other end cut similarly. It is best to have a slightly smaller chisel (say $\frac{1}{4}$-in. firmer) handy with which to clear the chips. Fig. 7 shows a sectional view of the operation in progress.

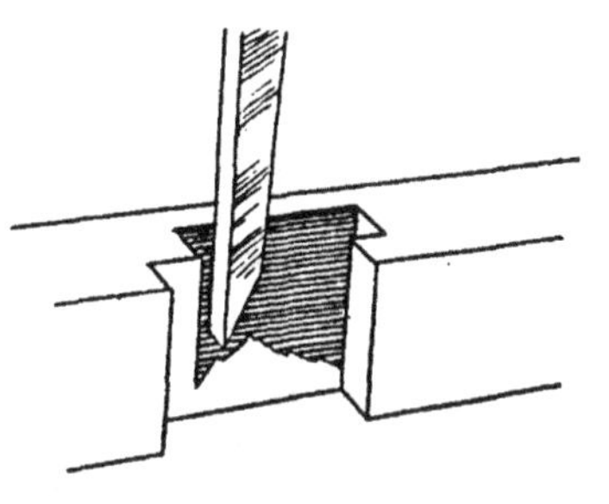

FIG. 7. SECTIONAL VIEW OF MORTISE.
Work downwards in steps from the centre outwards.

It is inevitable that the levering over of the chisel both in general chopping and in clearing the chips will round over the ends of the mortise, and it is for this reason that the chisel is not taken right up to the ends. When the main chopping has been completed it leaves just a single cut to be made at each end, this taking out the roundness and leaving sharp corners.

BORING

The tool chiefly used is the brace, this being fitted with a bit to suit the work in hand. Apart from size, braces are of two kinds: the simple brace and the ratchet brace (see page vi). The advantage of the latter is that it can be used in a corner or close up to a wall, the ratchet being set so that by moving the handle back and forth in half strokes the bit is rotated in one direction only, the back stroke leaving it stationary. It costs rather more than the simple brace, but is worth its cost. In regard to size, a sweep of 8 in. is a good average.

Bits. These vary according to the work they have to do. For fairly large, shallow holes or holes in thin wood the inexpensive centre bit is the most useful, and you can obtain this with either plain centre point or with screw centre. The latter has an advantage in the larger sizes in that it draws the bit into the wood, so lessening the labour. The bit is inexpensive and for general recessing, etc., is perfectly satisfactory. It is of little value for deep holes or for boring into end grain, as it tends to drift.

For fairly deep holes, such as those used in dowelling, the twist bit is the more satisfactory, because if started properly it will keep in a straight line. The spiral portion of the bit, apart from allowing clearance for the chips, ensures this by bearing against the sides of the hole. It is a more delicate tool, however, easily damaged if brought into contact with a nail and more difficult to sharpen. In fact there is a limit to the number of times it can be sharpened.

FIG. 8. VERTICAL BORING.

It is easy to tell whether brace leans to left or to right. Square placed on wood indicates whether brace bears away from or towards you. When boring holes before mortising always stand at *end* of mortise. If brace should incline along length of wood it would not be important, but for it to lean sideways would throw mortise out of truth.

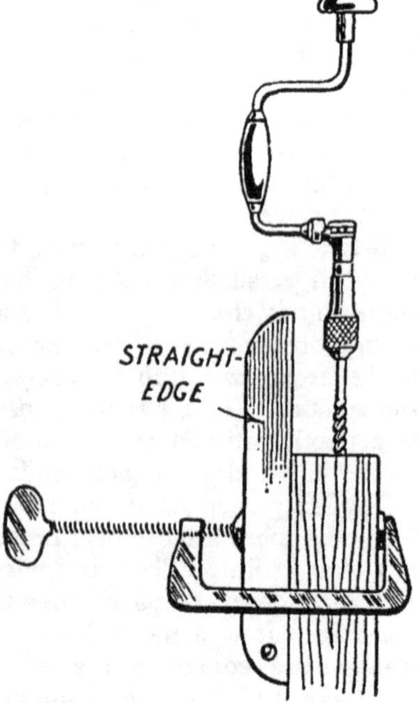

FIG. 9. STRAIGHT-EDGE USED TO TEST VERTICALITY OF BRACE.

This device is useful when boring into, say, the end of a leg to receive a dowel. In the workshop the general plan in important cases is for an assistant to stand at the side and indicate when the brace is upright.

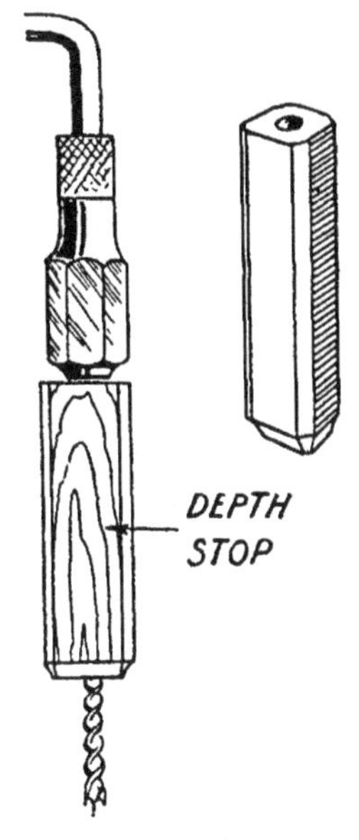

FIG. 10. SIMPLE DEPTH STOP.

Smaller holes such as those needed for screws are best bored with a shell bit (see page vi) or with a twist drill of the kind used by engineers. Gimlet or half-twist bits are best avoided because of their liability to split the wood. To countersink holes when screwing use the snail countersink (page vi).

Vertical boring. It is clearly important to be able to bore upright and at the same time it is difficult. It is easy enough to know whether the brace leans to the right or to the left, but is altogether more difficult to detect whether it leans away from or towards you. An experienced man is not likely to be badly out, but for an important job even he invariably asks someone to stand at the side and give him the tip when he is upright. One good plan is to stand the try-square on the bench near the brace as in Fig. 8. Once a start has been made it can be removed. Another plan, useful when the hole is to be bored in the end of the wood, is to cramp a straight-edge to the wood as in Fig. 9.

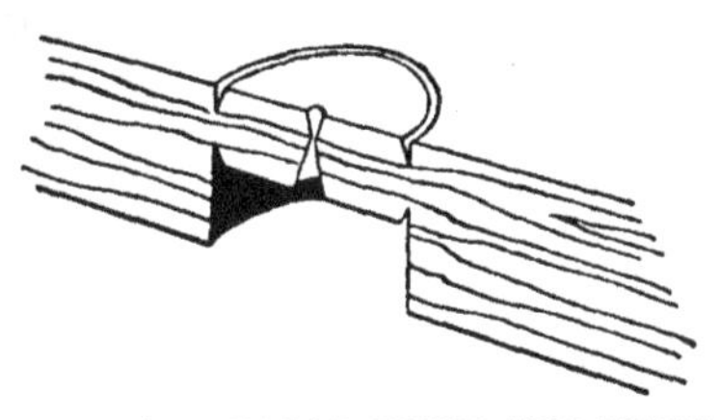

FIG. 11. BORING RIGHT THROUGH WOOD.

The hole should be bored from one side until the centre point projects beneath and the hole then completed from the other side.

Generally boring is best done with the brace in an upright position, though occasionally the wood can be fixed in the vice and the boring done horizontally. For small holes the left hand at the top of the brace will supply enough pressure, but for larger holes or those in hardwood the head can be brought to bear over the left hand, giving increased power.

When a number of holes has to be bored with the twist bit, all to the same depth, a simple stop can be made as in Fig. 10. It is simply a piece of wood with a hole bored right through it, its length being arranged to allow the bit a projection equal to the required depth of hole.

In the case of thin wood having a hole bored right through it, the simplest plan is to bore from one side until the centre point just emerges beneath. The wood is then reversed and the hole completed from the other side. Fig. 11 shows a sectional view of a piece of wood being bored in this way. An alternative method is to cramp the wood down on to a waste piece and bore right through from the one side. Done in this way there is no risk of the wood splitting out.

For making small screw holes (for the thread, not the shank) the bradawl is extremely useful as it is quick and handy. It should be

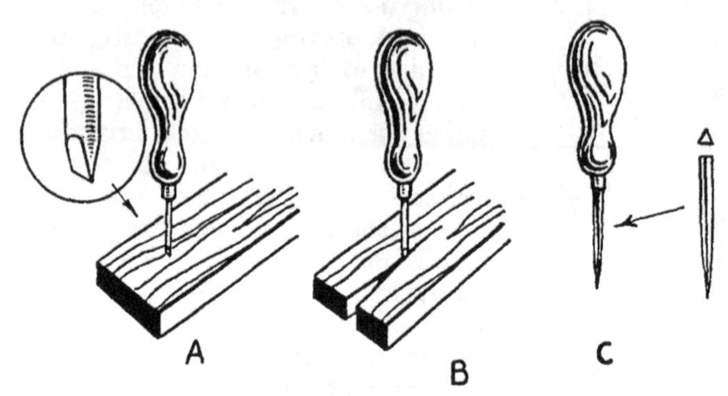

FIG. 12. POINTS TO NOTE WHEN USING THE BRADAWL.
The edge should be at right angles to the grain as at A. Otherwise the grain may split as at B. The birdcage maker's awl (c) is useful in that it will not split the wood.

used with the edge at right angles to the grain so that it cuts the fibres as at A, Fig. 12. If held the other way, near the edge it is liable to split the wood, B, owing to its wedge shape. An alternative is the birdcage-maker's awl, which is square in section and runs to a point, C, Fig. 12. Its advantage is that it can be used very near the edge without splitting. Both types are rotated back and forth, a steady downward pressure being maintained.

4. MARKING AND TESTING

ONE of the everyday uses of the square is that of testing the squareness of an edge when planing, and the first thing to be sure about is that the surface from which you are using the square is

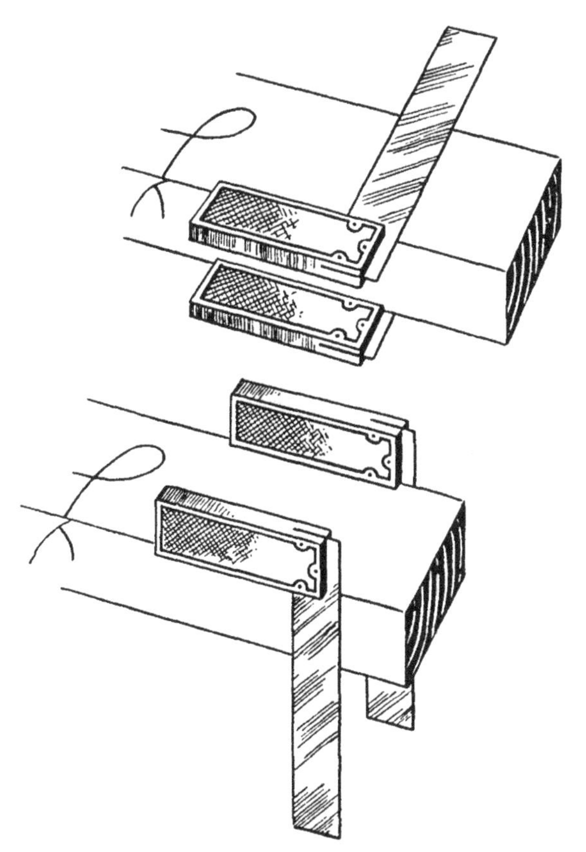

FIG. 1. USE OF TRY-SQUARE FOR MARKING AND TESTING.
The butt of the square is always against either the face side or edge.

itself free from winding. It is clear that if a surface twists in its length any adjoining edge, although true and square with it at one end, is bound to be out of square with it at the other. The truing up of a surface is dealt with on pages 103 to 107; also the method of testing for squareness at various positions along the length. The only further point to note is that when all four edges have to be planed up square, the butt of the square should always bear against either the face side or the face edge, as shown in Fig. 2.

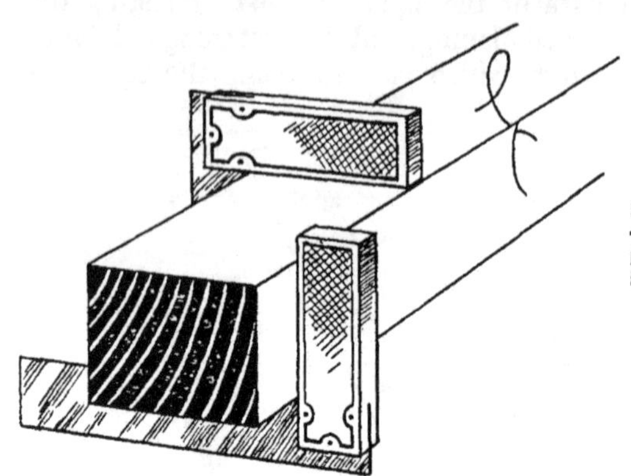

FIG. 2. TRY-SQUARE IN USE. The face side and edge having been made square the remaining surfaces are tested from one or other of these.

A similar idea applies when marks have to be squared around a piece of wood, as for instance when marking out the shoulders of a tenon. If the butt of the square is always used against either face side or face edge the marks are bound to meet (see Fig. 1).

One complication is that a square (especially one of the wood-metal type) is often inaccurate, so that it becomes more misleading than

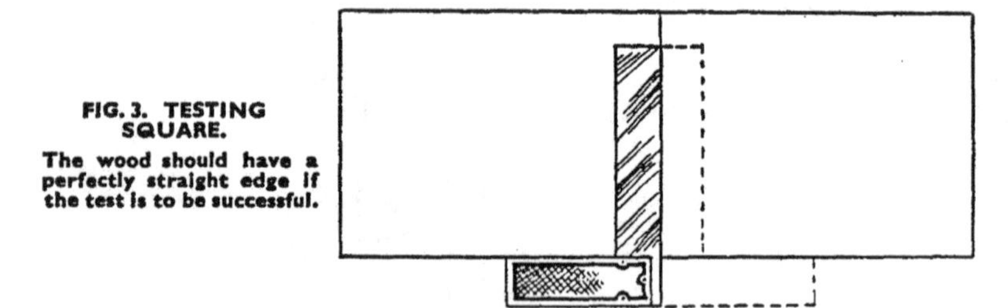

FIG. 3. TESTING SQUARE. The wood should have a perfectly straight edge if the test is to be successful.

helpful. To test such a square hold it against a board with an edge that you know to be dead straight and draw a knife along the edge. Reverse the square as shown by the dotted lines in Fig. 3 and if the square is accurate the edge will coincide with the mark.

Gauging. The gauge is an essential tool in the preparation of timber and in the marking out of joints, etc. Two kinds are available: marking gauge and cutting gauge. Most men in the trade have one of each because two are often needed on the same job, but if you can have one only it is better to have the cutting gauge, because it can be used for marking both *with* and across the grain, end grain, and for cutting. It is rather more tricky to use owing to its greater tendency to drift with the grain, but one soon gets used to it. The use of the marking gauge is confined to marking *with* the grain and end grain.

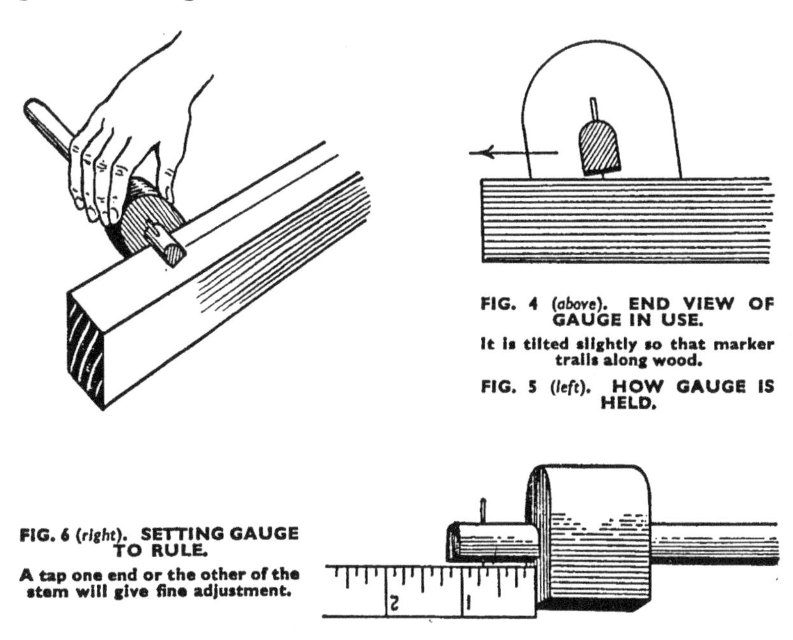

FIG. 4 (*above*). **END VIEW OF GAUGE IN USE.**
It is tilted slightly so that marker trails along wood.

FIG. 5 (*left*). **HOW GAUGE IS HELD.**

FIG. 6 (*right*). **SETTING GAUGE TO RULE.**
A tap one end or the other of the stem will give fine adjustment.

Fig. 5 shows how the gauge should be held. Forward pressure is given by the thumb and root of the first finger, downward pressure is maintained chiefly by the first finger, whilst the remaining fingers exert a strong inward pressure. The latter is most important because it is only by this that the tendency to drift is resisted. At the start of the stroke tilt the gauge forward as in Fig. 4 so that the marker trails along the wood rather than digs into it. Then when making a second stroke the gauge can be brought upright so that it marks to its full depth.

To set the gauge a rule is generally used, though when metal fittings are being let in, the gauge is set to the fitting itself. Fig. 6 shows how it is held up to the rule, the end of the latter touching the fence. When correct, half tighten the screw and place the rule against it to give a final check. Any slight adjustment can be made by striking one end or the other of the stem against the bench, this causing the fence to jolt slightly. When correct tighten the screw finally.

Mortise gauge. In the case of the mortise gauge, which has two markers, the distance apart of these is fixed by the size of chisel to be used for mortising. Place the chisel against the markers as in Fig. 7 and adjust the moveable marker as required. As a rule the mortise occurs in the middle of the wood, and a good guide is to set the fence approximately right and make a slight indentation from the face side. Reverse the gauge to the other side and make another slight mark. If there is a discrepancy between the two the gauge is re-adjusted to midway between the marks. Always use the gauge from the face side, however, because then the two parts will always go together level at the front, even though there may be a difference in the thickness of the wood.

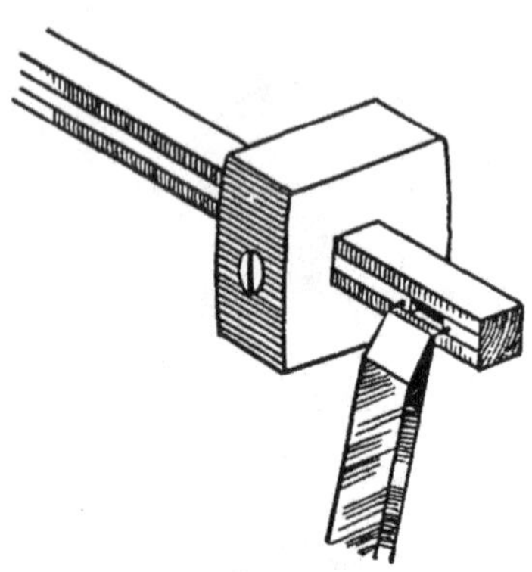

FIG. 7. SETTING MORTISE GAUGE.
The end screw is adjusted until markers equal chisel width.

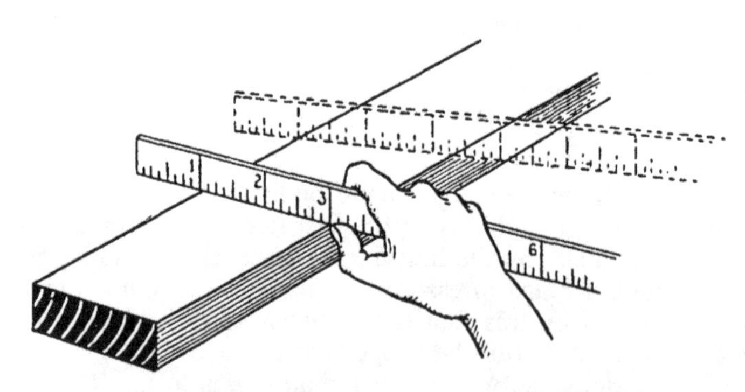

FIG. 8. MEASURING WIDTH OF WOOD WITH RULE.
Rule must be held square across the wood. By rocking the thumb one way or the other the rule can be made to slide slightly across the wood.

Rule. Except for the roughest work the rule should always be held so that the calibrations actually touch the wood as in Fig. 8. Otherwise it is quite possible for a reading to vary in accordance with the particular position from which the work is viewed, and the thicker the rule the greater the possible error. Another point is that the rule should be held square across the wood, or the reading may be greater than the true width, as shown by the dotted lines.

When measuring the width or thickness of a piece of wood it is more accurate to hold the rule with one of the inch calibrations opposite one edge, as in Fig. 8, rather than have the end of the rule

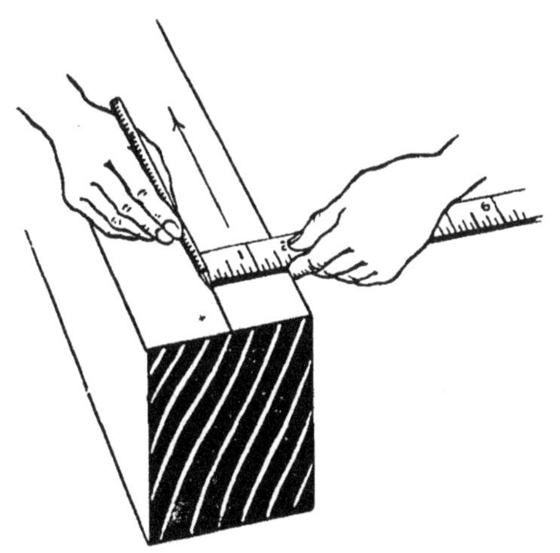

FIG. 9. MARKING LINE PARALLEL WITH EDGE.
The finger bears against the edge of the wood and acts as a sort of fence

level with it. It is easier to judge when the calibration is level with the edge than the rule end. Grip the rule with the thumb beneath and bearing against the edge of the wood as in Fig. 8. Then by straightening or bending the thumb the rule can be made to slide slightly one way or the other, so adjusting it exactly.

To draw a line parallel with an edge quickly and with reasonable accuracy the finger gauge method can be used as shown in Fig. 9. The important point to watch, apart from holding the fingers close up to the edge of the wood, is to keep the rule square with the edge.

5. SHARPENING TOOLS

THE basis of sharpening is a good oil-stone. It is one of those things on which you cannot economise. Pay the proper price for a stone made by a reputable firm and look after it, making a wood case to protect it, never using it dry, and wiping off old dirty oil when finished with. Reliable makes are the *India*, *Carborundum*, *Unirundum*, *Bauxilite*, and *Aloxite*, all of which are manufactured

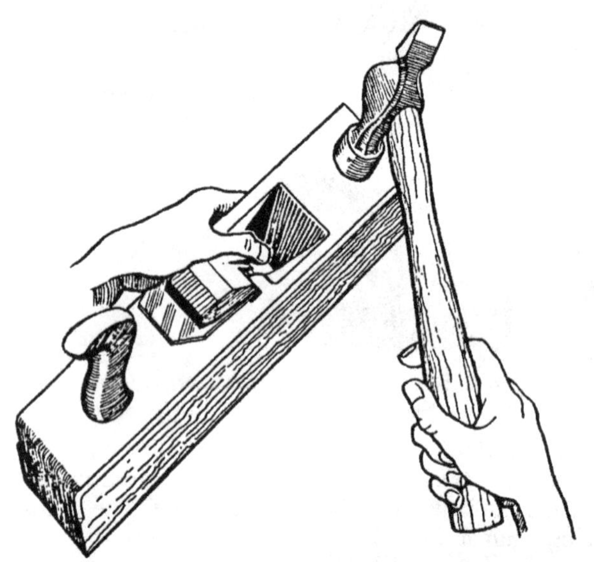

FIG. 1. REMOVING CUTTER AND WEDGE FROM PLANE
The front of the plane (striking knob if there is one) is struck smartly with the hammer.

stones. Of the natural stones the *Washita* is the best known. Use a thin machine oil of the kind sold in small tins and bottles. A drying oil such as linseed is fatal, since it dries hard in the pores and seals them. Three grades of stones are available: coarse, medium, and fine, and the last-named is the most generally useful. Carpenters who do fairly rough work prefer the medium stone as it is quicker cutting. The coarse grade is used only when a cutter has been gashed and needs rubbing down quickly. A good investment is the combination stone, fine one side and coarse the other.

The plane. Hold the plane in the left hand with the thumb passing down into the escapement (the recess where the shavings emerge) and on to the bolt which holds the cutter and back iron together as in Fig. 1. The fingers pass to beneath the sole. Strike the front of the plane smartly (on striking button if it has one) with the hammer, so releasing the wedge. The thumb will prevent the cutter from jolting out. Withdraw the cutter

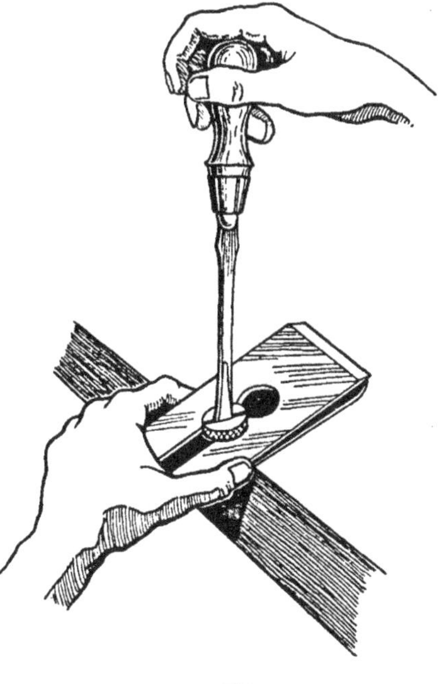

FIG. 2. RELEASING BACK IRON.
Hold the back end of the cutter and make sure that the screw is supported on the bench.

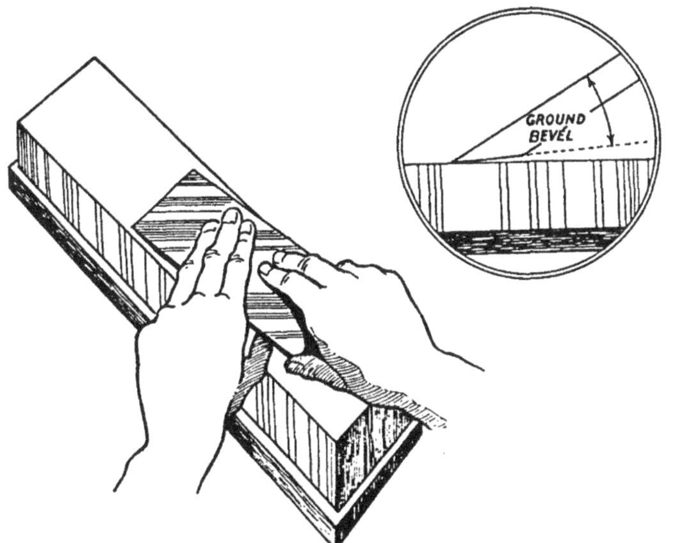

FIG. 3. SHARPENING THE PLANE CUTTER ON THE OILSTONE.
The sharpening angle is about 30 deg. As grinding bevel is at 25 deg. the back of the iron is raised slightly as shown in inset.

and back iron and undo the bolt. When doing this it is advisable to place the two on the bench and hold the end of the cutter as in Fig. 2 to prevent an accident. You can now slide the back iron along the slot in the cutter and separate the two.

A plane iron or cutter is ground on a grindstone to a bevel of about 25 degs. This, however, gives a coarse edge and it is necessary to finish off on an oil-stone. Put a few drops of oil on the stone, hold the cutter with the bevel flat upon it, and raise the hands a trifle. This will give an angle of about 30 degs., which is about right.

FIG. 4. TESTING FOR BURR WITH THUMB.

The idea of the two angles is that it lightens the sharpening considerably, since only the edge touches the stone. After several sharpenings, of course, the sharpened bevel will become wide, so that there is more steel to remove when sharpening, and it is then time to have it ground afresh.

Work back and forth with either an elliptical or straight movement, whichever you find the easier, as in Fig. 3. This will turn up a burr on the back which can be detected by drawing the thumb *across* the edge as in Fig. 4. This gives a quick indication that the bluntness has been sharpened away, though it takes no account of any gash in the edge; neither does it reveal the shape of the edge or whether it is square. Turn over the cutter *flat* on the stone and rub it once or twice (Fig. 5). This will turn back the burr and make its subsequent release easy.

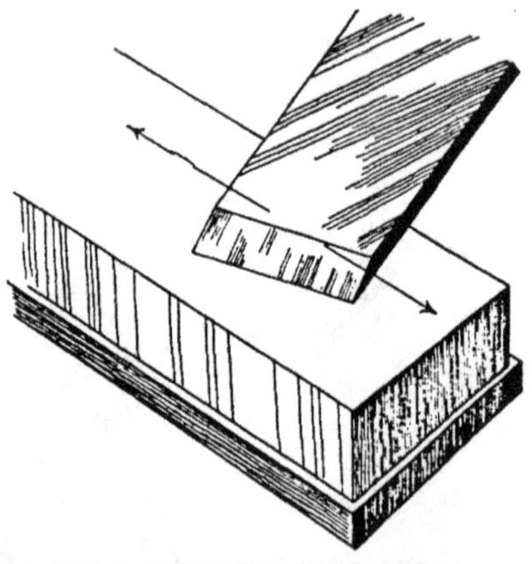

FIG. 5. TURNING BACK BURR. The cutter is reversed and held *flat* on the stone.

Stropping. A strop is used for this, a plain piece of soft leather held flat on a board. Give half a dozen rubs, first on the bevel and then flat on the back. A professional usually finishes off by stropping on his hand, but this is best avoided until you have had more experience. Now hold the cutter to the light. You cannot see a sharp edge, whereas any bluntness shows up as a thin line of white. Gashes show up similarly. The edge should be square with the sides of the cutter, and it should be *slightly* curved—not more than about $\frac{1}{32}$ in. all told.

Setting. Replace the back iron, reversing the procedure of removing it, and set it to within about $\frac{1}{16}$ in. of the edge. For coarse shavings this distance can be increased, whilst for fine work on awkward grain it can be lessened. Remember, however, that the closer you set it to the edge the harder it is to push the plane. The whole function of the back iron is to lessen the liability of the grain to tear out, but this is only attained at the cost of increased friction.

Once again use the thumb of the left hand to hold down the cutter when setting the plane. Look down the sole, as in Fig. 6, and adjust the cutter until it shows as a black line, the thickness of which depends upon the thickness of the shaving you wish to remove. Push in the wedge and tap it lightly home. Once again look down the sole and make any final adjustment. A tap one side or the other at the end will correct uneven projection, whilst a straight tap will give a coarser setting. To lessen the setting strike the front of the plane as when releasing the wedge. When all is in order give the wedge a final tap and the plane is ready for use.

FIG. 6. SIGHTING THE PLANE.
The paper on the bench shows up the line of the cutter which should be thin or thick according to the shaving required.

In the case of an adjustable metal plane the general procedure is similar, but of course no wedge is fitted. Instead there is either a lever cap or a screw. Such planes are never struck with the hammer, all adjustments being made by the screw or the lateral lever to the rear of the cutter. Rebate or shoulder planes are sharpened similarly, but the edge must be perfectly straight and square with the sides.

Chisels. The treatment is practically the same as for the plane and the angles are the same. The edge, however, should be straight and square. Mortise chisels and those coming in for heavy duty

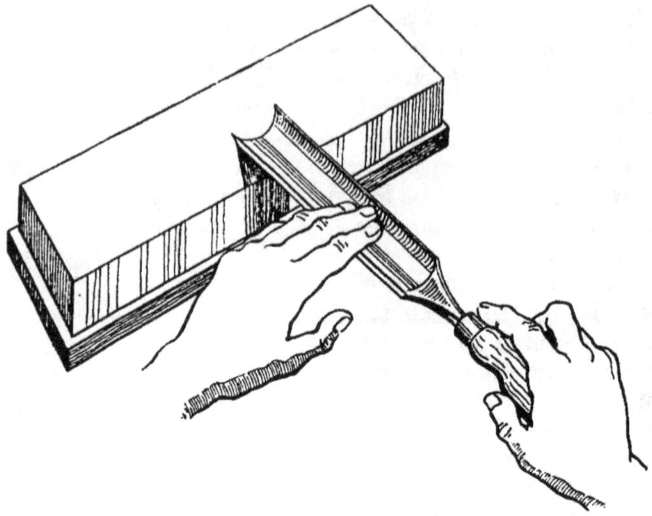

FIG. 7. SHARPENING FIRMER GOUGE ON OILSTONE.

The tool is given a rocking movement so that every part of the edge is sharpened. To turn back the burr the oilstone slip held *flat* on the inside can be used.

FIG. 8. SCRIBING GOUGE BEING SHARPENED WITH OILSTONE SLIP.

The slip should be of the same curvature as the gouge or slightly quicker. By rocking the outside of the gouge *flat* on the oilstone the burr can be turned back.

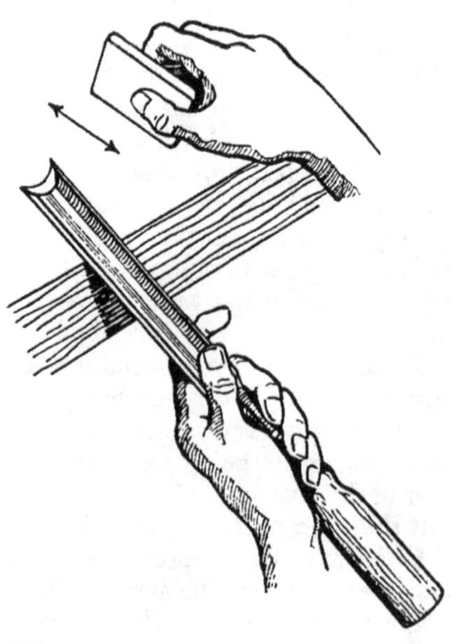

should be sharpened at a rather higher angle than those for paring as they need a stronger edge.

The position on the stone should be varied so that wear on the stone does not occur all in one place. An excellent plan is to keep a strop handy so that the edge can be restored quickly without using the stone. Keep the strop dressed with fine emery powder and oil and make it a habit to rub up a chisel little and often.

Gouges. These are of two kinds: the outside-ground, or firmer gouge, and the inside-ground, or scribing gouge. The former is sharpened on the oil-stone as in Fig. 7, a combined back-and-forth and rocking movement being employed. For the inside-ground gouge an oil-stone slip is used as in Fig. 8. The curvature of the stone should be the same as or rather quicker than that of the gouge,

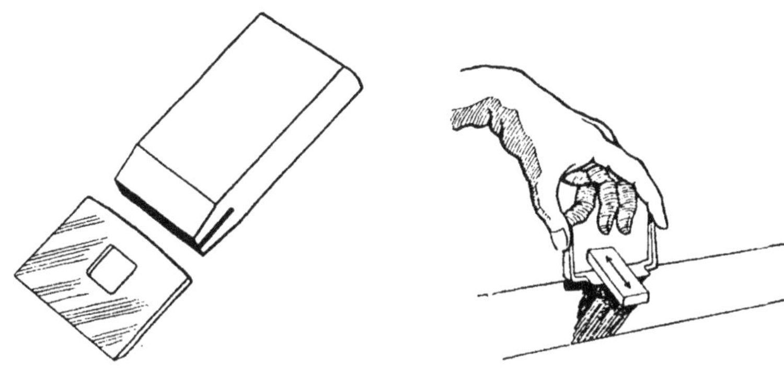

FIG. 9. HOLDER FOR CUTTER OF METAL SPOKESHAVE.

FIG. 10. SHARPENING WOOD SPOKE-SHAVE CUTTER.

and the endeavour should be to rub all parts of the bevel equally so that the edge is not made uneven.

Spokeshaves. In the case of the metal spokeshave the cutter is similar to that of a plane and it is sharpened in exactly the same way. Since it is much shorter, however, and is difficult to grip, the best plan is to make a holder for it as in Fig. 9. The wooden spoke-shave is a different proposition. It has projecting tangs which prevent the normal use of the oil-stone, and it is necessary to use either the edge of the oil-stone or the oil-stone slip, as in Fig. 10. Hold the cutter so that the edge slightly overlaps the edge of the bench and work the slip across it, retaining the same bevel as closely as possible. There should be no difficulty, since cutters are invariably hollow-ground, like a razor.

Bits. A fine file can be used for all bits. Taking first the centre bit, stick the point into a block of wood to steady it as in Fig. 11, and work the file across the cutter, maintaining the same angle. The nicker is sharpened at the inside, and the edge should be at an angle as at B, Fig. 12, so that it cuts, not scratches the wood. Note that to sharpen the nicker at the outside would cause it to cut a smaller

FIG. 11. FILING CUTTER OF CENTRE BIT.
The point of the bit should be stuck into a block of wood.

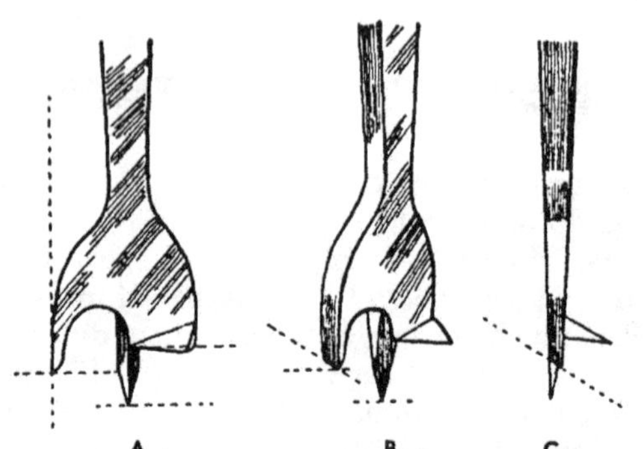

FIG. 12. ESSENTIAL FEATURES OF THE CENTRE BIT.

hole and would also cause binding, since the upper part of the bit would bind against the side of the hole. It is seldom that the centre point needs attention, but an occasional rub with the file will restore its triangular section. Note the essential order of projection in the three parts (A, Fig. 12).

A fine file is also used for the twist bit, but one with a safe edge is advisable, as it is essential that the centre screw thread is not touched. For the cutter stick the point into a block of wood as before (Fig. 11) and use the file on the bevel only. For the nickers hold the file on the inside at a slight angle.

As a last word, remember the bradawl. It can be very fatiguing driving in a blunt awl. Restore the main bevel with the file, and finish off the edge on the stone, keeping the edge square.

Saws. It is not advisable to sharpen your own saws. It is a tricky job, and a saw is easily spoilt. Have the sharpening done by a reputable sharpener.

6. PRELIMINARY MARKING

WOOD is often used in a wasteful way, not so much through carelessness as ignorance of certain practices in setting out which make for economy. These are learned from experience, but this takes time, and the following hints may be helpful.

Clearly a certain allowance for cleaning up is necessary, because saw marks, etc., have to be removed, joints cut, and so on. The general rule is to allow about $\frac{1}{2}$ in. extra in length, $\frac{1}{8}$ in. to $\frac{1}{4}$ in. extra in width, according to whether the work is large or small, and

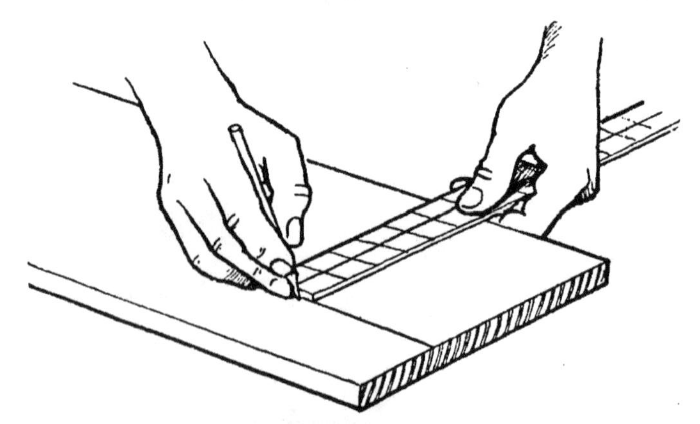

FIG. 1. MARKING LINE PARALLEL WITH EDGE USING RULE.
This method of marking is quick and is handy for work in which only approximate accuracy is needed.

$\frac{1}{16}$ in. to $\frac{1}{8}$ in. in thickness. As, however, most wood to-day is obtained ready planed on both sides, the usual plan is to put down the net thickness, since little more than a single shaving is needed to finish it. Another point to keep in mind is that length allowance may have to be greater in some cases and is entirely unnecessary in others. For instance, the wood for the stiles of a door having mortises cut near the ends should have extra allowance so that any tendency for the wood to split when being mortised is reduced to a minimum. On the other hand, the rails, having tenons at both ends, should be cut to the finished size, because otherwise a great deal of laborious and unnecessary sawing will be involved when tenoning.

Fig. 1 shows how the preliminary marking can be done with the pencil and rule. The edge is first made straight by planing and the marks then drawn parallel as shown. Cross lines are put in with the square. If it is not practicable to make the edge straight first or if the wood is not parallel at the edges, the straight-edge must be used.

Economical setting out. Suppose half a dozen pieces similar

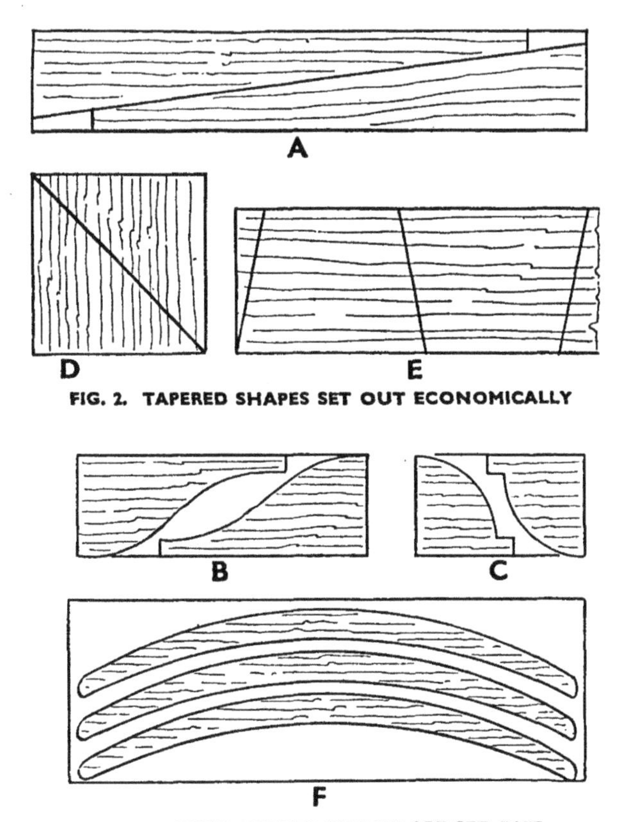

FIG. 2. TAPERED SHAPES SET OUT ECONOMICALLY

FIG. 3. HOW CURVED SHAPES ARE SET OUT

to Fig. 2, A, are required about 15 in. long and 2½ in. wide at the wide end. Do not jump to the conclusion that a 7 ft. 6 in. length of stuff 2½ in. wide is just what you require. Look at A and it will be seen that, by taking a board half an inch wider, two pieces can be cut from one length of 17 in. This means that six pieces could be cut from a board 4 ft. 3 in. by 3 in.—a considerable saving.

B and C, Fig. 3, are examples of bracket shapes which, arranged on the wood as shown (the grain in the right direction), can be cut with a minimum of waste. Triangular blocks when wanted are cut from squares, D, whilst parts like E can be sawn with practically no waste. Shaped items like coat-hangers, F, are arranged as shown, the waste being negligible if six or more can be cut from one board. In everyday work similar methods of economy in marking will suggest themselves.

Shaped parts. Sometimes the shape may be obtained with the

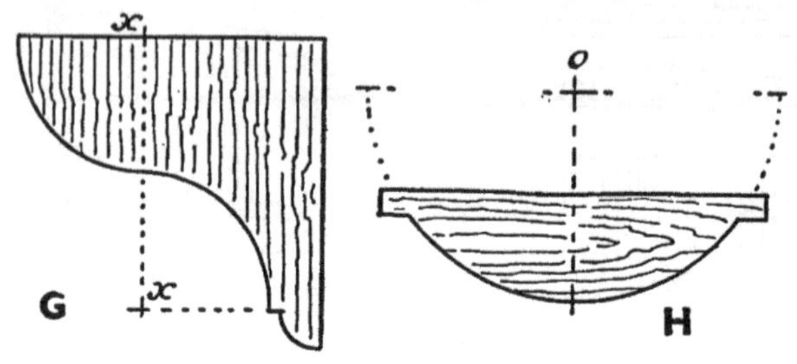

FIG. 4. CIRCULAR CURVES SET OUT WITH COMPASSES.

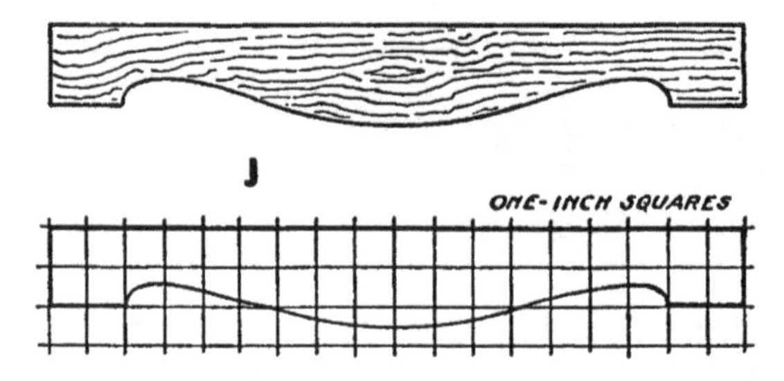

FIG. 5. SHAPES PLOTTED OUT MAP FASHION.

aid of compasses. In the case of a bracket, for example, which takes the familiar form shown in Fig. 4, G, the two curves are often quarter circles, with the centres at *x*, *x*. The small curve at the lower extremity can also be drawn with the compasses. Another example is seen in Fig. 4, H, where the centre of the curve will be found at *o*.

Plotting. Shapes which cannot be drawn with compasses, however, are more frequent. Curved rails and apron pieces like J (Fig. 5) are common, and when there is no full-size drawing or template, freehand drawing is unavoidable. Here the plotting (or mapping out) method is followed. Assume that J is 18 in. long and about 2½ in. wide. With the aid of a scale plot out the diagram into squares of 1 in. each, this being done by ruling in the horizontal and vertical lines indicated. On a sheet of paper draw the squares *full size*, 18 to the length and 3 to the width. By following the plotted diagram note where the curve intersects a vertical or horizontal line; mark with a dot; and then pencil in the shape. As a rule it is only necessary to draw in one half, as this may be reversed for the other side. Drawings of this kind should not be destroyed; they may be useful later.

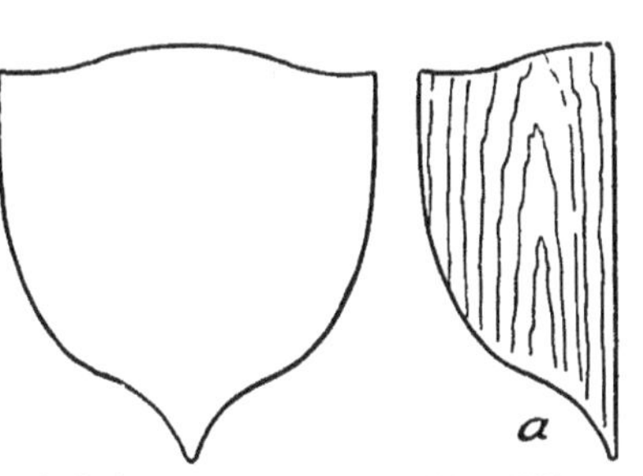

FIG. 6. TEMPLATE FOR MARKING.

Templates. When several similar shapes are wanted it is customary to make a template in thin plywood or stout cardboard from which to do the setting out. A shield form, such as Fig. 6, is troublesome to trace freehand, and if a number are likely to be required it saves time to have a template (*a*) which need be only one-half of the shield. When sawn, smooth the edges so that with a sharp pencil a clear line may be obtained for cutting. Before transferring, draw the centre line on the wood to be worked. The fact that the template is only a half ensures that both sides will be exactly alike.

Drawing an ellipse. For all practical purposes there is a simple

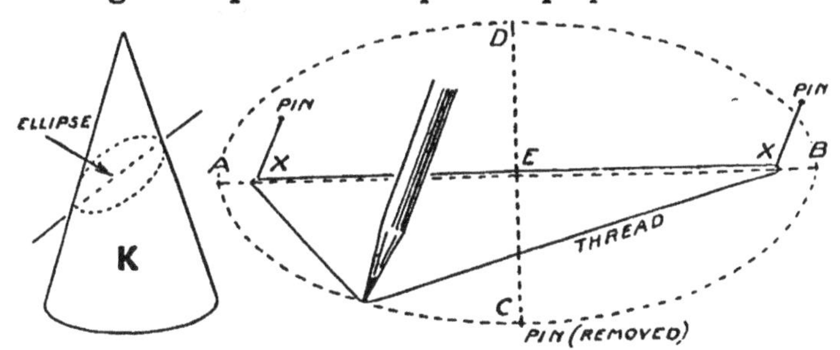

FIG. 7. ELLIPSE DRAWN BY PIN AND THREAD METHOD.
If string is used for a large ellipse it should be stretched first so that it does not give when drawing the shape.

method of drawing a correct ellipse which every woodworker should know. It is done with three pins, a short length of thread and a pencil (see Fig. 7). Assuming that the length and the width of the ellipse have been determined, draw AB and CD at right angles to each other, the point E being the centre of both axes. With the compasses take the length AE (which is *half* the *longer* axis) and with the point on C mark off X and X on the line AB. (Memorize this, as it is the clue to the method.) Knock in fine pins at X, X and C. Around the three pins tie a fairly stout cotton thread, taking care that the knot is tight. Withdraw the pin at C, leaving the thread loose on the two pins at XX.

If, now, the thread is strained tight with the pencil a perfect ellipse can be drawn as shown. Note three small points: do not lean the pencil sideways; see that the thread does not creep up the pin; keep the thread uniformly tight.

It is worth while to observe just how the ellipse is described. When using compasses there is *one* centre; here we have (because of the pins at XX) a *continuously changing* centre. The method is understood if you ask and answer three questions: (1) Why, when the thread is tight, does the pencil exactly reach the points A and B? (2) Why does it exactly reach the points C and D? (3) How do the intermediate curves come out perfect?

The answers are: (1) The total length of thread when knotted is the length of AB plus the length of XX. This is obvious, as you have already made each length from C to X equal to AE, which is half of AB. Thus it follows that the limit of the pencil's reach horizontally is exactly half its own length, which must be the length from right hand X to A, or left hand X to B. (2) As the thread has been tied around the pin which was originally at C, the limit of the pencil's reach on the shorter vertical diameter is C at one side and D at the other. (3) The line of the curve is automatic. There is no fixed centre, and but for any slight give in the thread or unsteadiness of the hand, the pencil could follow no other course.

7. NAILING AND SCREWING

FOR reasonably fine woodwork you rely mainly upon glue to hold wood together, and nails are used chiefly for less important parts, to hold a joint together whilst the glue sets, or sometimes to augment the strength of a glued joint. This calls for nails which, whilst having fair strength, will not make unsightly holes or be liable to split out the grain.

Kinds of nails. For wood up to about $\frac{3}{4}$ in. thick the best all-round nail is the panel pin at A, Fig. 1. It is of light gauge, making only a small hole, and grips hardwood sufficiently strongly when the parts are also glued. It can be obtained in lengths ranging from $\frac{3}{8}$ in. to 2 in. For very small work the veneer pin B is useful, as it is

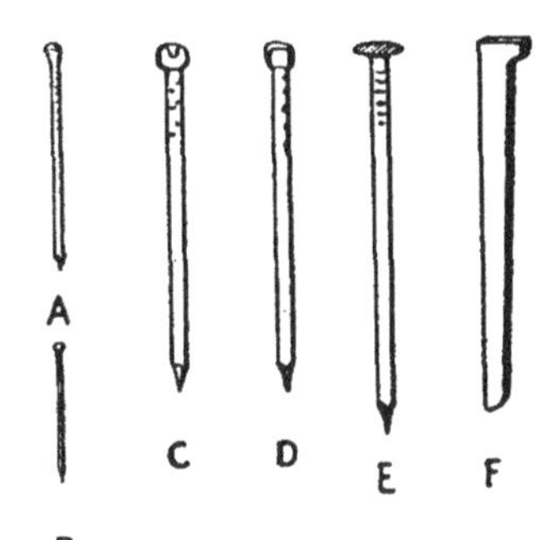

FIG. 1. KINDS OF NAILS IN COMMON USE.
A. Panel pin.
B. Veneer pin.
C. Oval wire nail.
D. Lost-head nail.
E. French nail.
F. Cut brad.

of very small gauge. It has only a light grip, however, and is of value only for holding parts whilst the glue sets. It is frequently used to hold small mouldings, being withdrawn once the glue has hardened.

For work requiring a stronger grip than that of the panel pin there is the oval brad shown at C. It has a small head, and when driven in with the length of its head parallel with the grain makes only a small hole. If used for a very hard wood it is inclined to bend, and the better nail is the lost-head at D. This is round in section and is stiffer than the oval nail, and leaves a hole not very much larger.

For woodwork in which strength is more important than appearance the french nail at E is useful. Its large head prevents it from pulling right through easily. Incidentally, you can make the head less unsightly and use it in place of the lost-head by holding the head on a block of iron and beating it flat, as in Fig. 2. It is a useful tip

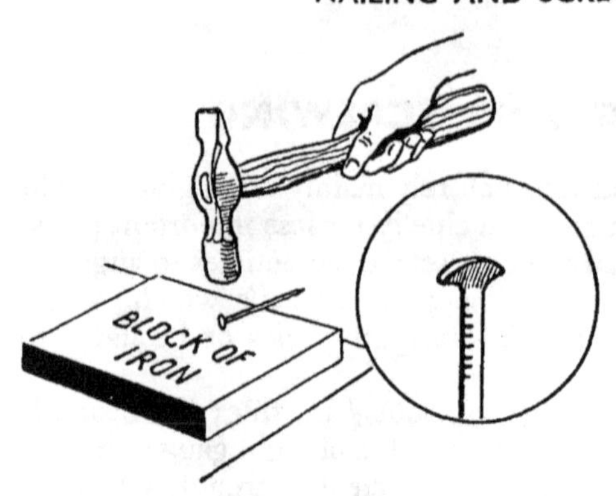

FIG. 2. FLATTENING FRENCH NAIL HEAD.
It should be driven into the wood with head in line with the grain.

to remember in case lost-heads should not be available. Cut nails, F, have a strong grip and when driven into softwood leave only a small hole. They are associated mostly with carpentry.

Driving a nail. One of the chief causes of a nail bending over when being driven is a dirty hammer face. Wet glue, paint, or oil upon it will almost certainly cause a nail to double up. Rub the face upon a sheet of fine glasspaper if in any doubt. Glue easily gets on to the hammer when nailing a joint which is also glued.

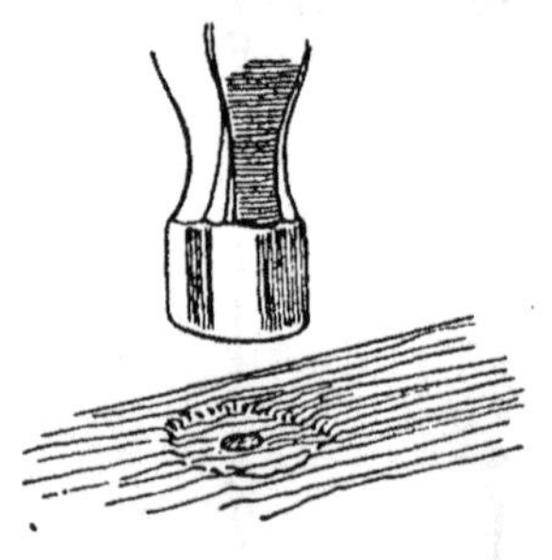

FIG. 3. BRUISE IN WOOD CAUSED BY HAMMER-HEAD.

As a blow from a hammer will bruise a wood surface easily, cease to strike a nail with the hammer when it is just proud of the surface. Otherwise an unsightly mark, as in Fig. 3, is inevitable. Final driving should be with the punch, as in Fig. 4; you will probably want to drive the nail below the surface anyway. Choose a punch which is rather smaller than the nail head, one with a hollow point preferably. It is not so liable to start away from the nail and make an unsightly hole.

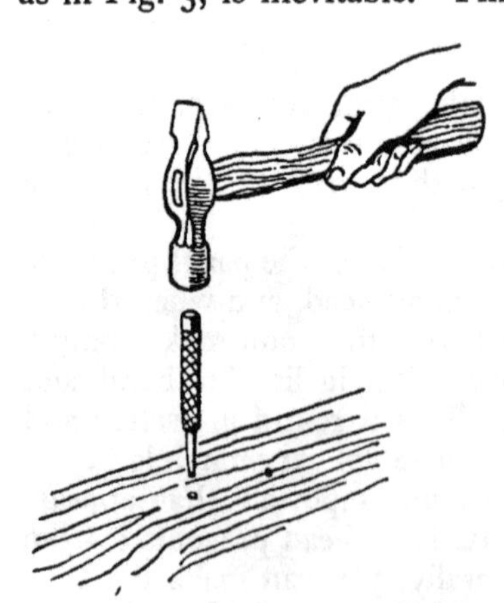

FIG. 4. PUNCH FOR NAIL.
This drives the head beneath the surface.

Some woods are specially liable to split, particularly when the nail is near an edge, and the safe plan is to make a pilot hole with a bradawl rather smaller than the gauge of the nail. It is also useful when the nail has to enter the grain at an angle. It ensures its starting in the required direction, after which it is much more likely to keep straight. In any case, give two or three light strokes to begin with, so that the nail is entered as required, before giving more powerful blows.

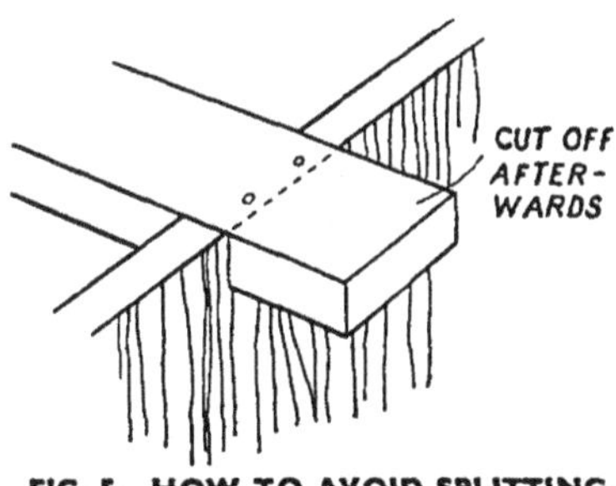

FIG. 5. HOW TO AVOID SPLITTING. The wood is left extra long and is cut off after nailing.

Another way of avoiding splitting is to allow the wood a projection and saw it off afterwards, as in Fig. 5. The nail is not then so near the edge when driven in and is not so liable to split the grain. Yet another device useful in some circumstances is to stagger the nails, as in Fig. 7. The drawing shows how two, three, and four nails can be arranged to each board.

A means whereby the strength of a nailed joint is increased considerably is "dovetailed" nailing. The nails are entered at an angle in alternate directions, and they thus exert considerable resistance to a direct pull. It is specially useful for work which has no mechanical strength and is not glued. Fig. 6 shows the idea. The first nail is put in upright so that there is no tendency for the top wood to move under the hammer blows.

It is sometimes possible to enter nails in positions where they are almost invisible. In Fig. 8, for instance, the nails at B are driven at an angle in the lower corner instead of being sent straight through

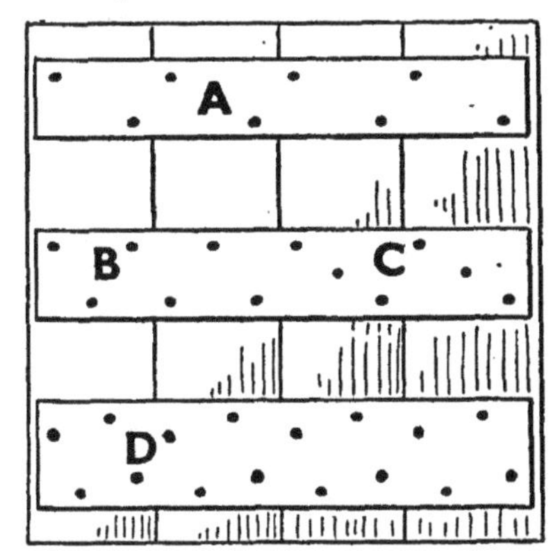

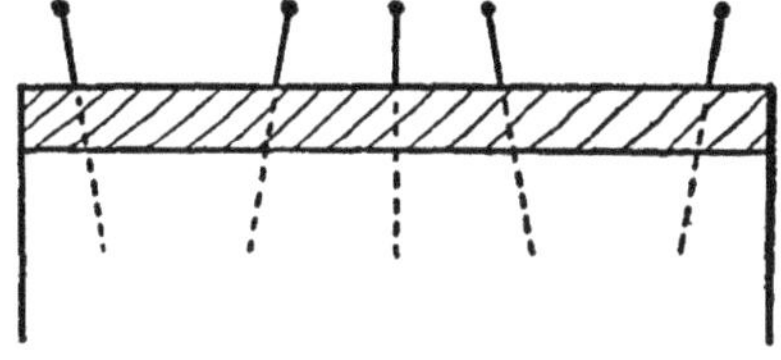

FIG. 6 (*above*). "DOVETAILED" NAILS. This helps to resist an outward pull.

FIG. 7 (*left*). NAILS STAGGERED TO AVOID SPLITTING.

the outside, as at A, where the holes are unsightly. When this is done it is essential that a cramp is put across the job whilst the nail is being entered, as otherwise the hammering will probably cause the parts to separate.

When a nail bends over, place a scraper or thin block of wood near it and lever over the pincers on this when withdrawing it (see Fig. 9). It avoids bruising the surface.

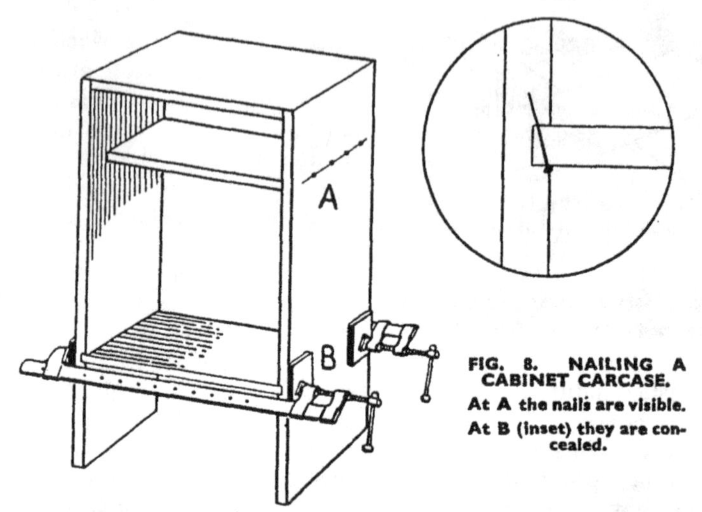

FIG. 8. NAILING A CABINET CARCASE.
At A the nails are visible.
At B (inset) they are concealed.

Screwing—kinds of screws. The screw most commonly used in woodwork is the flat-head or countersunk type shown at A, Fig. 10. It is intended to be let flush into the wood, the latter being countersunk to take the head. The length is taken over-all, as shown by the arrow. Round-head screws (B) come in occasionally, but are used chiefly in the smaller sizes for fixing certain metal fittings. The length here is taken from beneath the head. Occasionally what is known as the raised-head screw is used, this being countersunk and having the head slightly curved. It has a neat appearance, and is used generally with special screw cups.

FIG. 9. PULLING OUT NAILS.
The scraper avoids marking the wood.

Apart from length, screws are known also by gauge or thickness, and this gauge applies to all screws regardless of length. Thus, a No. 8 1-in. screw is of the same gauge as a No. 8 3-in. screw. There are also various metals and finishes, such as iron, brass, blacked, copper, bronzed, etc.

The only point to keep in mind when using brass screws is that, whilst strong enough when in position, they are liable to shear off if subjected to strong turning pressure when being driven in, especially the long, smaller gauges. The safest plan when brass screws have to be entered into hardwood is to drive in iron screws of the same gauge first. These can then be withdrawn and brass screws used. In this way the iron screws do the preliminary heavy work of cutting the thread in the wood.

Sizes of screw holes. When two pieces of wood are to be screwed together, two distinct sizes of holes are required: clearance hole and thread hole. Fig. 11 explains the reason for this. That in

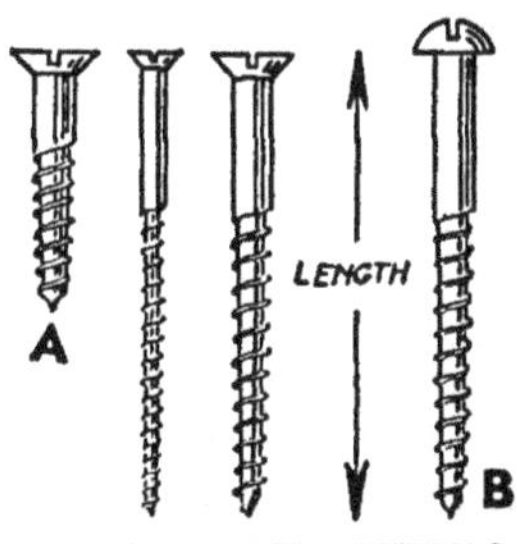

FIG. 10. SCREW DETAILS. Flat-head screws at A, and round-head at B.

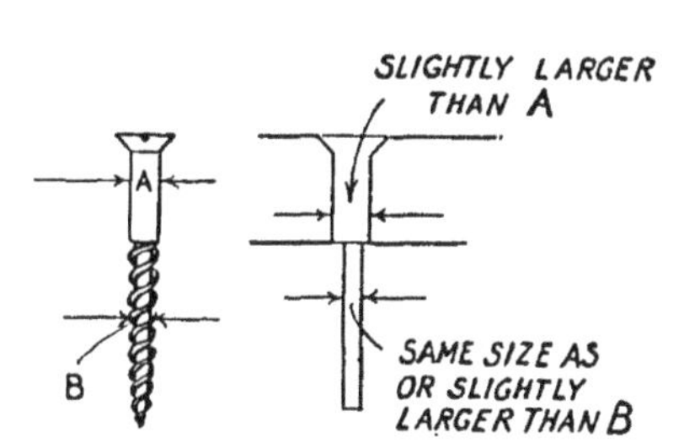

FIG. 11. SIZES OF SCREW HOLES. Clearance hole is larger than thread hole.

the upper piece of wood is to take the shank (A), and it should be an easy fit. The thread hole in the lower piece must clearly be smaller, because the thread has to bite its way into the wood. If a screw is examined closely it will be seen that there is a sort of centre rod with the thread projecting all round (B). Only the thread grips the wood, the centre rod forming merely the stiffening or strength of the screw. The thread hole then should be no smaller than the size of the centre rod and the depth should be a trifle more than the distance the screw will penetrate into the wood.

In practice one is not quite so particular about *exact* sizes, but it is important that the shank of the screw (A) is a free fit in the clearance hole. The thread hole is generally made with the bradawl, and it is just a case of picking the nearest to suit the gauge of screw being used. If you choose one which is about equal to the centre rod portion (B) you will not be far out.

Care is sometimes needed in the length of screw used for a job. For instance, suppose a fairly thin table-top is to be fixed with screws driven upwards through the rails. Clearly the maximum length of thread is desirable to enable the screw to grip properly, but if it is too long, even though it does not project, it may bend the top fibres up and so form a lump as shown in Fig. 12. In such a case, rather than use a shorter screw it would be better to nip off the point.

Recessed screws. Whilst on the subject of table-tops it is necessary to consider the method of screwing when the rails are

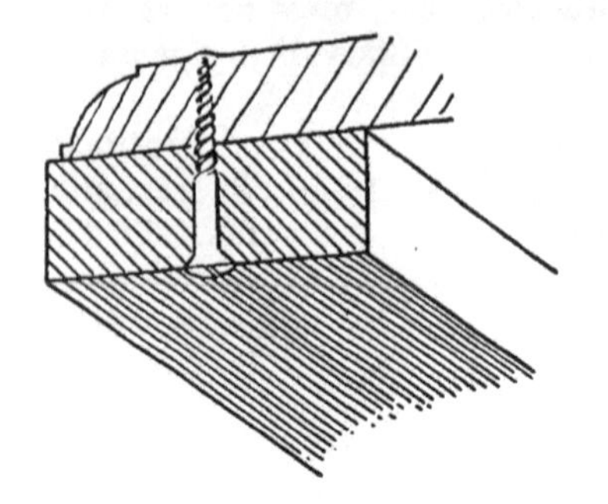

FIG. 12. SCREW TOO LONG CAUSES BUMP ON SURFACE OF WOOD.

upright rather than flat. To avoid using very long screws, recess holes can be bored as in Fig. 13. A depth stop should be fixed to the bit so that all holes are the same depth. The clearance hole is bored afterwards. Do not reverse the process, because there will be no wood in which the centre of the larger bit can engage.

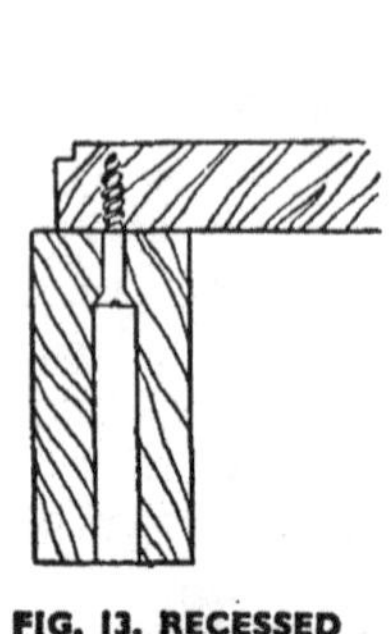

FIG. 13. RECESSED SCREW.

FIG. 14. POCKET SCREW.

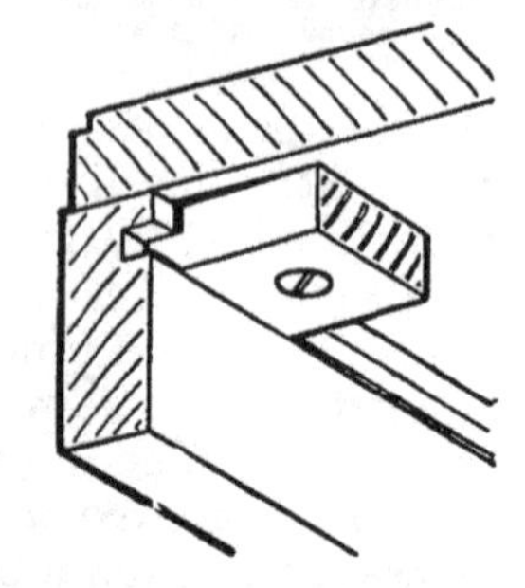

FIG. 15. BUTTON USED FOR TABLE-TOP.

Another method is the pocket screw, shown in Fig. 14. The clearance hole is drilled from the top edge at an angle so that it emerges at the inside of the rail. A gouge is then used to cut the pocket in which the screw-head fits.

Both the foregoing methods have the disadvantage that they make a rigid fixing which does not allow for possible shrinkage of the wood. When plywood or laminated board is used it does not matter, because there is no shrinkage, but solid wood would probably split if its shrinkage were resisted by rigid fixing. The usual plan, therefore, is to fix the front rigidly and use "buttons" at sides and back as in Fig. 15. These engage in grooves worked around the inner surface of the sides and are screwed to the top. They are thus free to slide in the grooves without allowing the top to move upwards. Note that the "step" of the button is slightly less than the distance between the groove and the top edge, so that there is a definite pull on the top when the screw is tightened.

Whilst it is unnecessary to have a different screwdriver for every size of screw, it is desirable for it to be of approximately the right size. At any rate, it is useless to try to use a small screwdriver for a large screw or *vice versa*. In the first case the tool itself would be ruined, and in the second the slot of the screw would be burred over. Always maintain a strong downward pressure in addition to turning the screw. Otherwise the tool will start from the slot and burr over the latter badly. Dip the thread of the screw into Vaseline, as this not only eases turning but prevents rust.

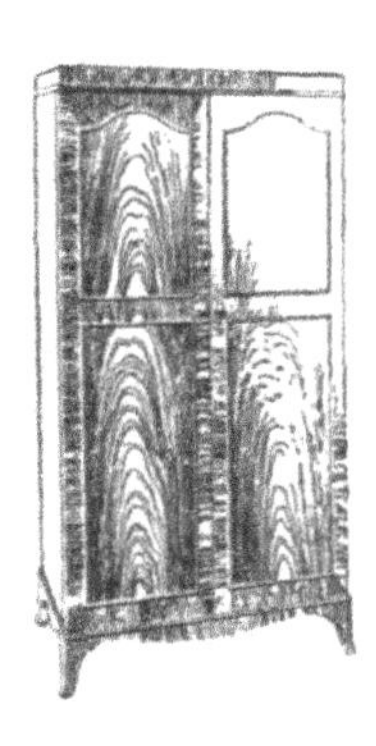

8. GLASSPAPERING

THE sole purpose of glasspaper is to remove marks made by any tools previously used and to make the surface smooth. It is not intended to make the work true, and it does not therefore replace the plane or any other tool. Properly used, it has its necessary place amongst the woodworking processes. Its abuse is when it is made

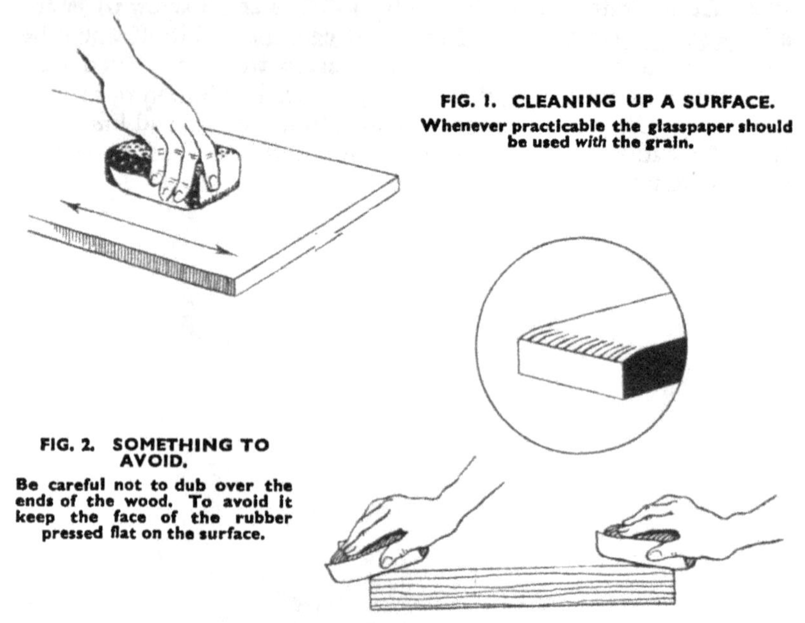

FIG. 1. CLEANING UP A SURFACE. Whenever practicable the glasspaper should be used *with* the grain.

FIG. 2. SOMETHING TO AVOID. Be careful not to dub over the ends of the wood. To avoid it keep the face of the rubber pressed flat on the surface.

to take the place of tools for operations for which it is unsuitable and for which it was never intended.

The danger with unskilled work is that the edges and corners of the work may become rounded over. To avoid this a rubber should always be used. For an ordinary flat surface a flat cork rubber measuring about 5 in. by 3 in. is used. If a sheet of glasspaper (which measures 12 in. by 10 in.) is cut up into either four or six, it will just comfortably cover the rubber with enough turn-up to enable the fingers to grip. Either two hands or one can be used, but a fair downward pressure should be maintained (Fig. 1). Take special care at the edges to avoid rocking the rubber as this inevitably leads to dull, rounded corners. The evils of this are shown in Fig. 2, and nothing looks worse. You can help matters by not allowing the rubber to pass the edge more than about an inch and keeping a firm downward pressure on the part bearing on the wood.

Work *with* the grain unless it is quite impossible. The point is that glasspaper does its work by scoring a number of fine scratches in the wood, and these are unnoticeable when they follow the grain, but show when they strike across it. Furthermore, it has an unfortunate effect on work which is to be stained since the stain takes more readily on wood on which the glasspaper has been taken across. It is thus liable to produce a patchy effect.

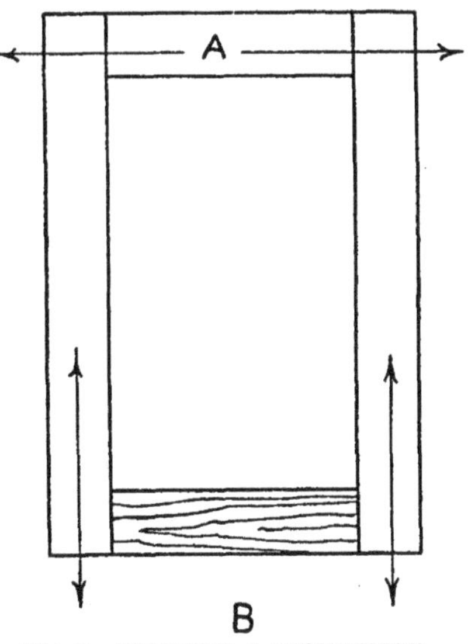

FIG. 3. CLEANING A FRAMEWORK.
Take the rubber straight across first as at A. Finish off level with the shoulders as at B.

There are a few occasions when it is unavoidable; for instance in quartered and other built-up patterns in veneer, in which the grain is bound to run in varying directions, and in such wood as burr walnut which has no definite direction in its grain.

In the former case the only plan is to work from end to end in one direction and finish off with extra fine glasspaper. For burr walnut a circular movement with the rubber should be followed and only the finest glasspaper (*flour*) used.

When a framework has to be cleaned up there is the slight added complication that the glasspaper must be taken across the grain in part, but there is no difficulty providing that it is used *with* the grain afterwards. Fig. 3 shows at A how the glasspaper is first used on the rails, being taken straight across the joints. Afterwards it is used on the stiles up to the shoulders only, thus obliterating the marks previously made.

Shaped surfaces. For a curved edge the best plan is to use a block of wood as in Fig. 4. Round over the edge of the block as at A, Fig. 4, for hollow curves, making the shape slightly quicker than that of the curve. Rounded shapes can be dealt with by using a flat block as at B.

Mouldings need specially made wood rubbers, these being worked to the reverse shape of the mouldings as at Fig. 5. Without them the corners would inevitably be rounded over. In the case of machine-made mouldings always damp with warm water first and allow to dry. This raises the grain and saves a lot of roughness in work to be stained later.

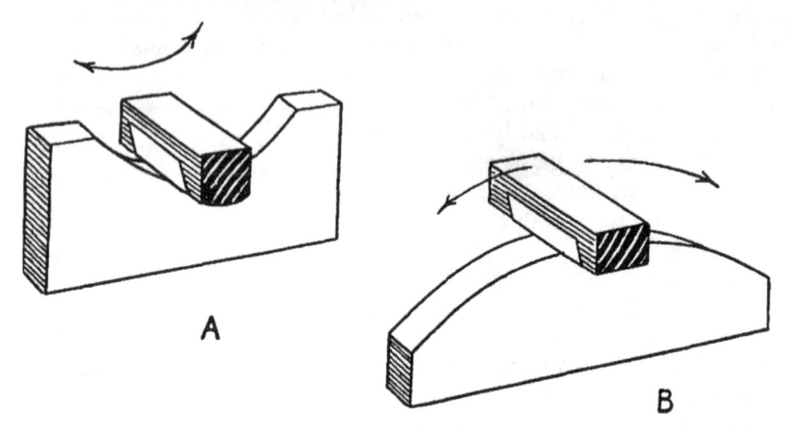

FIG. 4. CLEANING CURVED SURFACES WITH GLASSPAPER RUBBERS. For the concave shape a rounded rubber is needed (A). A flat rubber is used for the convex shape (B).

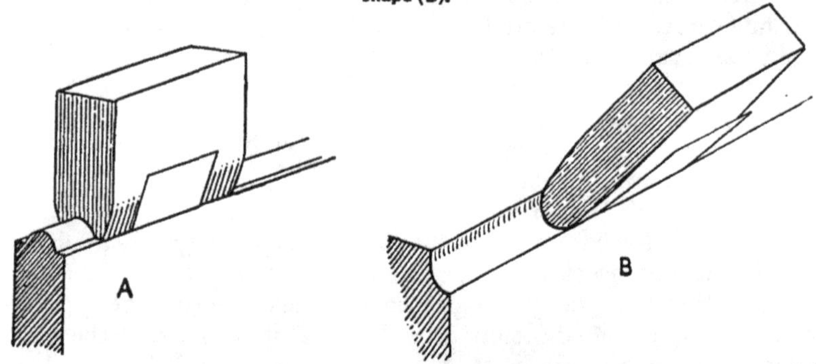

FIG. 5. RUBBERS FOR CLEANING UP MOULDINGS.

Grades of glasspaper. Woodwork to be painted needs nothing finer than middle 2 glasspaper, but polished woodwork requires a following rubbing with No. 1½ or No. 1. The first rubbing must be thorough because its purpose is to take out minor inequalities and to remove tool marks. When finished the surface should be completely flat and smooth. The purpose of using fine glasspaper to follow is simply to remove the large scratches made by the coarse grade.

9. GLUE AND ITS USE

ALTHOUGH the general tendency in the trade is to use proprietary glues of either the casein or the synthetic resin type, scotch glue is still widely used. Properly prepared and handled and kept free from dampness, it is extremely strong and has the advantage of being cheaper.

Preparation of scotch glue. This is manufactured from the skins and bones of animals, and is purchased mostly in flat cakes,

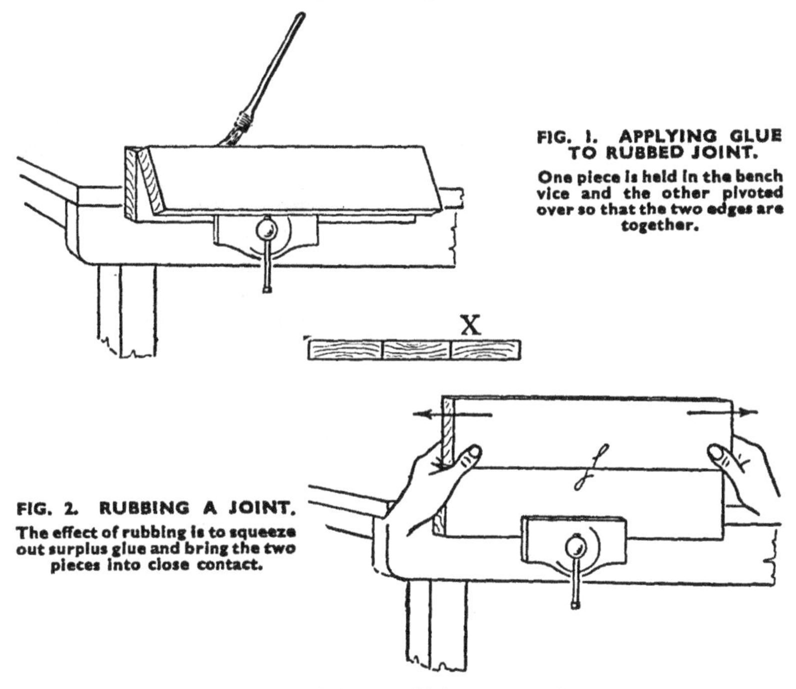

FIG. 1. APPLYING GLUE TO RUBBED JOINT. One piece is held in the bench vice and the other pivoted over so that the two edges are together.

FIG. 2. RUBBING A JOINT. The effect of rubbing is to squeeze out surplus glue and bring the two pieces into close contact.

though it can be obtained in small lumps or in a sand-like form. The advantage of the latter is the ease with which it can be prepared, since it liquifies much more quickly under heat. The cakes require to be broken up into small pieces, and since it is invariably brittle, it should be put into a piece of sacking to prevent flying. The crushed glue is placed in the *inner* can of the glue kettle with just enough cold water to cover it, and if possible allowed to steep overnight. The outer container of the kettle is then half filled with water and the glue slowly heated. Never place the inner container alone directly over the fire or gas burner. Stir periodically to remove all lumps and skim off any white matter. When the glue runs off the brush without dropping and at the same time is free from lumps, the consistency is approximately correct. If too thick, add a little clean warm water. Glue should not be boiled.

One of the functions of glue is to penetrate the pores of the wood so that the parts are virtually welded together. For this reason the glue is applied hot and before it has time to chill pressure is applied. Furthermore, the wood is warmed also to prevent chilling. The glue is forced into the pores and becomes part of the wood structure. At the same time, all surplus is squeezed out, no thickness of glue being left between the parts.

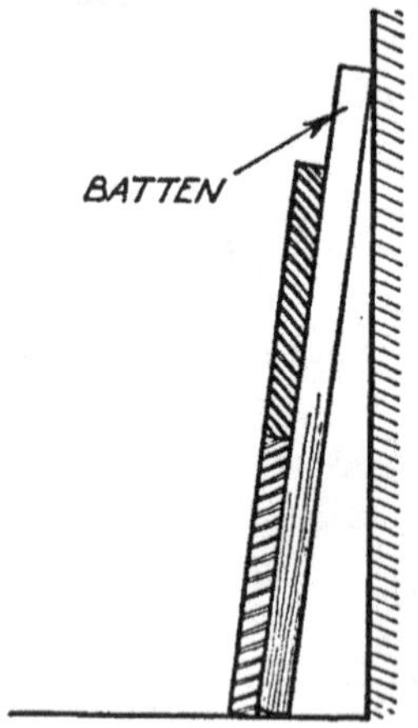

BATTEN

FIG. 3. STACKING JOINTS. The parts are supported across their entire width.

This means that the application of glue must be fairly rapid. Between the first operation and the final cramping there must be no delay; otherwise the glue may chill. Have everything ready—work, glue, cramps. When possible work in a warm room and heat the joints. Apply the glue liberally, but only on the part to be covered. The surplus glue squeezed out later should at once be wiped off with a damp swab. If allowed to set it will have to be chipped off with a chisel. It is much more easily removed when soft.

If a fairly wide table top (not veneered) is examined, it will usually be found that it has been made up of three or more boards. This is termed "jointed to width." Furniture timber of the required thickness is rarely available in very wide boards; and even if it were, some woods would be liable to twist unless securely battened. Not only is a jointed table-top more economical, but is more durable than one in a single width. The boards are arranged with the heart sides alternately up and down, as at X, Fig. 1, the edges planed true, and after gluing *rubbed* together. It is this rubbing back and forward till all surplus glue has been squeezed out that has given to the joint its common name, "rubbed."

The edges to be joined are marked (for guidance later) and planed perfectly true either in the vice or on the shooting-board. In the latter case one piece is laid on the board face downwards and the other face upwards to ensure their going together in alignment.

The two are warmed before a fire (without burning the edges) and one board is secured in the vice. The second board is held as indicated in Fig. 1 and glue liberally applied to the edges. When turned edge to edge, Fig. 2, hold them level on the face side by using the thumbs as a guide, then (keeping the hands low) rub back and forth. Test with the thumbs to see that all is flush, and lay aside in an upright position for about twelve hours until the glue sets. The work should rest across its entire width upon a batten, as in Fig. 3.

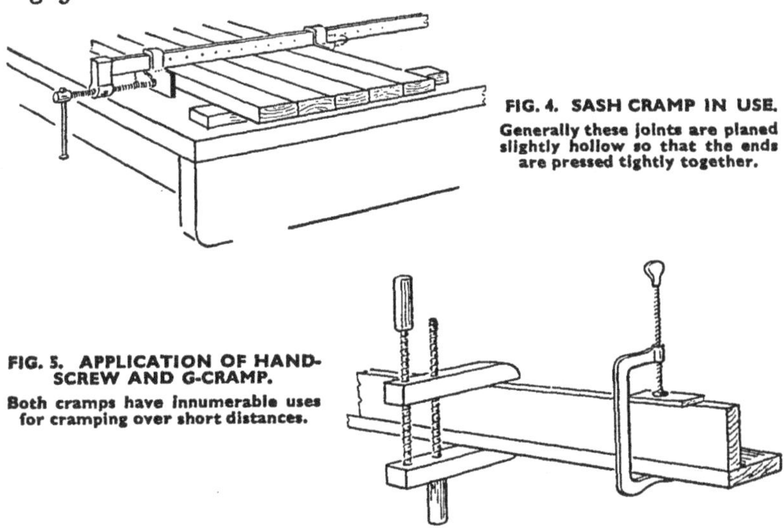

FIG. 4. SASH CRAMP IN USE.
Generally these joints are planed slightly hollow so that the ends are pressed tightly together.

FIG. 5. APPLICATION OF HAND-SCREW AND G-CRAMP.
Both cramps have innumerable uses for cramping over short distances.

Jointed boards up to 30 in. or 36 in. do not need cramping. In the case of larger boards it is common workshop practice so to plane the edges that there is just a perceptible hollow in the centre. When glued and rubbed these are then firmly cramped across the middle. In this way the ends, which are the most vulnerable places, are pressed firmly together by the natural spring of the wood after the cramps have been released.

When jointed work is wide, necessitating three or more boards, it is customary to apply pressure with a sash cramp (Fig. 4). The work is allowed to rest on a couple of battens, as indicated. The gluing of pieces edge to face (Fig. 5) calls for little comment, but the illustration shows the method of cramping. As there is a tendency for the wood to float on the liquid glue when pressure is applied, it may be necessary to readjust the cramps. Alternatively it may be possible to knock in a temporary nail at each end or at one side to prevent movement.

Cramping. Apart from squeezing out surplus glue, the purpose of the cramp is to pull up the joint. Remember, however, that the cramp does not remedy a defective joint; in spite of all cramping, the badly made joint will eventually gape when the cramp is removed.

One of the most useful forms of cramp is the wooden handscrew (see Fig. 5), which can be used in endless ways, not only for cramping joints but for holding work. It is particularly useful for jointing

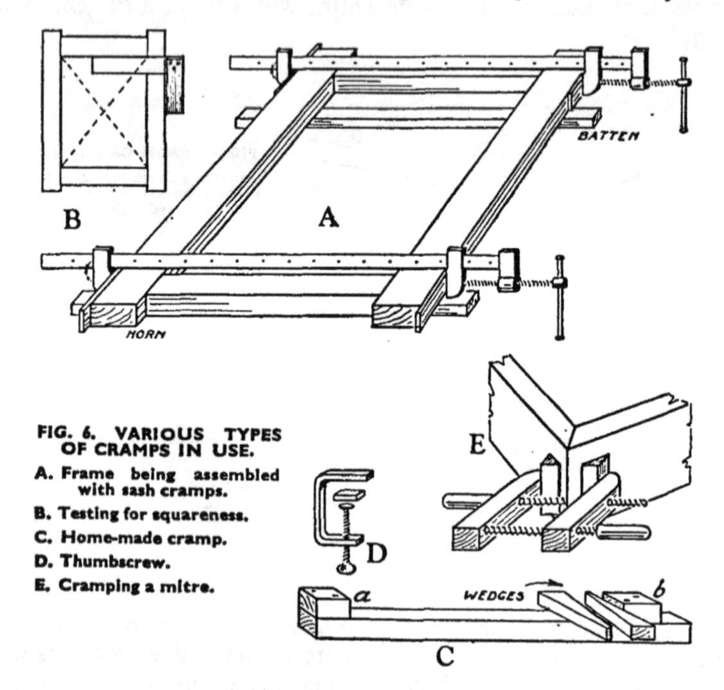

FIG. 6. VARIOUS TYPES OF CRAMPS IN USE.
A. Frame being assembled with sash cramps.
B. Testing for squareness.
C. Home-made cramp.
D. Thumbscrew.
E. Cramping a mitre.

boards face to face, for lipping and for applying mouldings or other narrow pieces of wood to larger work.

One instance of this use has been shown in Fig. 5, an example of edge-to-face gluing. Another is given in Fig. 6 (E), where a mitred plinth is cramped. As the jaws of the handscrew cannot grip the wood direct, two triangular blocks of wood are temporarily glued on. The handscrew is applied as shown and in this way exercises the necessary pressure. Later the triangular blocks are chiselled off and the surface cleaned.

In using the handscrew the jaws are opened to a trifle more than the width to be cramped. This is done rapidly by gripping a handle in each hand and rapidly revolving the one about the other. Place over the wood and tighten the screw nearer the work. Finally tighten the outer screw, the effect of which is to lever over the jaws on to the wood. When tightening is completed the jaws should be parallel. It is the tightening with the outer screw that gives the real pressure.

G-cramps (see Fig. 5 at right) in different sizes are useful when the bulkier handscrew might be awkward to handle. Smaller iron thumbscrews (Fig. 6, D) are also extremely handy for all kinds of small work. In using G-cramps and thumbscrews, always place a scrap of waste wood between the screw and the work to prevent injury to the surface when the cramp is tightened.

The joiner's sash cramp (see Fig. 6, A) comes to be essential when large work is tackled. Its advantage is that it will take work of any width from a few inches up to 4 ft. 6 in. or more, according to the size of the cramp. The ordinary run of lengths ranges from 24 in. to 48 in., heavier size from 48 in. to 60 in.

When cramping make sure that pressure is applied where it is needed. Take A, Fig. 6, which represents a mortised and tenoned framework. The ends of the stiles (called the "horns") have been left projecting to be sawn off later. The frame, too, is resting on a couple of battens, this to prevent glue from being smeared on to the bench and also to facilitate the handling of the screw. Pressure is at the points immediately opposite the rails. Place the cramp so that the long bar is in line with the centre of the width of rails; also adjust the shoes (or jaws) so that the axis of the screw is in line with the centre of the thickness of stile and rail.

It may be necessary to adjust the cramps to correct the frame if it is out of square or is in winding; lowering one end or the other will correct the latter, whilst shifting the shoes horizontally will enable a framework to be pulled square. To protect the edges of the stiles thin strips of wood are placed between the shoes and the wood.

Before and during cramping all work must be tested for squareness (see B, Fig. 6). In small work this may be done with the try-square, which is held in turn at all four corners. In the case of larger frames, carcase work, etc., the piece is measured diagonally from corner to corner (see dotted lines at B). If square, the two diagonals will be the same length. Use a strip of wood to test. Point one end to fit into the corners and mark the length with a pencil. Reverse into the other corners and again mark the length. Adjust until the length is midway between the two marks.

A common type of home-made cramp is shown in Fig. 6, C. To a batten is screwed a block (*a*). At a point about ½ in. more than the width of work to be cramped screw another block (*b*). By means of a couple of hardwood wedges the work may be cramped tightly.

10. DEALING WITH CURVED EDGES

WHEN cutting around a curve much depends upon the thickness of the wood being sawn. It is disastrous, for instance, to attempt to cut a shape in $\frac{1}{8}$ in. wood with a bow or keyhole saw; the teeth are too coarse and the result would be a badly ragged back surface and possibly an annoying split. The tool must be chosen in

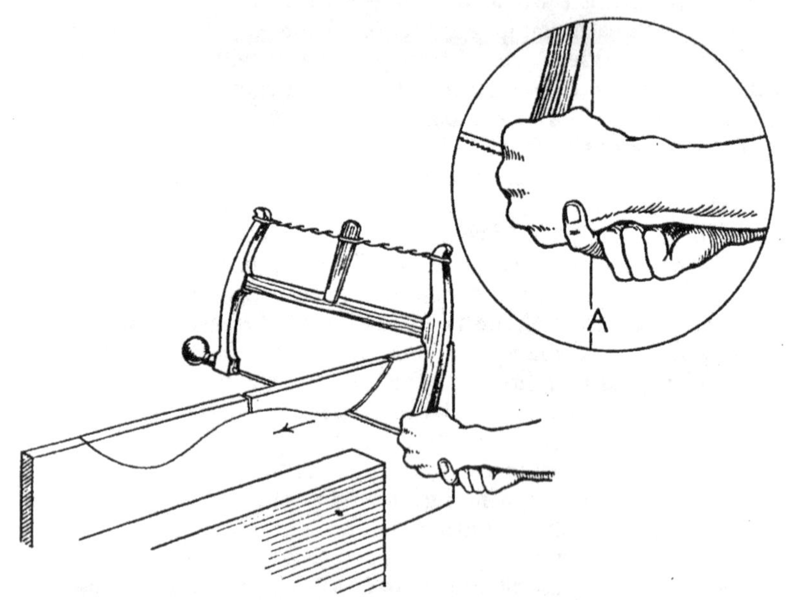

FIG. I. CUTTING A SHAPE WITH THE BOW-SAW.
Generally both hands are used as shown inset at A. The wood should be held low in the vice to avoid vibration.

accordance with the wood. In some cases it is better to avoid sawing altogether, and to waste away unwanted parts with chisel or gouge, just making straight saw cuts at intervals to cut up the grain.

Bow-saw. For the majority of work in wood from, say, $\frac{3}{8}$ in. up to 1 in. or so, the best tool is the bow-saw. Its blade is narrow so that it will negotiate fairly quick curves, and its teeth are of a size to give reasonably quick cutting without extensive ragging at the back. It can be used for inner as well as exterior cuts, one rivet at the holder being withdrawn to enable the blade to be passed through a hole bored in a waste part of the wood. Furthermore, the handles can be turned in the frame so that the cross bar will clear the edge of the wood—unless the cut is a long way in. In Fig. 1, for instance, the blade is turned to cut at right angles with the frame, and it can thus cut along the whole length without hindrance. Obviously both handles must be turned to the same extent, as otherwise the tool is liable to wander from the line. Test this by holding the saw so that the eye looks across the blade. Any twisting will be obvious.

Generally the wood is fixed in the vice, and an essential point is to fix it as low as possible so that undue vibration is avoided. This

FIG. 2. CUTTING LARGE CIRCLE IN A PANEL OF WOOD.
The short grain at XX is necessarily weak and needs care.

is specially important when the wood is thin and the part to be left is narrow and has short grain. Take as an example Fig. 2 in which a circular hole has to be pierced. It is desirable constantly to alter the position of the wood in the vice so that the saw is never working high up. Furthermore, the cut should be started at the long grain. Otherwise considerable strain would be thrown on the short grain at the completion of the cut when the circle had been practically finished.

Use two hands to the saw as at A, Fig. 1 and endeavour to keep it square with the wood both horizontally and vertically. It is generally easy to tell whether the blade leans to the right or left, but more difficult to see whether the hands drop or are too high. It does not matter so much when the cut happens to be vertical, but an error is disastrous when the cut runs across at an angle. And matters are still more complicated when the blade is fixed in the frame at an angle. There is no positive guide in this beyond judgment, though you can place a square against the wood occasionally at the start. Eventually, however, you will have to learn square cutting by experience. Test the edge after cutting to see whether you have a bias one way or the other.

FIG. 3. ORDER OF PROCEDURE WHEN SAWING A SHAPE.
Note that the straight portions are cut with the back-saw.

Clearly the saw must cut on the waste side of the line to allow for cleaning up, but it is a sign of poor craftsmanship to leave a lot to be cleaned off. It indicates the man who has no confidence in his sawing. Keep, then, just to the side of the line and gradually turn the saw to follow the curve.

When a shape has some square cuts in it it is advisable to cut these with the back-saw. In Fig. 3, for instance, the black portion could be bow-sawn first in the direction shown by the arrows. Next the straight cut B could be made with the back-saw. Cut C with the bow-saw follows, this just stopping short of cut D, which is made with the back-saw. The corner between B and C could be chiselled. Finally the cut at E is made with the back-saw, leaving the curve to be chiselled away.

Keyhole-saw. This is not a very practical tool for cutting shapes owing to its liability to buckle. Its chief use, as the name suggests, is for occasional inner cuts as when cutting the straight part of a keyhole. It would be too much of a business to disconnect the bow-saw blade and use this. Sometimes, however, the keyhole-saw is necessary when an internal cut is too far from the edge for the bow-saw to reach. At best it makes a rather coarse cut—the blade has to be fairly thick to give it rigidity—and the root of the blade is somewhat wide for the same reason, and this makes it difficult to cut quick curves. The best plan is to allow the blade the minimum projection which will give reasonable working movement. This enables the narrow part of the blade to be used without danger of its buckling.

Fret-saw and coping-saws. These are ideal for thin wood, since the rag is negligible. The fret-saw is the finer of the two, but the cut is necessarily slow. Normally several grades of blades are available, and for cabinet work the medium and coarser ones are generally the more useful, being quicker cutting and easier to control.

Thick wood. When really thick wood has to be shaped it is frequently an advantage not to use a saw, except to make cuts with the back saw to ease the wasting away of the wood with the chisel. As an example take the stretcher foot shown at A, Fig. 4. The shape should be set out on both sides, and lines squared in where the straight members occur, as at B. A series of saw cuts with the back-saw should be made at these lines. This will straightway remove the black portion shown at C, and this is followed by that shown black at D. The chisel could be used from each side for this if preferred if the initial cut across the grain is made first. A series of intermediate cuts across the grain as at D enables the waste to be chopped away in steps, after which the steps can be removed from each side with chisel and gouge (E). A bullnose or shoulder plane is useful in the final levelling and shaping. Rasp and file followed by scraping give the final shaping.

Cleaning up. The spokeshave, wood or metal, is generally used to clean up curves. Two kinds are available: flat face for convex

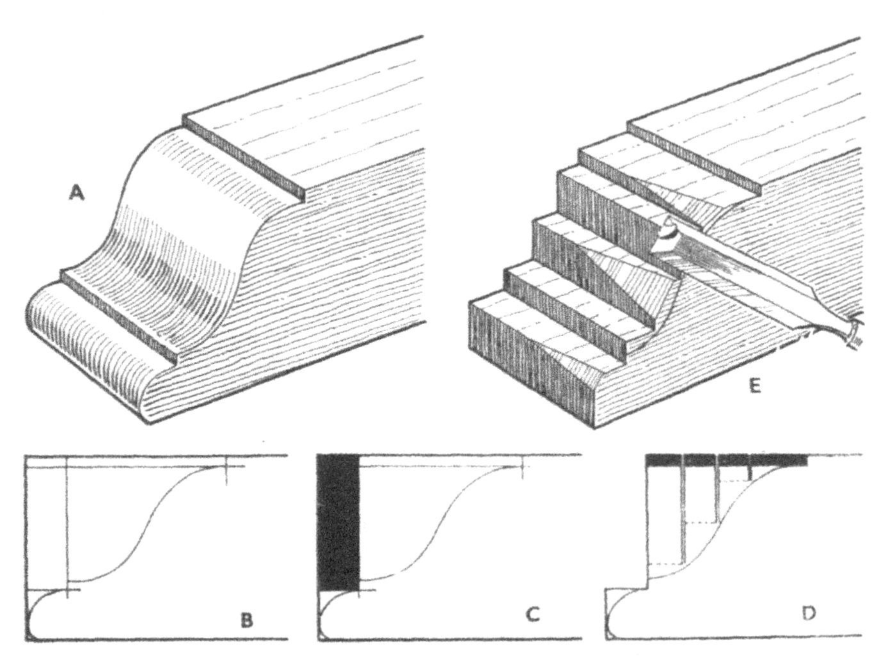

FIG. 4. SHAPED FOOT IN THICK WOOD, AND ORDER IN WHICH WORK IS CARRIED OUT.

FIG. 5. CLEANING SHAPE WITH THE SPOKESHAVE.
Direction of grain should be watched.

or rounded shapes and round face for concave or hollow curves. Set similarly to a plane and use with two hands, as in Fig. 5. Examine the grain beforehand and work always with it (see arrows in Fig. 5). The idea is to take out any lumps first, and you can generally detect these by the run of the tool. Test with the try-square to see that the edge is true before reaching right down to the line, so that any correction can be made without overrunning. Sometimes it is helpful to use the tool at an angle so that it has a slicing cut, though this cannot be done in the case of acute curves.

Small curves which are too sharp for the spokeshave to enter need the use of rasp and file. The former gives a coarse cut, but it wastes down the wood rapidly. It is used for the preliminary work, being followed by the file, which is much finer. Even this leaves some marks and these should be taken out with the scraper (if available) or a thorough scouring with glasspaper.

FIG. 6. FINISHING WITH GLASSPAPER.
The wood block prevents dubbing over the sharp edges.

11. HOW TO MAKE A DOOR

THE first point to decide when making a door is the way in which you propose to fix the panel. If it is to fit in grooves it will have to be inserted when you glue up the framework, and it will be impossible to remove it. If, however, it rests in a rebate you can insert it later, and this is an advantage for work to be french polished. In a glazed door or one with a mirror the rebate method is clearly essential. You have to decide this at once because it affects the joints.

To take a practical example, assume that you have to make the cupboard door shown in Fig. 1, the panel being of wood and fitting

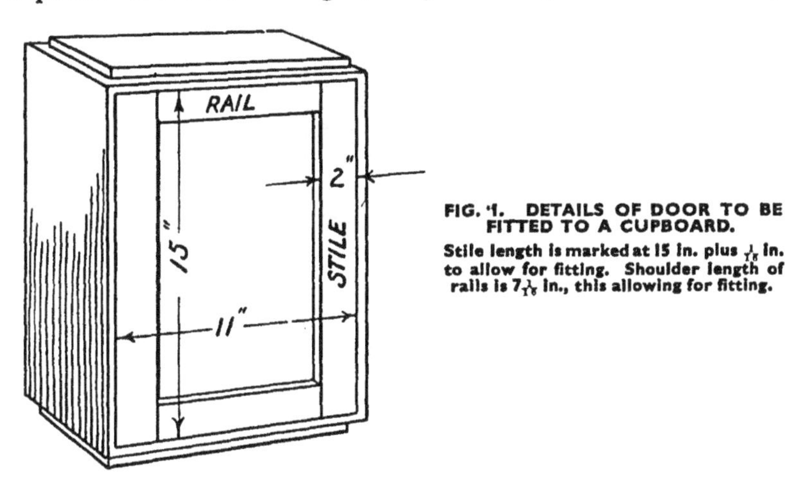

FIG. 1. DETAILS OF DOOR TO BE FITTED TO A CUPBOARD.

Stile length is marked at 15 in. plus $\frac{1}{16}$ in. to allow for fitting. Shoulder length of rails is $7\frac{1}{16}$ in., this allowing for fitting.

in grooves in the framework. Rails and stiles both finish 2 in. wide by $\frac{7}{8}$ in. thick, whilst the panel is $\frac{3}{8}$ in. thick. Cut out the four pieces for the framework, making the stiles at least 1 in. longer than the finished size, and the rails the finished over-all size including the tenons. Plane them to finish slightly full 2 in. width, being specially careful to make the edges square.

Marking out. Fig. 2 shows how the shoulder size of the rails is ascertained. The stiles are laid across the bottom of the cupboard hard up against the sides, the rail placed upon them, and pencil marks made opposite the inner edges of the stiles. Both rails are now fixed together temporarily with a thumbscrew (remember to put a slip of wood beneath the shoe to prevent damage), and the shoulder size squared across both with chisel (or knife) and square. About $\frac{1}{16}$ in.

is added over the pencil marks so as to give allowance for trimming and fitting. Beyond the shoulder lines by an amount equal to the groove depth other lines are put in, these representing the haunch size. As the face edges are inwards when the door is assembled the

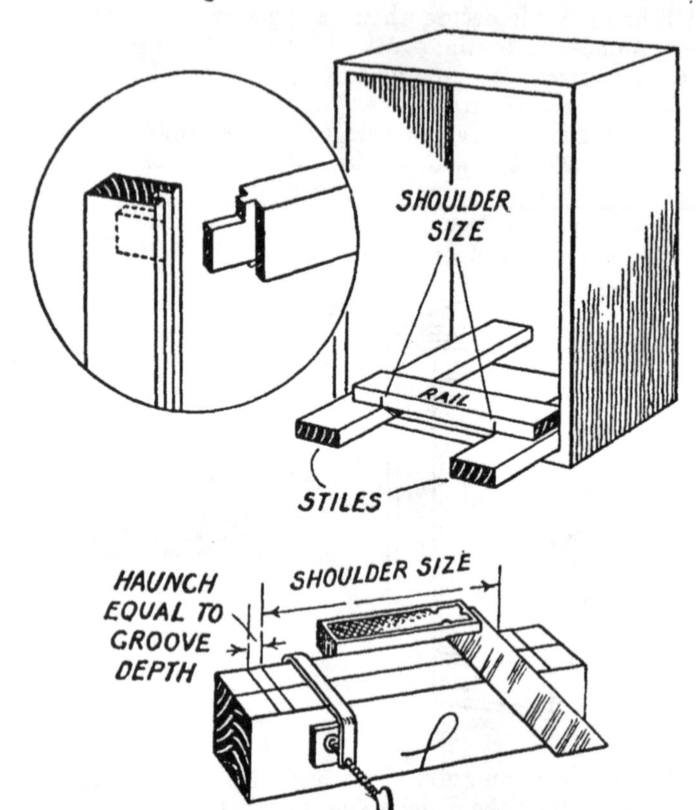

FIG. 2. HOW RAILS ARE MARKED OUT.
These marks should be put in with chisel and square.

marks should be on the outer edges as shown. The rails are separated and the shoulder lines squared round on to both sides and edges.

Stile sizes are taken from the cupboard itself, as in Fig. 3, the $\frac{1}{16}$ in. allowance being added as before. By fixing both together the marks can be squared across both, thus ensuring both being alike (Fig. 3). The face edges are marked in this case. Inside the overall marks other lines are put in marking the rail width, and between them again are further lines giving the groove depth and haunch

(Fig. 3). The shaded parts at the ends are waste and are removed later. They are desirable because, apart from trimming, they lessen any liability for the wood to split when chopping the mortises and fitting the joints. Such allowance is undesirable in the case of the

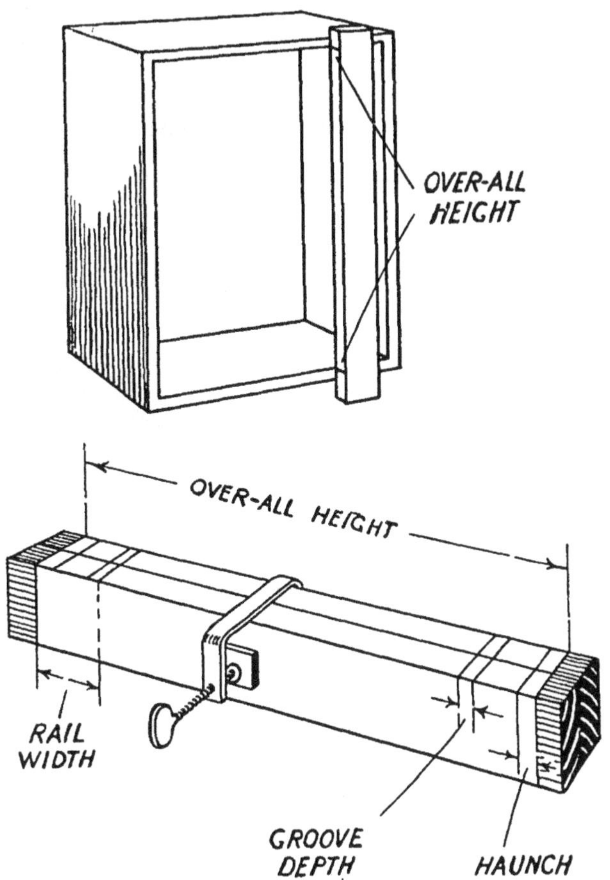

FIG. 3. ASCERTAINING OVER-ALL STILE LENGTH.
All these marks should be made with pencil and square.

rails because it would have to be cut off either before or after tenoning, and would have no advantage.

The cutting of the joint is dealt with in Chapter 16, and here we need no more than note that each joint should be fitted independently and tested to see that it goes together square and without twist. If each mortise and tenon is marked with corresponding numbers, as shown inset in Fig. 4 (thus: 3·3, 4·4, etc.), the joints can be replaced in their correct relative positions quickly without danger of their becoming mixed. Note that the marks are put on the face sides in every case so that the possibility of their being reversed is avoided.

Testing. Fig. 4 shows how the door should be tested for truth. The test at A is made when gluing up and is for squareness. Note that the square is used at *both* sides because it sometimes happens that the reading at one side will show the frame to be square, whilst that at the other will reveal it to be untrue. Theoretically, of course,

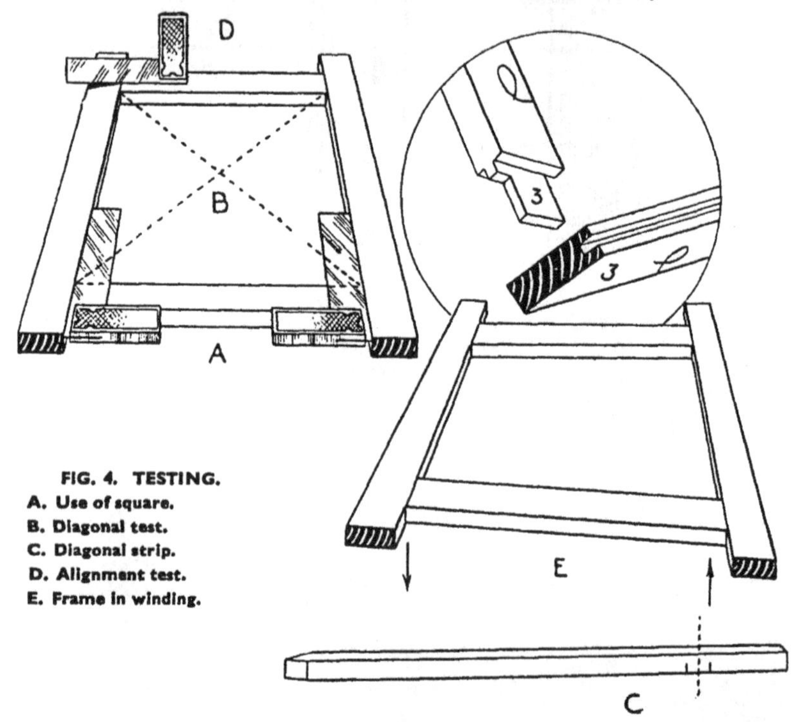

FIG. 4. TESTING.
A. Use of square.
B. Diagonal test.
C. Diagonal strip.
D. Alignment test.
E. Frame in winding.

this should not happen if the workmanship has been accurate, but as a practical matter it does sometimes occur, and it may be due to inaccurate marking out or jointing, to the wood not being planed true, or to the wood being forced into a curve by pressure of the cramps. The best plan in a small door is to divide the inaccuracy, but in a larger door it is safer to use the diagonal test B. If the door is true the same length will be registered in both directions. The strip is pointed at one end as at C so that it fits right into the corner. A pencil mark is made opposite the other corner. When reversed into the opposite corners another pencil mark is made, and the frame then adjusted until the length falls between the two pencil marks (see dotted line).

The test with the square or straight-edge at D should be made

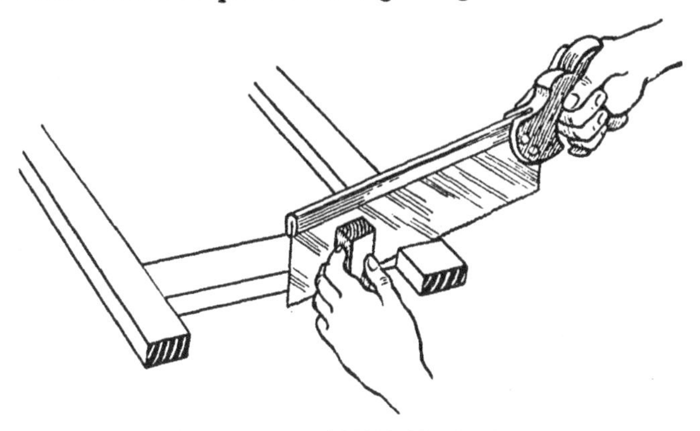

FIG. 5. SAWING OFF HORNS AFTER ASSEMBLING.
The piece of wood held against the saw-blade keeps the latter in line with the frame.

when the individual joint is being fitted as well as after gluing, its purpose being to test whether the parts are in alignment. The winding test at E must also be made when the framework is put together dry so that any inaccuracy can be put right before gluing.

Since in this case the panel fits in grooves in the framework, it will clearly be necessary to insert it during the gluing operation. Assuming it to be of solid wood it is imperative that it is not glued in, as otherwise it may split in the event of shrinkage.

Fitting. To fit the door saw off the horns as in Fig. 5, using a block of wood against the blade to keep it square. Plane the hingeing edge straight and square, and, offering the door in position, plane the bottom edge so that it makes a close fit with the cupboard, as shown in Fig. 6. Now plane the top edge also to make a close fit and then, holding

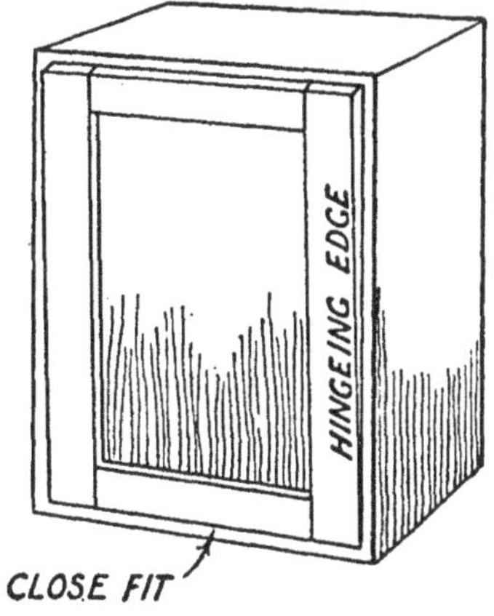

FIG. 6. FITTING DOOR.
Hingeing edge and bottom are fitted first.

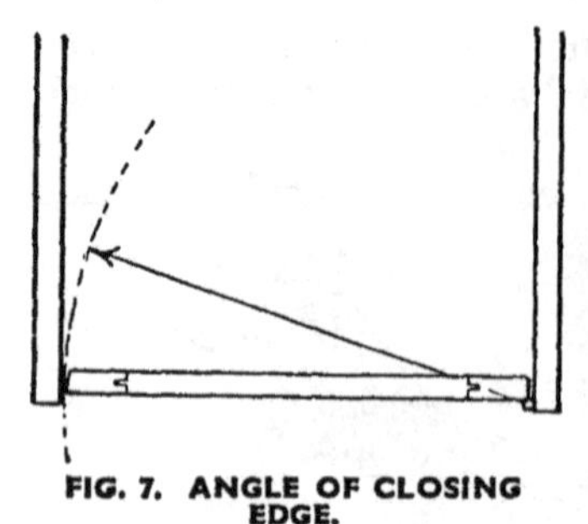

FIG. 7. ANGLE OF CLOSING EDGE.
This is at a slight angle (shown in exaggeration) so that it clears cupboard side.

the door in position, note how much too large it is and remove the surplus equally from both top and bottom edges. Do not make the mistake of removing all the shavings from one rail. It will make them look odd. The same thing applies to the stiles. Plane both edges square, then plane the closing edge at a *slight* angle so that it clears when opened. There should be a slight clearance all round, say the thickness of a piece of brown paper for work to be polished and rather more when paint is to be the finish.

12. HOW TO MAKE A BOX

THE joints you use for a box depend largely upon the use to which the box has to be put. If, for instance, strength is of first importance, as in a tool chest, the dovetail is the best. A simpler if not so strong alternative is the lapped joint, which requires the use of nails as well as glue. For quite light boxes the tongued joint is reasonably strong; whilst for a small box to be veneered the keyed mitre is the most satisfactory.

Dovetailed corners. If the box is fairly deep it may be necessary to joint pieces together to make up the width, and it is desirable to stagger the joints so that they are not opposite each other at the corners. Fig. 1 shows the idea at A. This also shows how the parts are laid out in a row (B), just as though they were the sides of a cardboard box opened out (C), and the joining ends numbered. This enables the parts to be assembled in the correct order without hesitation. Note that all the face edges are downwards. Square the edges and make the length of all parts the finished outside size. Make sure that the opposite sides are exactly the same length. It is a good plan to put them together and feel around the edges, when any inaccuracy will be at once noticeable.

DOVETAILING THE BOX

The dovetailing now follows, and the process described on page 185 can be followed. If the lid is to have an edging it can be sawn off after assembling, though in this case it is essential that the dovetails are specially spaced to allow for it, as shown at D, Fig. 1. E shows the lid being sawn. Note that the saw is held at a fairly low angle,

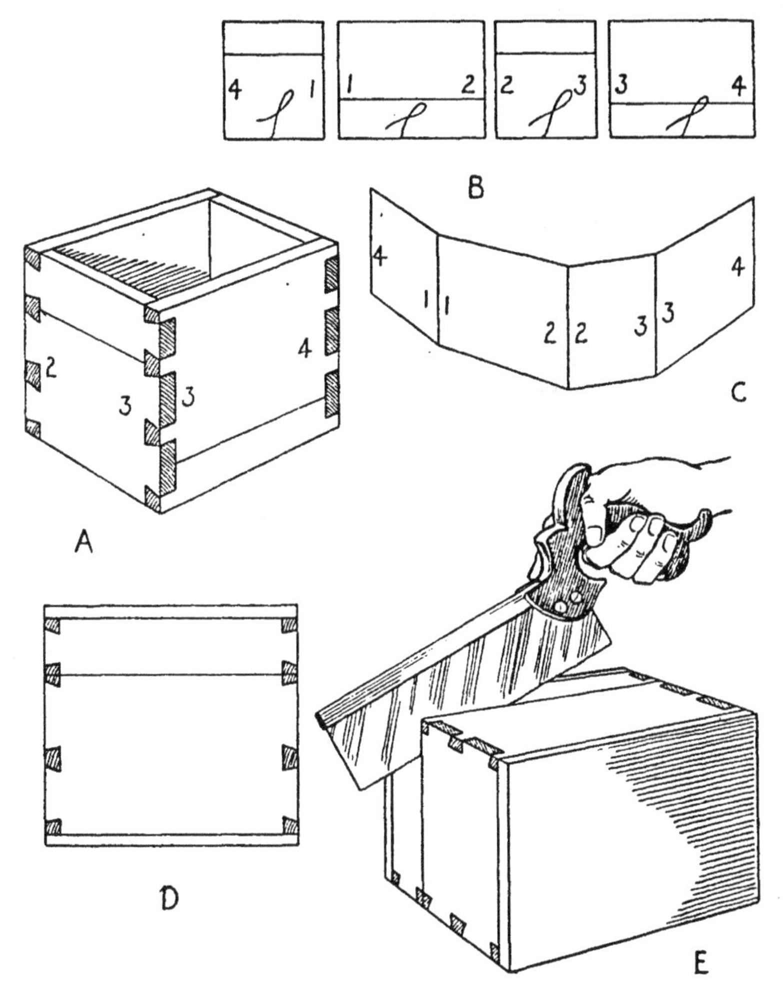

FIG. 1. STAGES IN MARKING OUT AND MAKING A BOX.

A. How corners are marked. Note also the staggered joints.
B. Identification marks on joining corners.
C. How parts resemble sides of cardboard box opened out.
D. Side view showing joints.
E. Sawing away lid.

as this enables the line to be followed more easily. After sawing down a fair way the box can be turned over to the adjacent side and the saw worked in the other direction.

Lapped joint. For a box which needs to be reasonably strong and in which nails are not an objection the lapped joint, at A, Fig. 2, is effective. Square up the wood to size, but make the ends shorter

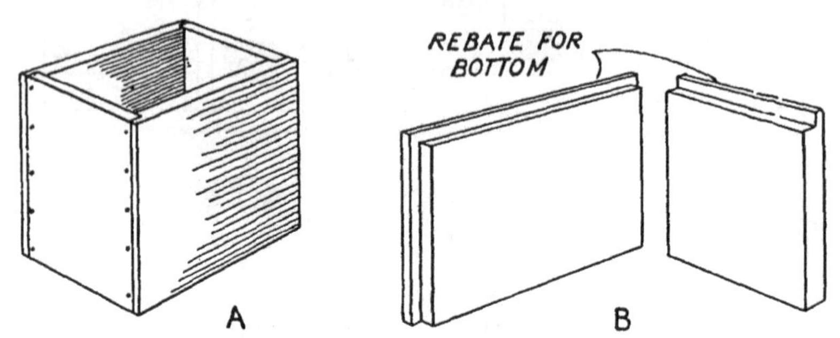

FIG. 2. BOX MADE WITH SIMPLE LAPPED JOINTS (A).
How rebate for bottom lines up with end joints (B).

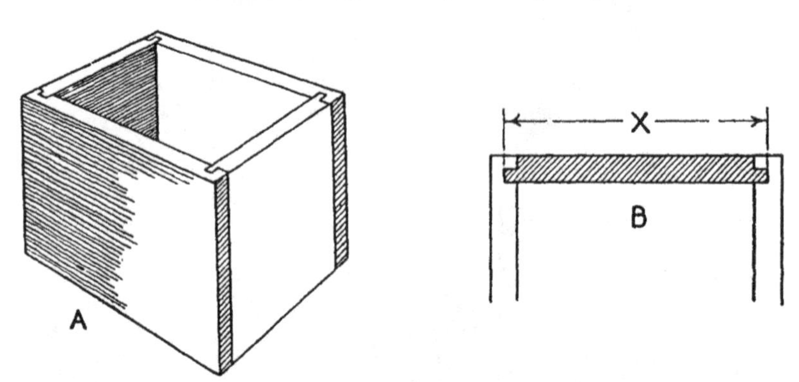

FIG. 3. TONGUED AND GROOVED JOINT USED FOR A BOX.
Over-all length of tongued piece is given at X.

than the finished size by the thickness of the laps on the long sides. Mark out the laps with the cutting gauge, and cut the joints by sawing across the grain and removing the waste with the chisel. If a rebate plane or shoulder plane is available, this is handy to finish off. When assembling, glue the joint and drive in a nail upright at the centre. The remaining nails can be at an angle, dovetail fashion. Should the lid have to be sawn off as at E, Fig. 1, the nails must be placed so that the line along which the saw has to be taken is clear. The bottom is usually screwed straight on beneath, but if it is desired to conceal it a rebate can be worked along the bottom edge in line with that at the ends, as at B, Fig. 2.

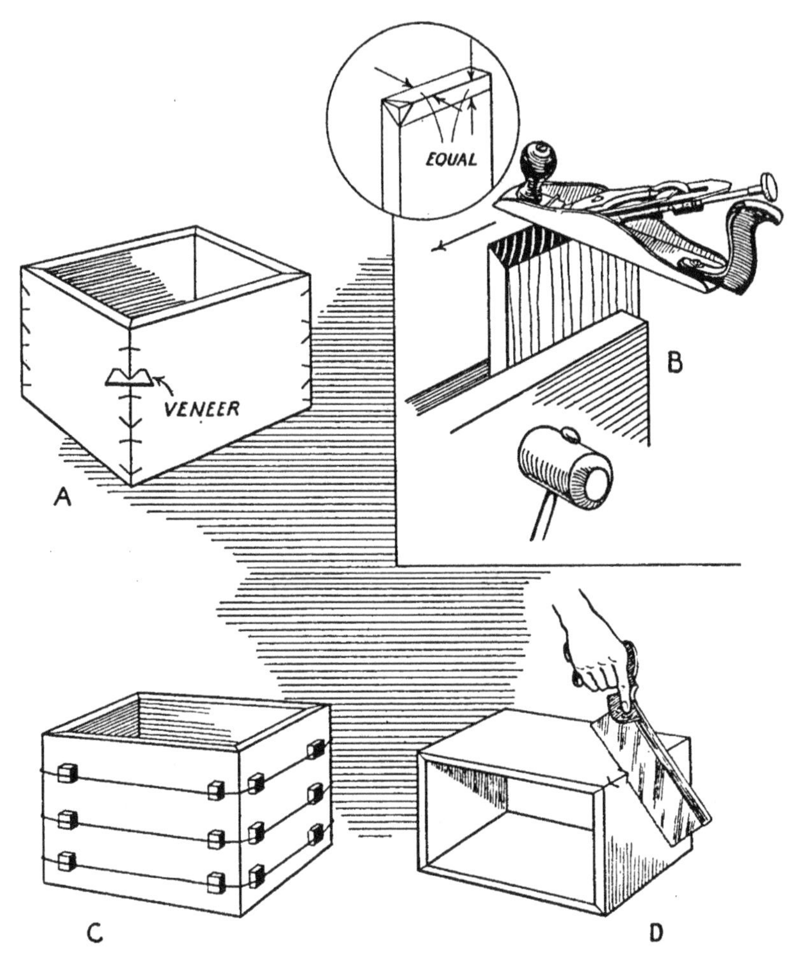

FIG. 4. BOX WITH MITRED AND VENEER KEYED CORNERS.
A. How veneer keys are added. B. Planing the mitres. C. String and block cramping. D. Sawing kerfs for keys.

Tongued joint. When nails must be avoided the grooved joint as at A, Fig. 3, is a simple alternative. It is not a specially strong joint, but there are purposes for which it is strong enough. The sides are cut to the finished outside size, but the length of the ends has to be calculated in accordance with the depth of the grooves (see *x* at B, Fig. 3). Mark out both the groove and the tongue with the cutting gauge. Cramps are desirable when gluing, but no nails are needed.

Keyed mitre. When a box is to be veneered it is advisable to avoid dovetails because these are liable to show through to the surface eventually owing to the shrinkage in the timber. The mitred joint is preferable in this respect, but it has little strength in itself. If keyed as at A, Fig. 4, however, it is strengthened considerably. The mitres are glued together, and when the glue has set saw cuts are made across the corners. Little slips of veneer are glued in these cuts, these being levelled after setting.

The four parts are squared to the finished outside size, each in turn is fixed in the vice, and the mitre planed as at B, Fig. 4. If the far corner is chiselled off down to the mitre line, as shown inset, the liability to split out will be reduced considerably. It is a help, too, if the plane is held at an angle to give a slicing cut.

The mitre square should be used to test the angle, though a good general guide is to draw a pencil line at a distance from the edge equal to the thickness of the wood. This represents the extent to which the wood has to be planed away and is shown inset at B, Fig. 4.

To assemble the parts the string and wedge method is satisfactory. The parts are glued and put together as at C, Fig. 4. If the joints are lightly rubbed as they are assembled they will hold together whilst the string is added. Tie two, three, or four pieces of string round, according to the size of the box, and insert little blocks of wood in the middle of each side. If the blocks are pushed towards the corners they will have the effect of forcing the joints tightly together.

The glue having set, a series of saw cuts is made at an angle across each corner as at D, Fig. 4. Slips of veneer with the grain running lengthwise are glued and rubbed into them. When the glue has set the veneer is levelled.

13. HOW TO MAKE A DRAWER

A DRAWER is virtually a sort of box, but it must have certain special qualities if it is to be successful. For instance, it must resist the pull to which it is constantly subjected ; it must have the bottom raised so that it does not scrape as it is moved ; it must have its bearing surfaces broad enough to resist wear ; and it must look

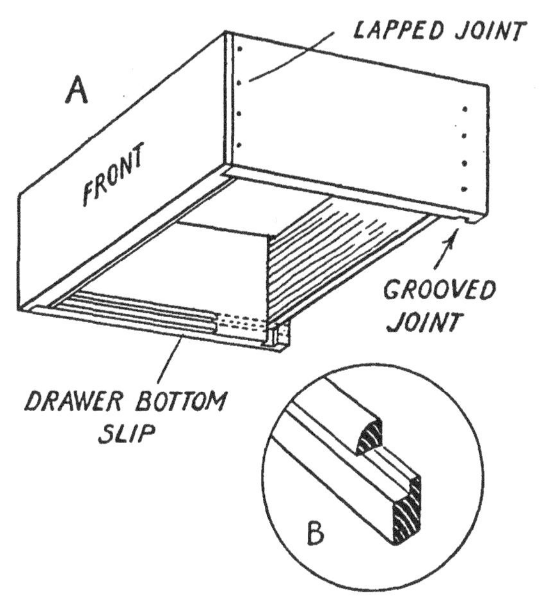

FIG. 1. SIMPLE DRAWER WITH LAPPED AND GROOVED JOINTS.

The sides join the front with a lapped joint, and the back with a grooved joint. B shows how the drawer slip is cut away to fit beneath the back.

neat. The dovetailed drawer meets these requirements, though a rather special arrangement of dovetails is called for. First, however, let us take a simpler construction which, whilst not so strong nor so neat, is satisfactory for an unimportant piece of work.

Simple construction. As shown in Fig. 1, a lapped joint is cut at the front, whilst the back fits in grooves across the sides. To hold the bottom, grooved drawer slips are glued to the sides and front, the back finishing level with the top of the groove to enable the

HOW TO MAKE A DRAWER

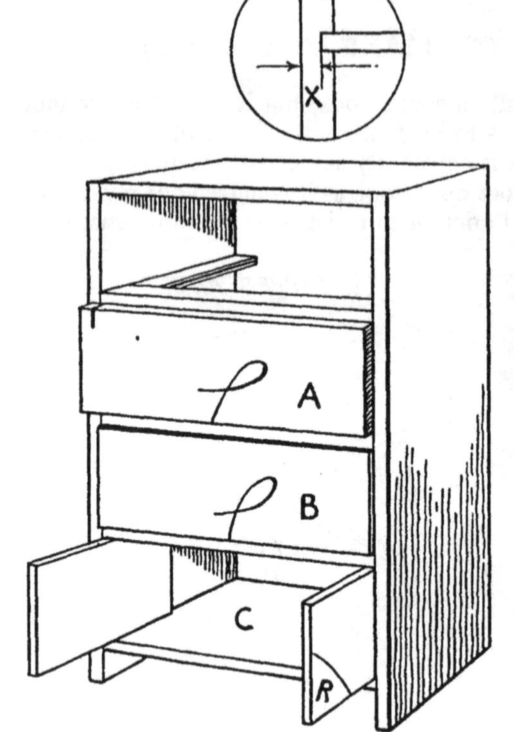

FIG. 2. FITTING DRAWER FRONT AND SIDES.

At A the bottom and right hand edge have been fitted and the length has been marked.

All four edges have been fitted at B.

C shows how the sides are planed to a hand-tight fit and are given identification marks R (right) and L (left). The inset drawing shows how the length of the back is calculated when it is grooved in.

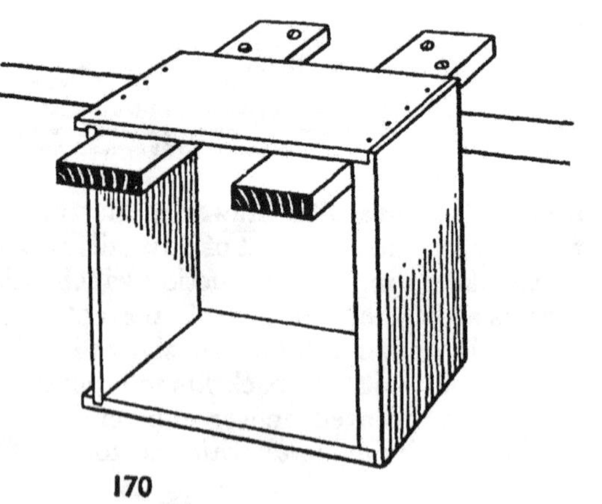

FIG. 3. HOW DRAWER IS SUPPORTED WHEN BEING PLANED.

By resting it over two battens the drawer sides can be planed without danger of racking.

bottom to pass beneath it. Apart from supporting the bottom, the slips increase the bearing surface of the underside and so reduce wear. The front might conveniently be $\frac{3}{4}$ or $\frac{7}{8}$ in. thick, and the sides and back $\frac{3}{8}$ in. As the slips are usually grooved $\frac{3}{16}$ in. the bottom might be of this thickness. If a little more it could be bevelled at the underside.

The front is first prepared to size, being trimmed to fit accurately the opening for which it is intended. It is a help if the edges are planed at a *slight* angle so that they can be just entered without going right in. There should not be more than the thickness of a piece of brown paper difference, however. Plane the bottom edge first and trim one end so that it makes a close fit. Mark the length as at A, Fig. 2, and cut off and trim. The width follows so that the whole thing can just be entered as at B, Fig. 2.

Clearly the back must be smaller than the front, and to find the exact length it is necessary to decide on the depth of the grooves to be cut across the sides (see inset, Fig. 2). The length equals that of the front less double the size X. Proceed as in the case of the front, planing the bottom edge straight and planing one end to fit. The length is marked and trimmed to fit the other end. In width it has to stand above the bottom, and it is usual also to let it stand down at the top.

A fairly tight fit is desirable for the sides. Plane the bottom edge straight, square the front, cut to length, and trim square. Set a gauge to the width and plane so that it is a trifle full. You can then remove single fine shavings until the side can just be passed in with a tight fit. Mark each outer bottom corner *R* or *L* so that there is no doubt as to where it goes. When a chest has several drawers of the same size it is advisable to mark all the parts with a number also so that each drawer can be correctly assembled. There are bound to be slight variations in size and the drawers should be made and fitted individually.

The parts should be glued together as well as nailed. Nailing alone has little strength, especially in softwood. The nails should be " dovetailed " (see page 141) and punched in. Fitting and cleaning up follows after the glue has set before the bottom is added, and the best plan is to fix a couple of wide battens to overhang the bench edge, as in Fig. 3. The drawer rests on these whilst being planed, all racking tendency being thus avoided.

Glue and fine pins are used to fix the drawer slips. At the front the corners are mitred, but at the back it is necessary to cut away the top part so that it passes beneath the back. This enables the bottom to be slid in from the rear.

Fitting. When fitting a drawer make sure of exactly where it is tight before removing any shavings. You can generally tell by the feel just where it is binding, and another indication is the presence of shiny patches. These are caused by rubbing and give an indication of where the wood needs easing. Do not apply any lubricant until after the work has been polished because stain will not strike through this. Candle-grease is the best to use. One point to be ascertained at the outset is whether the drawer runners are free from winding, because this can upset the whole running. Even though the drawer sides clear everywhere in width the drawers will bind if the runners wind. The same thing can apply of course if the drawer winds, though this would not happen in a properly made drawer.

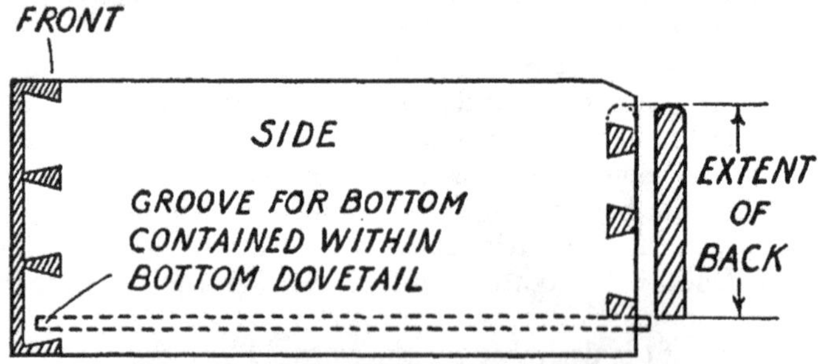

FIG. 4. SETTING OUT OF DRAWER DETAILS.
At the front the pins are run almost to a point.

Dovetailed drawer. No better method of construction than dovetailing has ever been found for a drawer, and even in this machine age drawers are still dovetailed by hand in the best work. The general fitting is as already described, but a rather special arrangement of dovetails is necessary. This is partly to suit the particular construction and partly because a neat appearance is desirable.

Fig. 4 gives the setting out of the joints. Note that at the front lapped dovetails are cut, and that the pins between the dovetails are narrow and run nearly to a point. At the front the bottom fits in a groove, and it is essential that the bottom dovetail is arranged to contain it. Otherwise a gap will show if the groove emerges at the pin. The back stands up above the bottom, and the bottom edge runs right through to form the bottom pin. This necessitates the bottom "dovetail" being cut square, as shown. It is usual to allow the top edge to stand down slightly and round it over. This means that the top pin must be set down enough to enable the plane to be taken right through when rounding without affecting the pin.

FITTING THE DRAWER

The general procedure in the preparation of the parts is much the same as that already given, except that the backs are necessarily the full length of the opening. Fig. 5 shows the fitting. If each side alternately is pressed lightly it is generally easy to tell where it is binding. Faults in a drawer are shown in Fig. 6. At A the slack fit enables the drawer to lodge at an angle, causing it to jam. When pressure is applied to the other side it usually results in this going in suddenly and causing it to jam the other way. At B the sides have been planed too much so that the drawer drops badly when opened.

FIG. 5. FITTING A DRAWER, TESTING FOR TIGHT RUNNING.

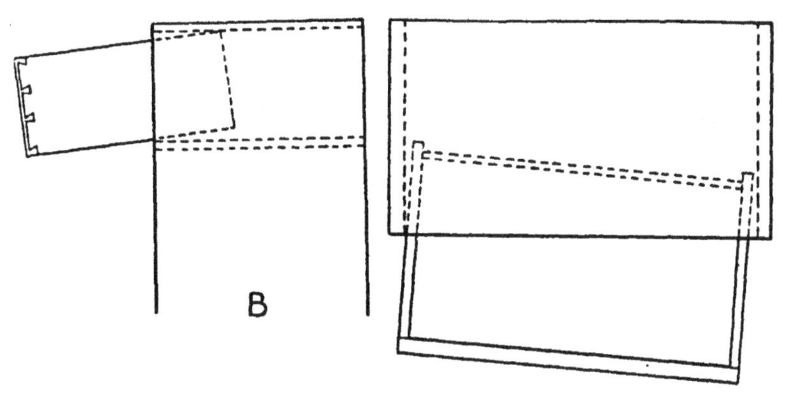

FIG. 6. FAULTS IN BADLY FITTED DRAWERS.

14. HINGEING

THE type of hinge most generally used for furniture and other small doors is the butt hinge shown in Fig. 1. It requires to be let into the wood, and it is upon the accurate and neat cutting of the recesses that the success of the work largely depends. The great point to remember is that it is the position of the knuckle that counts. The wing or outer edge is far less important. As a rule the hinge is let wholly into the door, with just a shallow sloping recess in the cupboard to hold the wing edge, as shown in Fig. 2. In this way all complications are avoided even when the door is made to stand in slightly, as shown.

Plane the door-frame to make an accurate fit in the cupboard, and with pencil and try-square mark on its edge the position of the hinges. There is no definite rule on this point, but they are generally set in about their own length from the end. Set the gauge to the distance from the wing edge to the centre of the knuckle (A, Fig. 3) and mark between the pencil lines as shown. Do not overrun the

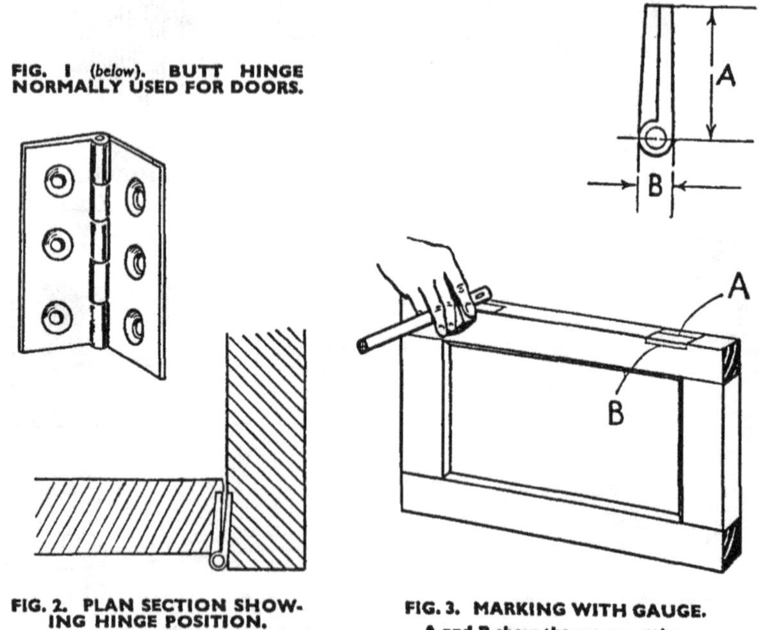

FIG. 1 (*below*). BUTT HINGE NORMALLY USED FOR DOORS.

FIG. 2. PLAN SECTION SHOWING HINGE POSITION.

FIG. 3. MARKING WITH GAUGE. A and B show the gauge setting.

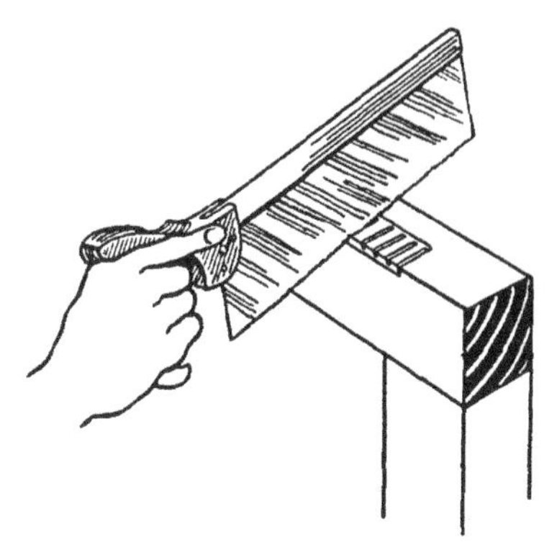

FIG. 4. CUTTING RECESSES.

The ends are sawn as far as the diagonal. The intermediate saw cuts break the grain and prevent a split from developing when the chisel is being used.

FIG. 5. REMOVING WASTE WITH THE CHISEL.

The ends are cut down vertically (B) and the waste pared as at A. Note the block of wood beneath the recess to give support.

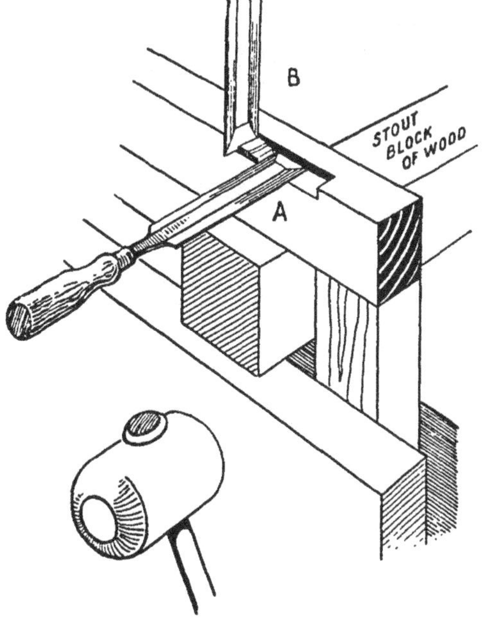

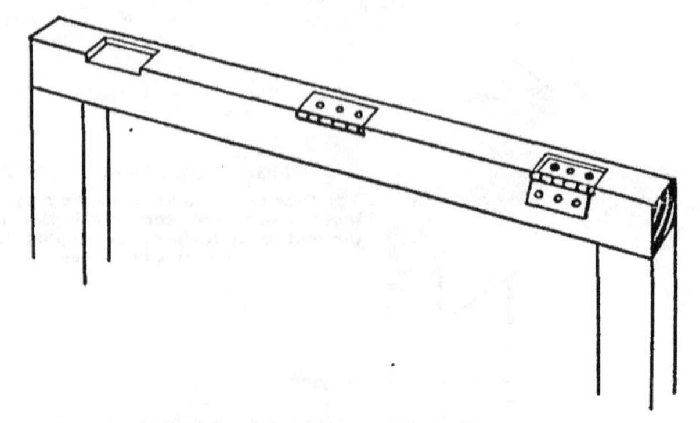

FIG. 6. HOW THE HINGE IS SCREWED IN POSITION TO DOOR.

The recess is shown to the left. At centre the hinge is closed. Open hinge is given to the right.

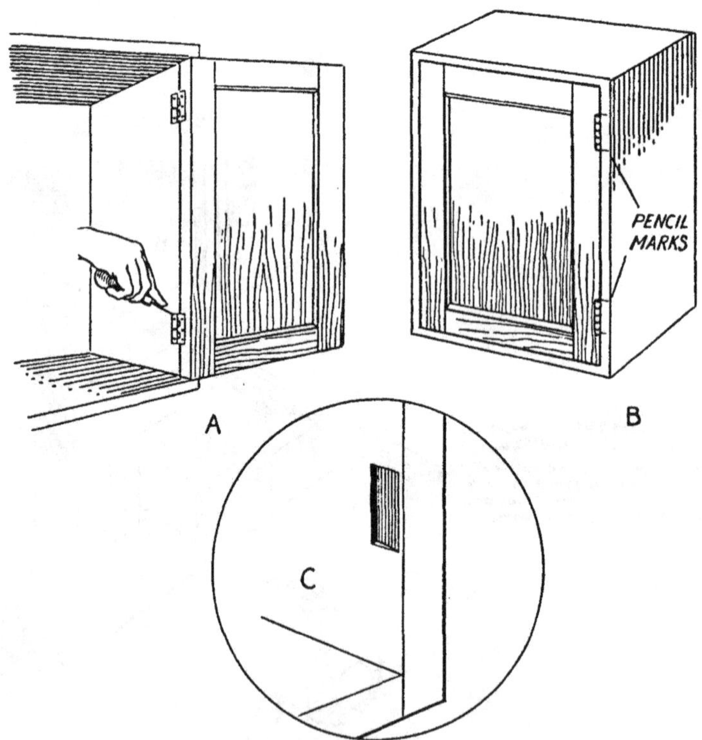

FIG. 7. MARKING HINGE POSITIONS ON CUPBOARD.

Two methods are given at A and B. Sloping recess is shown at C.

lines, because such marks look ugly. The gauge is now reset to the thickness of the knuckle (B) and the face of the door marked as in Fig. 3.

Cutting. Preliminary cutting is with the fine back-saw. Make a cut at just inside the line at each end down to the diagonal, and a series of cuts in between, the purpose being to cut up the grain short and so stop splitting as far as possible. Take special care not to cut beyond either gauge line, since such marks are a blemish and are the sign of a poor workman. Cutting is shown in Fig. 4.

The waste is removed with the chisel, and after the preliminary paring away with the chisel held at a slight angle, the ends and the gauge line are deepened by downward cuts, the mallet being used. The framework is best held in the vice during the operation, with a piece of felt at the front to prevent bruising. Sometimes it is possible to put a block beneath the recess as in Fig. 5 so that the wood has good support beneath. If the inner edge is moulded, however, the block must reach only into the rebate, as otherwise the moulding may be damaged.

Now deepen the recesses right down to the gauge line. If a slicing movement is followed it will be possible to make the bottom perfectly level. Note from Fig. 2 that the recess is slightly shallower towards the back. The exact slope is not important, the purpose being simply to avoid a big drop-in when the hinge is fixed. Take special care not to cut beyond the gauge line at the outside.

Fix each hinge with two screws only. Then if any adjustment is needed later there is still one position in which a fresh hole can be made. Fig. 6 shows the framework with two hinges in position. Note how the knuckle is flush when the hinge is closed.

Put the door in the position it is to occupy and make pencil marks at each side of the hinges. When the top and bottom of the cupboard project it is simpler to open the hinges and mark as at A, Fig. 7. Otherwise the hinges can be closed, the door dropped right in, and the ends marked as at B.

If the door has to finish flush with the edges of the cupboard use the gauge with the same setting as when marking the door recesses. For a door to be set in increase the setting by the required amount. Chisel away the sloping recesses as at C, taking care not to cut away the wood where the knuckle beds down. In this connection note that if the door is set in, say $\frac{1}{8}$ in., the recesses will begin $\frac{1}{8}$ in. from the edge or a little more.

Put a single screw into each hinge and try the closing. If any adjustment in position is needed put a screw into a different hole and try again.

15. FITTING A LOCK

MOST locks require to be let into the wood so that they finish flush with the surface. The chief kinds are for doors and drawers, and the fitting of both is practically identical. In both kinds remember to work to the position of the keyhole, not to the body of the lock. The reason for this is that the keyhole is not always in the centre of the lock, and clearly the keyhole must be centred. In the case of a door the lock has to be chosen in accordance with whether it closes to the right or the left. To tell which you need face the door from outside. If the bolt has to shoot to the right to lock you need a right-hand lock, and *vice versa*

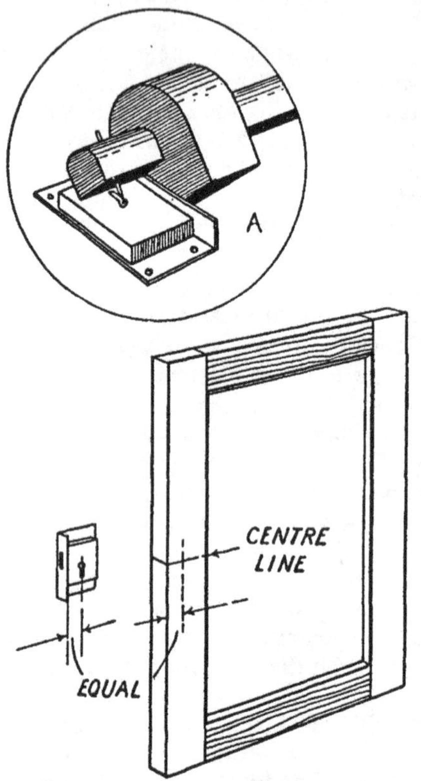

FIG. 1. MARKING KEYHOLE POSITION.
A shows how the gauge is set to the lock pin.

Marking keyhole.—With pencil and square mark a centre line midway from top to bottom (or wherever it is wanted) on the stile to receive the lock as in Fig. 1, returning it at the edge. Now set a gauge from the plate of the lock to the centre of the pin as at A, Fig. 1, and with it cut the pencil line just marked. At this point a hole is bored to form the rounded part of the keyhole. If a brass escutcheon is being used, this gives the size of hole to be bored. Take the hole right through.

Place the escutcheon on the hole, keeping it perfectly upright, and give a light tap with the hammer. This will form a slight indentation in the wood, indicating the position of the recess to be cut. Fix the frame in the vice and saw down just inside the lines, as in Fig. 2. With a small chisel or sharp bradawl cut away the waste. Smear the edges of the escutcheon with *Seccotine* and tap home. It should be a reasonably tight fit, but not so tight as to cause distortion.

The notch to receive the body of the lock has now to be marked, and to do this hold the lock in position with the pin exactly level with the pencil line. Mark on to the wood with pencil where the edges of the lock body occur, as in Fig. 3, and square these around both the edge and back face. The width and depth of the lock can be gauged in.

Cramp the door face downwards on to a flat piece of wood so that it is not bruised and saw down the pencil lines as far as the diagonal as in Fig. 4. The saw can go right on the lines, as it is desirable to make the recess *slightly* full so as to allow a small amount of adjustment. A few saw cuts in between serve to cut up the grain. They should stop short of the gauge lines. Pare away the waste, chopping down the ends where the saw cannot reach.

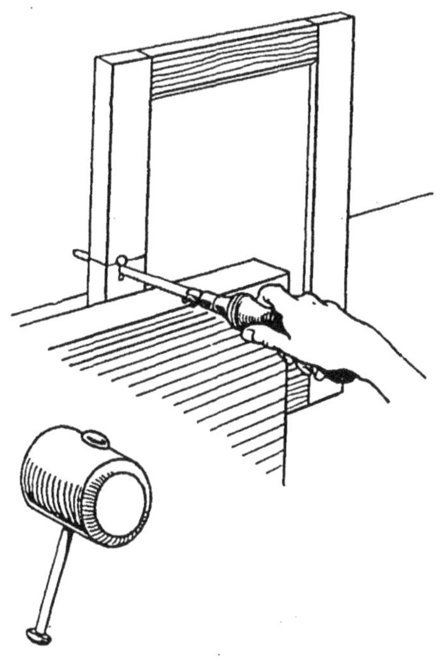

FIG. 2. SAWING SIDES OF KEYHOLE.
After the hole has been bored the lower straight portion is sawn in.

The plates of the lock have now to be recessed in flush, and to mark these hold the lock in position, looking through the keyhole to see that the pin is at the right height (it will, of course, be slightly to one side owing to the plate recess being yet uncut). Then mark the sides with a knife as in Fig. 5. Top and bottom cannot be marked in this way, because the lock is not yet in its final position. The gauge can be used for this, but take special care to stop the tool at the lines at both ends. Tap carefully around the lines with the chisel and ease away the waste, trying in the lock from time to time to see that it makes a flush fit. Finally drive in the screws.

To mark the slot to receive the bolt when the door is locked, put

FITTING A LOCK

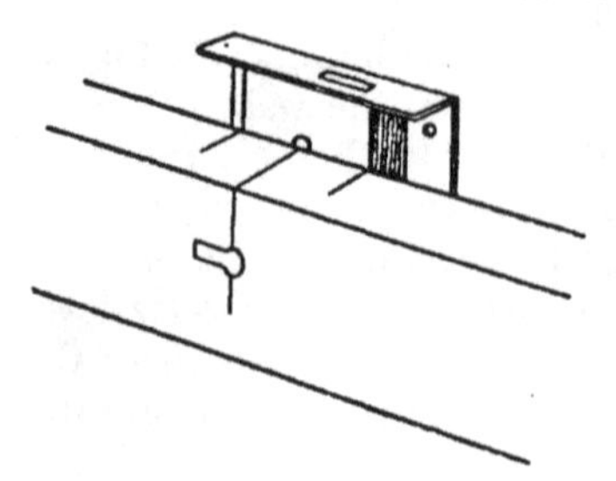

FIG. 3. MARKING POSITION OF RECESS FOR BODY OF LOCK.

Note the pin opposite the squared line.

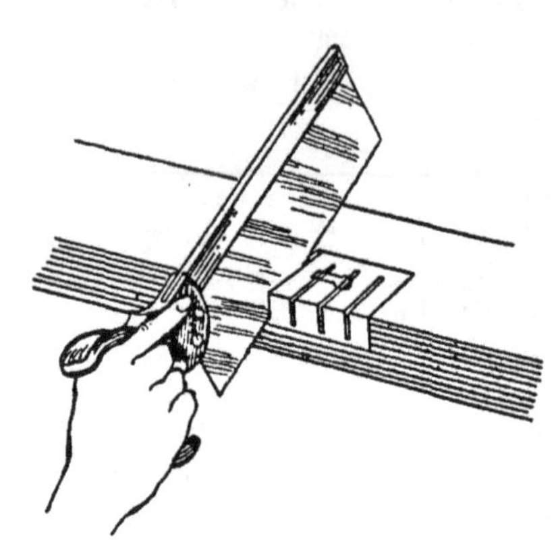

FIG. 4. CUTTING WITH SAW.

Cuts are made as far as the diagonal. The intermediate cuts help to prevent splitting.

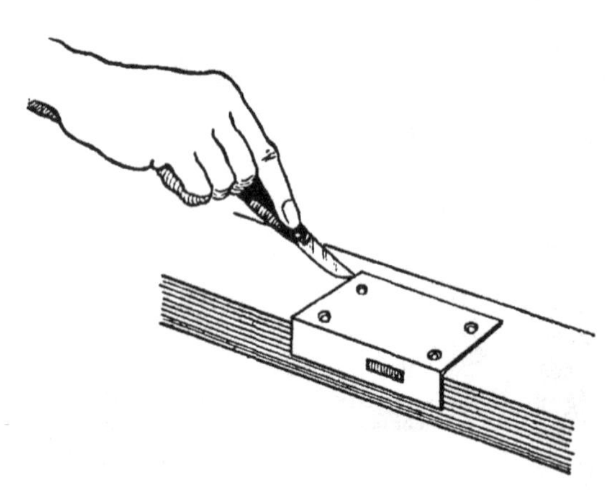

FIG. 5. MARKING SIDES OF PLATE.

Make sure that the pin is exactly opposite the keyhole before marking.

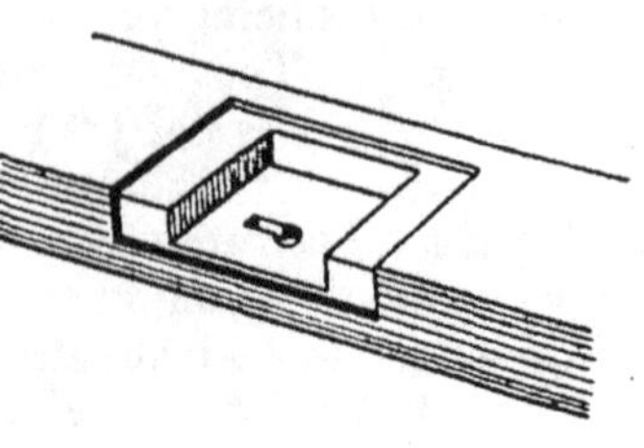

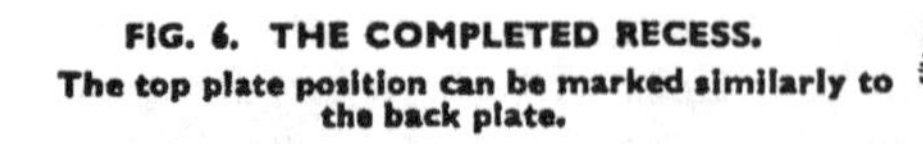

FIG. 6. THE COMPLETED RECESS.

The top plate position can be marked similarly to the back plate.

a smear of dirty oil from the oil-stone on the edge of the bolt. Close the door and turn the key so that the bolt, in trying to shoot, leaves an impression on the wood. Chop in the recess with a narrow chisel or a bradawl.

16. BASIC JOINTS

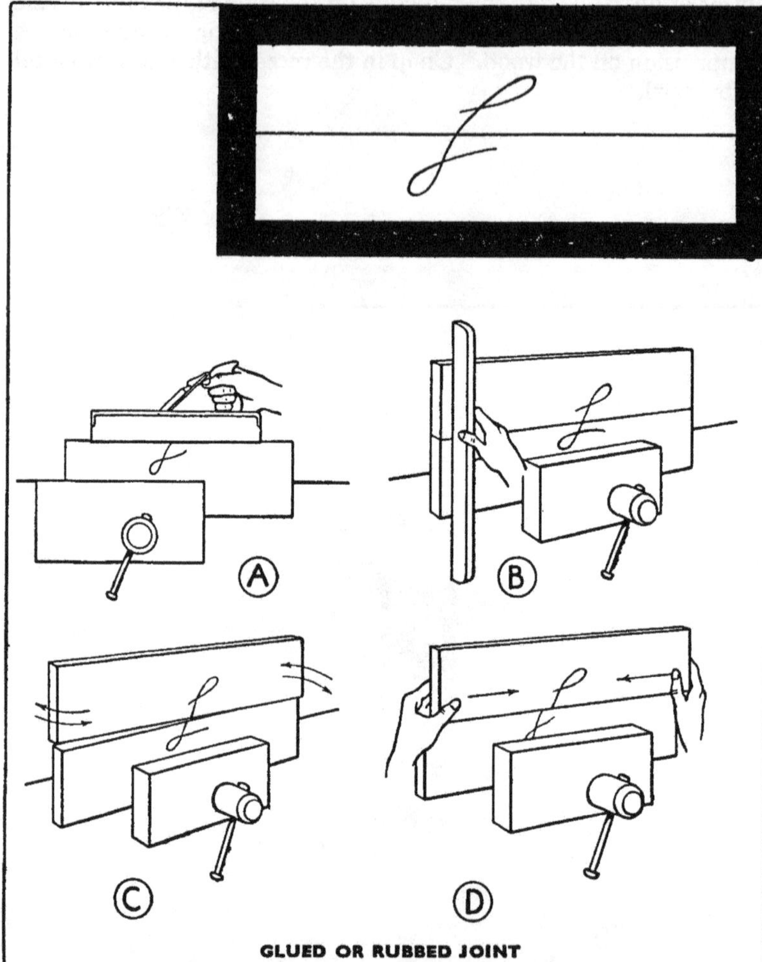

GLUED OR RUBBED JOINT

Used to increase the width of a board. Joints up to about 3 ft. can be planed to a perfect joint and rubbed. Longer joints are planed slightly hollow and cramped at the centre.

A. Planing joint in the bench vice. Thin wood is planed on the shooting-board.

B. Testing alignment of pieces with straight-edge.

C. Swivelling wood to test whether joint is round (a fault). There should be friction at the ends.

D. After heating joint and gluing, the top piece is rubbed back and forth, squeezing out glue and making close joint.

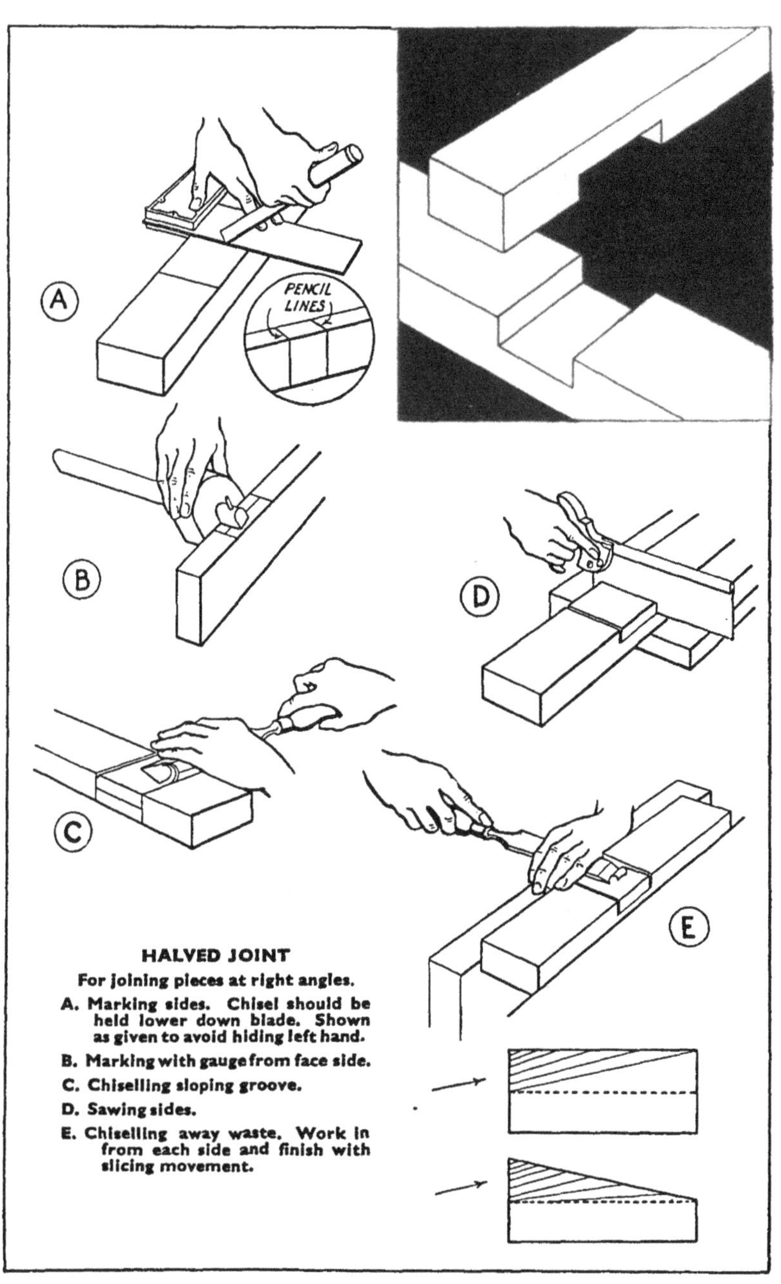

HALVED JOINT

For joining pieces at right angles.

A. Marking sides. Chisel should be held lower down blade. Shown as given to avoid hiding left hand.

B. Marking with gauge from face side.

C. Chiselling sloping groove.

D. Sawing sides.

E. Chiselling away waste. Work in from each side and finish with slicing movement.

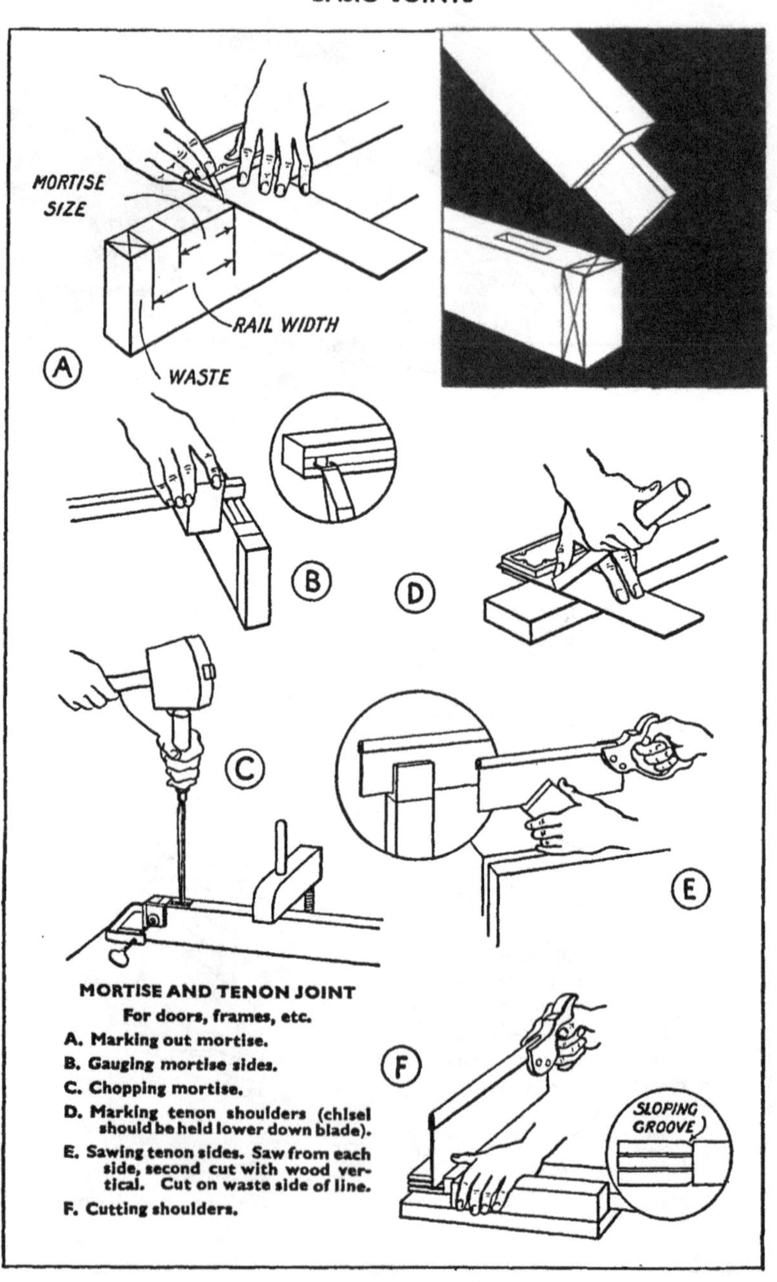

MORTISE AND TENON JOINT

For doors, frames, etc.

A. Marking out mortise.

B. Gauging mortise sides.

C. Chopping mortise.

D. Marking tenon shoulders (chisel should be held lower down blade).

E. Sawing tenon sides. Saw from each side, second cut with wood vertical. Cut on waste side of line.

F. Cutting shoulders.

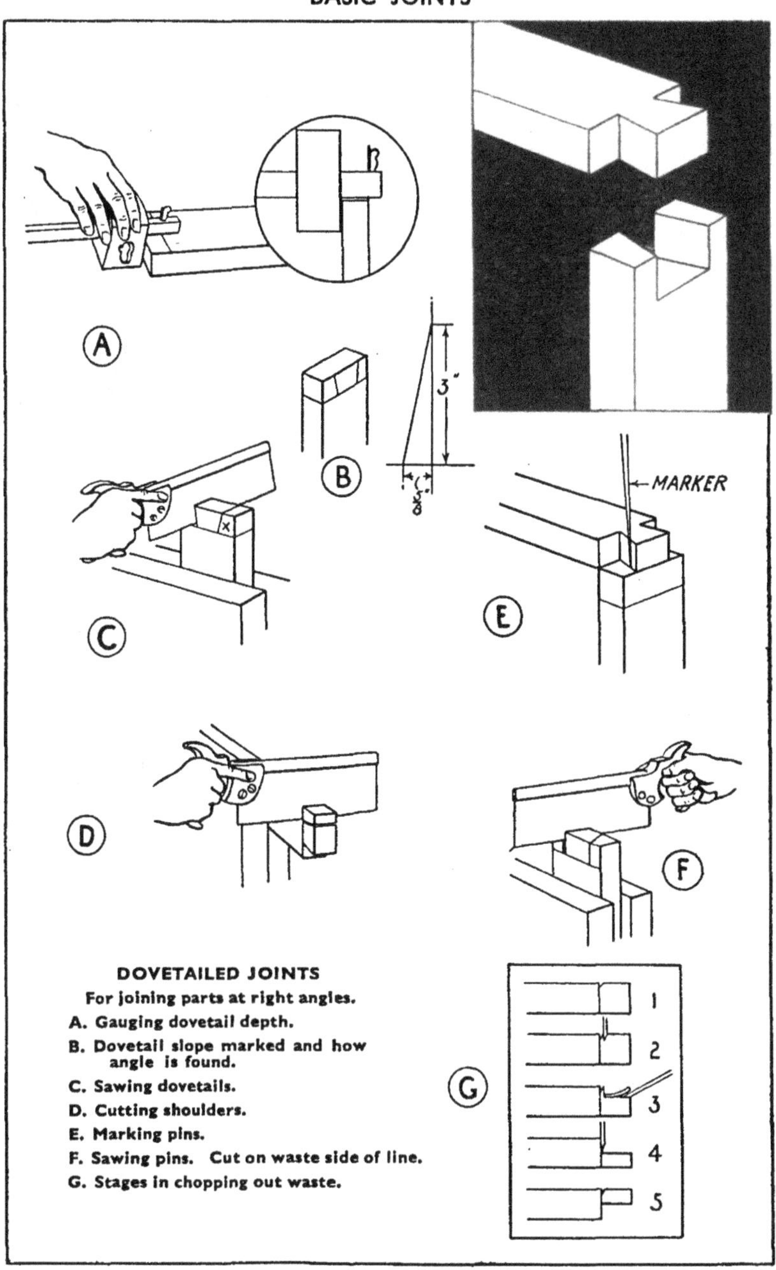

DOVETAILED JOINTS

For joining parts at right angles.

A. Gauging dovetail depth.
B. Dovetail slope marked and how angle is found.
C. Sawing dovetails.
D. Cutting shoulders.
E. Marking pins.
F. Sawing pins. Cut on waste side of line.
G. Stages in chopping out waste.

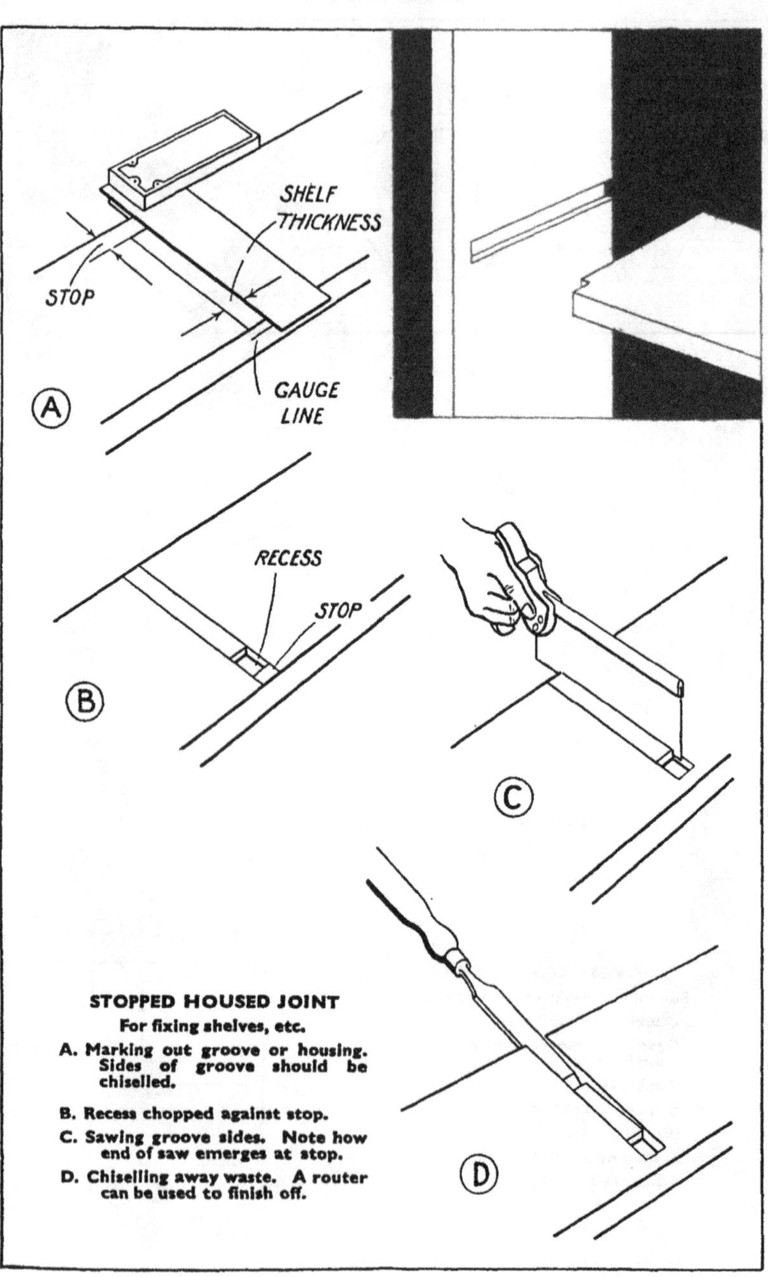

STOPPED HOUSED JOINT

For fixing shelves, etc.

A. Marking out groove or housing. Sides of groove should be chiselled.

B. Recess chopped against stop.

C. Sawing groove sides. Note how end of saw emerges at stop.

D. Chiselling away waste. A router can be used to finish off.

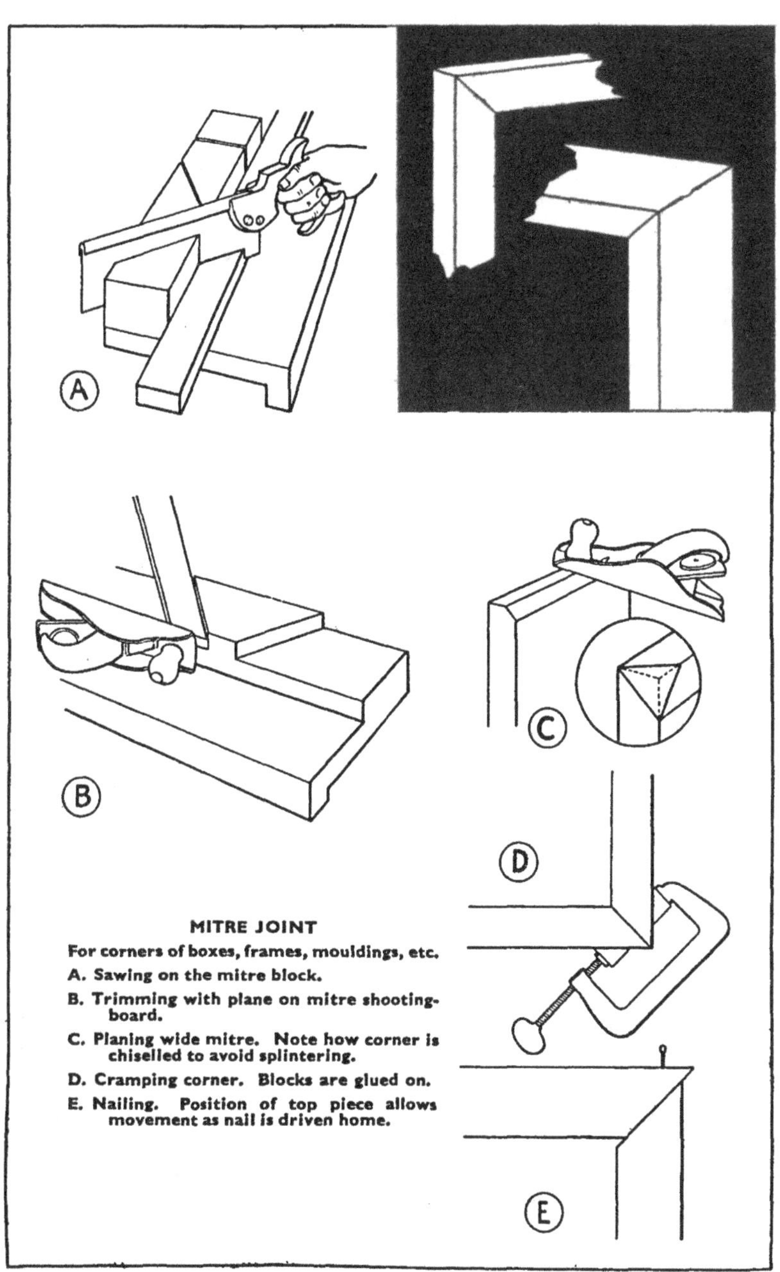

MITRE JOINT

For corners of boxes, frames, mouldings, etc.

A. Sawing on the mitre block.

B. Trimming with plane on mitre shooting-board.

C. Planing wide mitre. Note how corner is chiselled to avoid splintering.

D. Cramping corner. Blocks are glued on.

E. Nailing. Position of top piece allows movement as nail is driven home.

17. THINGS TO KNOW ABOUT WOOD

THE timbers of commerce are known under two wide varieties, the Softwoods and the Hardwoods. The terms *soft* and *hard* may be misleading, as certain of the softwoods are harder, heavier and more durable than many of the hardwoods; but there are differences in structure, and the designations have been in use for so long that they are accepted all over the world.

Softwoods are those which are obtained from the cone-bearing trees and include the various pines, the spruce, the larch, and woods such as pitch-pine, Douglas fir, and certain cedars. Generally speaking, they are the timbers known to the carpenter and joiner. Hardwoods are those which we cut from trees other than conifers: those of the broad-leaved families. Here again it does not necessarily follow that the leaf itself is either broad or large. The word "broad" is used to distinguish the leaf from the needles of the pine or the spiked tufts of the larch. Among the well-known hardwoods of this country are the oak, ash, beech, birch, elm, chestnut, sycamore, etc. Imported hardwoods are the mahoganies, walnuts, canary (American whitewood), satin walnut (gum), and scores of others. Many of these are Empire timbers.

SOFTWOODS

These are employed for all classes of building construction. For the home they provide the rafters, joists, floor-boards, skirtings, doors, panelling, kitchen and scullery fixtures, and window-frames. For gardens they give greenhouses, garages, tool or work sheds, shelters, fences, pergolas, trellis screens, clothes posts, garden seats, poultry houses, rabbit hutches, dog kennels, and endless other items.

Pine. Bear in mind that in the names of softwoods there is world-wide confusion. It is not only that the names in use differ from those known on the Continent and in America, but that even in this country different localities apply varying names to the same wood. The Scots pine, for example, is often called a fir, and in any case is known as red Baltic pine, red fir, and redwood. Often the name degenerates to "deal": in certain districts it is called yellow deal and in others red deal.

On account of its scarcity and prohibitive price Canadian (or Quebec) yellow pine—fifty years ago the favourite softwood—need not be mentioned. The most widely used is the red Baltic (or Scots), which has held its own for three centuries. Light and easily worked, it is normally obtainable in every dimension and size. Do not be misled if the local yard man refers to it as red *deal.* "Deal" is really a term loosely applied to any small plank not over 9 in. by 3 in.

Douglas fir (alternatively known as British Columbian or Oregon pine) is a different timber, more suitable for large constructional work than for incidental carpentry. The tree is one of the stateliest in the world, rising in many cases to a height of 300 ft. The timber is heavier and harder than Baltic pine and its special value is that it may be procured in very large sizes. A considerable quantity is now grown in this country.

Pitch-pine, again, is a wood chosen for its strength and durability. Generally speaking it is not suitable for indoor work, although it has always been a favourite for church furniture. As a timber for garden seats, however, it wears well.

Spruce is the timber to which the convenient all-round term "whitewood" is usually applied. If of American origin it is simply called spruce, whilst if from Northern Europe it is often spoken of as white fir. It is a clean white timber and may be used for kitchen tables, dressers, and all kinds of indoor fitments. When selecting the wood it is wise to avoid boards with a multiplicity of knots.

Larch to-day is one of our most valuable softwoods, and in country districts (especially in the north) is one of the most easily obtained. For outdoor work of every kind it may be used, whilst for chimney-pieces, doors, cupboards, kitchen furniture it makes an excellent substitute for hardwood. Much heavier than spruce and nearly twice the weight of pine, it is now extensively used for entrance gates, summer-houses, and other garden woodwork.

Western red cedar. Very light in weight and easy to work, the home craftsman will find this a most useful wood, especially for outdoor purposes. It leaves a nice silky surface from the plane, and as it resists dry rot and is practically immune from insect attack it requires no finish when used out of doors. Large boards free of defects are obtainable, and it may be used indoors without risk of warping. Complete houses as well as sheds, garages, etc., are now constructed from this timber.

It may be added that, at a builders' yard, sound softwood of some kind is always there. Unless tied to a specific timber it is wise to take this, no matter under what particular name it is sold. If the wood is sound it is worth procuring.

THINGS TO KNOW ABOUT WOOD

HARDWOODS

These may be divided into three general classes: (1) the prime furniture woods; (2) minor hardwoods; (3) empire timbers and other imported decorative varieties.

Oak is, of course, a constructional wood, and much of the smaller British oak cut is used for this purpose and for gate-posts, casks, barrels, and similar work. The wider timber is imported—American, Russian, and Japanese. British oak is the strongest and heaviest, but is definitely hard to work. The Japanese variety is milder; but the great bulk of oak used in this country is American. The reader should learn early to handle oak, as for furniture of all kinds, large or small, it can hardly be surpassed. It is, too, capable of endless alternative finishes from natural colour to the darkest tones, all showing the distinctive grain of the wood.

Mahogany still holds the premier position as a hardwood for decorative purposes. It is in no sense a carpentry wood, but is indispensable for light cabinetwork as well as for high-class furniture. It is a timber of excellent working qualities and for two hundred years its rich figure has been prized above that of any other wood.

Walnut (the furniture variety known as "black" walnut) is of a rich, deep brown with very dark streaks. Whilst hard and heavy, it is not difficult to work. Clean under the tool, it will take a beautiful polish.

Among other hardwoods which have been used wholly or in part for furniture are rosewood, satinwood, satin walnut (gum), sycamore, teak, padauk, ebony, and boxwood. At times, if procurable, they are excellent for small items of furniture, cabinetwork, and ornamental articles. To the home worker satin walnut is one of the most useful, being light and easy to work and showing a pleasant grain. It is also moderate in price.

Hardwoods spoken of as "minor" are not so called because of any inferiority in quality, but simply because they are more suitable for constructive purposes than for decorative woodwork. Thus all who engage in carpentry should make early acquaintance with such timbers as birch, beech, canary (American whitewood), ash, sweet chestnut, sycamore, maple, and others. One or other might not be deliberately selected for a particular purpose, but it often happens that timber-yards have occasional small lots of lesser-used woods, and if the quality is good the stuff is worth securing. It is of great advantage to understand the working qualities of different timbers and their usefulness for special jobs. Sound home-grown wood can often be picked up in this way in a country yard.

Beech. To any one who owns a plane, beech-wood is familiar. We know it also in tool handles and in sundry domestic articles. Its close, even texture and fine, silky grain are the qualities that have proved its usefulness for such purposes. For cabinetwork generally it is not suitable, but for chair frames and legs, stools, turned work of every kind, garden seats, wheelbarrow frames, and similar work it is excellent. It is worth while remembering that beech oddments provide us with one of the best of firewoods.

Birch is more generally useful, although except in narrower lengths it is chiefly the Canadian birch that is procurable. Many of us know the wood best from the excellent birch plywood on the market. Like beech, it is widely used for chair-making, and we find it employed for such purposes as cart and carriage building, heavy panelling, deck-chairs and small bobbins and spools. For all kinds of light cabinetwork, fittings and fitments it may also be used when the object does not call for a prime furniture hardwood. It takes stain well and is often used (with lipped edges) for the less prominent parts of larger furniture.

Ash, in certain respects the most valuable of our home-grown timbers, we see regularly in chisel and garden tool handles, in tennis rackets, hockey sticks, cart and wheelbarrow shafts and felloes, motor body work, etc.; indeed, wherever strength combined with resilience is required. For long it was a favourite for cheaper furniture, but the home worker should reserve it for those purposes for which its remarkable elasticity has made it indispensable.

Sycamore (generally referred to as plane in Scotland) must not be confused with the well-known London plane of the south. One of the first trees to leaf in early spring, its dense foliage is unmistakable. Very light in colour, the wood has a silky and lustrous surface when planed. The grain is hard and tough, and to those with a lathe it will be found serviceable for all kinds of turnery. Commercially it is in general use for printing and mangle rollers, dairy utensils, bread-boards, and brush backs.

Lime will be used chiefly by those who go in for carving, although it is also serviceable in the construction of certain musical instruments.

Canary (known previously as American whitewood) is the timber derived from the majestic tulip tree of North America. It must not be confused either with our spruce whitewood or with the decorative tulipwood so often seen in inlaid stringings. It is essentially an indoor wood, and when procurable can be used for less important cabinetwork and for kitchen furniture and fittings. It has always, too, been regarded as a reliable foundation for veneering.

Other familiar hardwoods used in commerce, but which are less likely to be of service in the home workshop, are alder, sweet chestnut (a useful substitute for oak), elm, hornbeam, maple, poplar, willow, etc. Experimental work is always instructive, and if in a yard oddments of such woods (or others, like box, holly, pear, cherry or plum) happen to be lying about they can frequently be bought at a nominal figure. For incidental work they will be useful, especially to a man of ideas and initiative.

EMPIRE TIMBERS

Of the more recently imported Empire woods there may not be many which will be used by the home carpenter, although commercially they take a prominent place. Of course for generations we have imported heavily from the Dominions and Crown Colonies: softwoods from Canada; box, cedar, ebony, greenheart, lignum vitæ, mahogany, satinwood, and others from the British West Indies; valuable hardwoods from West Africa; jarrah, black bean, silky oak, and many others from Australia; kauri pine from New Zealand; boxwood, cedar, laurel, padauk, rosewood, teak, sandalwood, etc., from India, Burma, and the Andaman Islands.

Timber, it will be remembered, grows where it will and knows no state frontiers. Thus many woods drawn from the Dominions or Colonies are also obtained from neighbouring countries. From Scandinavia, Russia, and from the United States we import vast quantities, and we draw also from Central European and Black Sea states, from Central and South America, from the Dutch East Indies, and from tropical West Africa. The timbers need not be listed, as mainly they are woods for the cabinetmaker.*

HOW TIMBERS ARE SOLD

The sale of timber in large quantities does not concern the home worker. What he should know is how, at a timber yard or saw-mill, the prices are calculated. Taking softwoods first he should familiarise himself with the accepted terms applied to cut timbers. Several of these are used loosely, but it is a help if the buyer understands them.

CUT TIMBER is wood which has been partly converted; that is, sawn into planks, boards, etc. This is almost invariably square-edged.

* The handbook *Timbers for Woodwork* deals fully with the world's principal softwoods and hardwoods.

PLANK. A length 11 in. or over in width and from 2 in. to 4 in. or more thick. Average thickness is 3 in.

DEAL. Smaller than a plank. A common dimension is 9 in. by 3 in., but thickness may be from 2 in. to 4 in.

BATTEN. From 5 in. to 8 in. wide, thickness being from 2 in. to 4 in.

BOARD. Over 4 in. wide (no limit), but under 2 in. thick. The term covers floor-boards, match-boards, etc.

SCANTLING. Small timber from 2 in. to 4½ in. wide by from 2 in. to 4 in. thick.

STRIP. Under 4 in. wide and under 2 in. thick.

These dimensions must be taken as approximate, but the buyer will find himself at an advantage if he can make it clear that he knows what he wants.

MILLED TIMBER applies to partly manufactured stuff; that is, boards with tongued and grooved edges for jointing, rebated or chamfered lengths, moulded goods, etc.

SQUARE. This is a trade term which represents a hundred superficial feet—the equivalent of 100 ft. of stuff 12 in. wide.

The word, however, has another meaning. "Squares" are stuff where width and thickness are alike (such as for a table leg), the dimensions ranging from 1 in. by 1 in. to 6 in. square.

TIMBERS as a rule are sold in two ways: "per foot run" and "super." Lighter goods such as matchboarding, scantling and strip are priced at so much per lineal foot. The calculation here is simple, and if the purchaser is buying an odd lot and is not stipulating for equality in length he may find that a few odd pieces are thrown in.

If sold "super" this means according to superficial area, or in other words per square foot. Of course the thickness determines the price. The length multiplied by the width gives the number of square feet, and it is well that the buyer should accustom himself to quick mental arithmetic. A board 12 in. by 12 in. is one square foot (144 sq. in.). So also are pieces 24 in. by 6 in., 18 in. by 8 in., 16 in. by 9 in. and so on (all equivalent to 144 sq. in.). Examples of larger boards are:

12 ft. by	15 in. wide:	equals	15 sq. ft.
16 ,,	9 ,,	,,	12 ,,
18 ,,	7 ,,	,,	10½ ,,

When multiplying the length (if given in feet) by the width (if in in.) divide by 12 to bring the total to square feet.

Hardwoods are invariably sold in this way except in the case of stripwood—thin stuff from ¼ in. square upwards. This is used chiefly for toy and model making and other light work.

Hints on buying. In buying, however, there is much to learn apart from the calculation of prices. It is obvious that, on account of the labour, planed wood is more costly than unplaned. This, too, raises another point. A board from the saw may be (nominally) 1 in. thick, but when this is planed on both sides it will hold up only to $\frac{7}{8}$ in. This applies to all sawn stuff and must be taken into consideration when the finished thickness is specified.

Then again, wide boards are invariably sold at a proportionately higher price than narrow ones, the difference (especially in hardwoods) often being considerable. If stuff from 3 in. to 6 in. wide is required it is no economy to purchase a 10-in. or 12-in. board and rip the pieces from this. Indeed, in the case of wide shelving (say, for a cupboard) it is cheaper to buy narrow stuff and joint it to the width desired. No loss in strength is involved.

Where, too, a novice frequently feels that he is being over-charged is when buying planed timber to a stated size. As an example, suppose that a board 3 ft. 8 in. long by 9$\frac{1}{2}$ in. wide is wanted for a particular purpose, the finished thickness being $\frac{3}{4}$ in. Now, in the yard the nearest piece available may be 5 ft. by 11 in., this in 1 in. unplaned. The dealer has to rip off a strip 1$\frac{1}{2}$ in. wide and cut the length to size, and will charge accordingly. The waste is of no use to him. When a cutting list is sent by post to a firm which specialises in this work it is always wise for the purchaser to *make his own allowances in length and width.* Any trimming he may do himself.

Needless to say, a personal visit (which permits of inspection) is preferable, especially when good hardwoods are required. The buyer may then pick what he wants without being too particular as to detail dimensions. If he has any imagination he will know how to utilise the surplus. If, too, he takes a peep into odd corners where apparent "waste" is lying about, he may often strike a good bargain for job lots of excellent timber for miscellaneous work.

PLYWOOD AND LAMINBOARD

PLYWOOD is a manufactured commodity, but neither it nor laminboard is a wood *substitute.* Both are made entirely of wood. The simplest form of plywood is "three-ply," which consists of three sheets of rotary-cut veneer glued or cemented together with the grain of the centre layer lying at right angles with that of the outer layers. This centre sheet (the core) is usually a shade thicker than the outer two. Finished thicknesses range from 1 mm. to 25 mm. (approximately from $\frac{1}{32}$ in. to 1 in.), the stouter material being built up of five, seven, nine, or more sheets of veneer, each alternating in the direction of the grain.

The three great advantages of plywood are: (1) that width-strength is equal to length-strength and the board is thus unsplittable; (2) that shrinkage is practically eliminated and in this way the risk of warping is avoided; (3) that it is procurable in very large sizes, boards being manufactured up to 7 ft. or 8 ft. in length and up to 5 ft. or more in width.

An incidental disadvantage is that the edges are rather unsightly, this due to the cross grain of the alternating layers. In the case of cabinet doors or table tops, however, the difficulty is overcome by "lipping" the edges—that is, gluing on strips of thin, solid hardwood to hide the raw plies. When used for panels or for drawer bottoms the edges are not seen.

LAMINBOARD differs in construction and is not manufactured in the lighter thicknesses. The range is from ½ in. to 2 in. The inner core consists of a number of narrow strips of wood glued one to the other. At each side there is a facing, the grain of this running at right angles with the core. As in the case of plywood, shrinkage is reduced to a minimum, and for carcase work, doors, etc., laminboard is in great demand, especially as it provides an excellent groundwork for veneering.

Blockboard and battenboard are other forms of laminated board, the chief difference being in the width of the core stock.

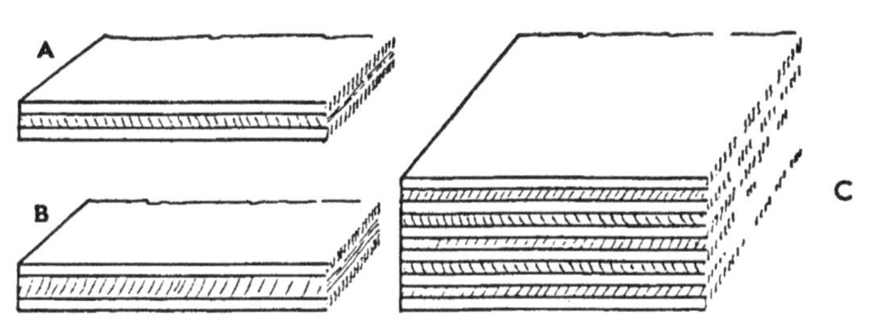

FIG. 1. EXAMPLES OF PLYWOOD.
A. Equal-layer ply. B. Stout-heart ply. C. Multi-ply.

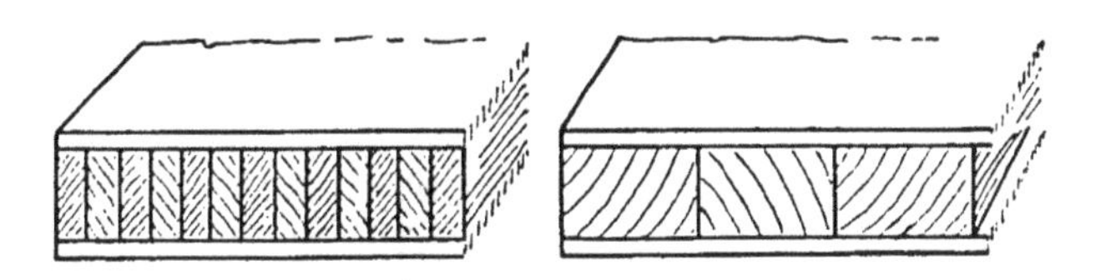

FIG. 2. LAMINBOARD. FIG. 3. BLOCKBOARD.

INDEX

INDEX

INDEX